Security through Freedom:

American Political Thought and Practice

As long as we may think as we will, and speak as we think, the condition of man will proceed in improvement.
—THOMAS JEFFERSON

Books by Alpheus Thomas Mason

Organized Labor and the Law, 1925

Brandeis and the Modern State, 1933

The Brandeis Way, 1938

Bureaucracy Convicts Itself, 1941

Brandeis: A Free Man's Life, 1946

The Fall of a Railroad Empire (with Henry L. Staples), 1947

Free Government in the Making, 1949

The Supreme Court: Vehicle of Revealed Truth or Power Group, 1953

American Constitutional Law (with William M. Beaney), 1954

Security through Freedom, 1955

Security through Freedom:

American Political Thought and Practice

★

ALPHEUS THOMAS MASON

Cornell University Press, Ithaca, New York

To the memory of Lloyd Irving Gibbons

Foreword

THE American political tradition is complex, many-faceted. It has been said that we do not understand, nor do others, what our system really means. A deliberate effort to explore it evokes fear and trembling. Conscious of the difficulties that beset us, I have focused these chapters on one narrow segment—the continuing conflict between political and judicial control of government.

Americans, unlike most free peoples, are disinclined to rely on political checks as adequate for obliging government to control itself. Our most characteristic devices—written constitutions, bills of rights, separation of powers, judicial review, federalism, and states' rights—all these reflect ancestral distrust of government. Except in times of crisis, fragmentation of political authority has been our primary safeguard for liberty. Nor is the special deposit of power we entrust to judges an exception to the general rule; for their authority is usually thought of as negative, as protective of individual rights, especially economic, against arbitrary infringement by government. When judicial authority becomes positive, determining vital issues of the day, as under Jefferson, Jackson, Lincoln, and the two Roosevelts, judges also fall under criticism. Nevertheless, the judiciary is still valued as a bulwark against the danger that has always terrified Americans—unrestrained majority rule. The view that "law emanates solely from the will of the majority of the people and can, therefore, be modified at any time to meet majority wishes" has been described as "absolutely totalitarian." Justice David J. Brewer defined despotism as "the control of the many over the few." In some parts of the free world, this definition suggests democracy rather than despotism.

The conflict now, as always, is between reactionary methods that restrict freedom and democratic procedures that safeguard the individual, between political demagogues who vainly seek to maintain the status quo and the dissenter, sometimes starry-eyed, who envisions a better life for all. Society's twofold danger is ignorant change and ignorant opposition to change. Heretofore, these contending drives, at least in their lesser gradations, have been thought of as attesting the strength of our society. They have been our guarantee that the resulting unity would be based on that most solid of all foundations—diversity. Now, however, certain thoughtful observers see signs of decay at the foundations. Summing up his indictment of the security program, Vannevar Bush declared: "Suspicion and distrust are rampant in the land. We have nearly lost our greatest advantage over the enemy—our mutual regard and trust as a people."

It may be that the difficulties we experience in stating as well as in holding to our creed are inherent in the nature of free government itself. If it consists in *how* a society conducts its business as well as in the particular decisions reached, we can understand why Justice Holmes thought that its essence could be better conveyed by contagion than by argument and exegesis. These essays are grounded in this belief. The approach is pragmatic. The validity and reality of the values we profess are portrayed primarily in actions taken, things done, at a given time and place. Although experience has proved the superiority of its methods, free government is still on trial. In the opening number of *The Federalist*, Hamilton remarked that "it seems to have been reserved for the people of this country, by their conduct and example, to decide the important question, whether societies of men are really capable or not of establishing good government from reflection and choice, or whether they are forever destined to depend for their political constitutions on accident and force." That responsibility rests even more squarely on America today.

One piles up debts to generous people and institutions in preparing a work even of modest dimensions. I am happy to record the debt owed to the research of former graduate students, especially that of Mr. William C. Gibbons, congressional interne, American Political Science Association, Washington, D.C.; Dr. Sam Krislov, instructor, Hunter College; Dr. Lloyd M. Wells, assistant professor, Southern Methodist University; Mr. Robert Tienken and Mr. Richard L. Sklar, graduate students, Department of Politics, Princeton University. My talented undergraduate research assistant, James H. Duffy, did the laborious task of checking documentation against original sources. Miss Helen Fairbanks, Public Administration Section, Princeton University Library, cheerfully responded to numberless calls for help in tracking down elusive sources. Miss Hope Gibbons read the galley proof and offered suggestions so persuasive as to incline me to make changes more extensive than usual in the proof. The Princeton University Research Fund furthered the project by financial assistance. Prentice-Hall, Inc., and the Boston University Press allowed me to draw on previous writings published under their imprint. I am grateful also to individuals and publishers who permitted quotation from their printed works.

One of the pleasant concomitants of the Messenger Lectureship at Cornell University is the opportunity it affords the lecturer to live on campus for an extended period. For two weeks I enjoyed the hospitality of that unique student organization—the Telluride Association. The faculties and administrative officers of Cornell University extended innumerable kindnesses and courtesies, making my stay there an altogether pleasant and stimulating experience.

A. T. M.

Princeton
June 15, 1955

Contents

Security through Freedom:

American Political Thought and Practice

Political versus Judicial

Control of Government

AMERICANS are now under special urgency to interpret their guiding doctrines both for themselves and for others. The demand for this grows in part out of recent recognition that a nation's strength lies in ideas no less than in armies and munitions of war. Ideas, as the saying goes, are weapons. "One person with a belief" has been rated "a social power equal to ninety-nine who have only interests." [1] "The ideas

[1] J. S. Mill, *Utilitarianism, Liberty and Representative Government* (Everyman ed.; New York: Dutton, 1910), p. 183. "We ought not to forget," Mill writes, "that there is an incessant and everflowing current of human affairs toward the worse, consisting of all the follies, all the vices, all the negligences, indolences, and supineness of mankind; which is only controlled, and kept from sweeping all before it, by the exertions which some persons constantly, and others by fits, put forward in the direction of good and worthy objects" (*ibid.*, p. 191).

of economists and political philosophers," John Maynard Keynes declared, "both when they are right and when they are wrong, are more powerful than is commonly understood. Indeed the world is ruled by little else. . . . Soon or late, it is ideas, not vested interests, which are dangerous for good or evil." [2]

It was not battalions and billions that empowered the frail and shrunken Gandhi to win out in India; it was belief in a principle which even Great Britain at last had to respect. By sitting quietly and holding tenaciously to his faith, one man aroused political consciousness and finally dominated 350 million people whom others with far greater physical and economic strength had failed to move. "In the history of the world," Alfred North Whitehead wrote, "the prize has not gone to those species which specialized in methods of violence, or even in defensive armour." Nature early produced animals encased in hard shells for defense against the ills of life. It also experimented in size. "But smaller animals, without external armour, warm-blooded, sensitive, and alert, have cleared these monsters off the face of the earth. . . . There is something in the ready use of force which defeats its own object." "Its main defect," Whitehead concludes suggestively, "is that it bars cooperation." [3]

A significant shift in strategy continues today under our own eyes—the change from tanks to ideas, from stress on military might to so-called psychological warfare. The "assembling of the wise men of the State, instead of assembling armies," which greatly impressed Jefferson in 1787,

[2] J. M. Keynes, *General Theory of Employment, Interest and Money* (New York: Harcourt, Brace, 1936), pp. 383–384.
[3] A. N. Whitehead, *Science and the Modern World* (New York: Macmillan, 1925), p. 297.

may in time become standard practice.[4] American experience in explaining our "way of life" has not, however, been conspicuously successful. Unlike totalitarians, right and left, we cannot confidently point to any particular gospel or hero as expressing the essence of our tradition. The Army's World War II experience illustrates the difficulty. Believing that information on the background of the war would induce better attitudes among our soldiers, the Army chiefs staged an intensive mass communication campaign on "Why We Fight." When asked what they had learned about the results, a psychologist who had worked on the program answered: "Nothing . . . just about nothing. And to be honest we still don't know the answer." [5]

The Voice of America programs still plague the producers. Small wonder! Even scholars are disagreed as to the meaning of our political tradition, or whether there is any such thing as American political thought. To pattern lovers, to neat minds, it presents a bewildering jungle. Our way of political life cannot be ticketed and pigeon-holed. Irregularities and confusions make for such an indescribable complexity as to disqualify any single source of influence. Nevertheless, on any roster of authoritative names considered influential, John Locke's would more than likely head the list. Many factors made Locke's individualistic norms meaningful to pre-Revolutionary American society. The frontier was "a veritable state of nature," and the Mayflower Compact a living example of Locke's hypothetical

---

[4] Thomas Jefferson cited this as the most hopeful aspect of the Federal Convention of 1787. See letter to David Humphreys March 18, 1789, in *Writings of Thomas Jefferson* (ed. by Henry A. Washington; Washington: Taylor and Maury, 1853), III, 10. Hereafter cited as *Writings of Jefferson.*

[5] Quoted in "Is Anybody Listening?" *Fortune*, 42 (Sept. 1950), 81.

social contract.[6] During the Revolutionary period, Locke was referred to deferentially as "the ingenious Mr. Locke," "the incomparable Mr. Locke." Jefferson incorporated in the Declaration of Independence several basic sentences from his *Second Treatise of Civil Government*. As late as 1921 George Sutherland, formerly a United States Senator, and later a Supreme Court Justice, praised Locke's "golden words." And yet one may question whether the dauntless champion of England's Glorious Revolution of 1688 did in fact provide the constitutional blueprint for America.

Locke, like latter-day Americans, was trying to solve the ages-old conundrum of liberty versus authority. His concern for the first is reflected in all he has to say about natural law and natural rights. In a state of nature all men are in a condition of "perfect freedom to order their actions and dispose of their possessions and persons, as they think fit, within the bounds of the law of nature." [7] The state of nature is also a condition of "perfect equality." [8] "All being kings," as he put it, there is no superiority of one individual over another in interpreting and enforcing natural law.[9] In the transition from a state of nature to civil society, the individual inevitably loses some freedom, and equality vanishes completely. The former is given up "to be regulated by laws made by the society, so far forth as the preservation of himself and the rest of that society shall require." Executive power, equally enjoyed by all, the individual "wholly gives up." [10]

[6] See Louis Hartz, "American Political Thought and the American Revolution," *American Political Science Review*, 46 (June 1952), 321.

[7] "Of Civil Government," *Works of John Locke* (London: Otridge, 1812), V, 339–340 (par. 4).

[8] *Ibid.*, p. 342 (par. 7). [9] *Ibid.*, p. 412 (par. 123).

[10] *Ibid.*, pp. 413–414 (par. 128–130).

Despite this enormous surrender, the most striking feature of Locke's system is the number and variety of restraints imposed on government. Constitutional prescription compels the legislative power to rule according to "promulgated, standing laws." [11] Structural limits, notably separation of power, proscribe the fusing of legislative and executive authority. Finally, civil government, like individuals in a state of nature, is bound by natural law. Right of revolution is posited as a natural right.

But all these limitations pale beneath the absolute necessity for enough power to govern in the public interest. Promulgated standing law is not an absolute barrier to power. The very definition of "prerogative" in the executive is "discretion" to act "for the public good, without the prescription of the law, and sometimes even against it." [12] Likewise separation of powers, though partly justified because there is "too great a temptation to human frailty, apt to grasp powers," [13] serves not as a restriction to enfeeble government, but rather as the mark of "well-ordered Commonwealths." It remained for the Frenchman Montesquieu to develop this principle into a power-breaking device acceptable to Americans. Even the right of revolution, which our fathers translated into reality, appears in Locke's pages as primarily a recipe for avoiding it. A government that betrays its trust is in rebellion and thus renounces its claim to obedience: "This . . . power in the people of providing for their safety anew by a new legislative, when their legislators have acted contrary to their trust, by invading their property, is the best fence against rebellion, and the probablest means to hinder it." [14] Thus, promulgated standing law, natural law and natural

[11] *Ibid.*, p. 419 (par. 136).　　[12] *Ibid.*, p. 435 (par. 160).
[13] *Ibid.*, p. 424 (par. 143).　　[14] *Ibid.*, p. 472 (par. 226).

rights, along with structural barriers and the right of revolution, are largely paper safeguards, verbal admonitions against abuse of power.[15] The idea of checking Parliament by any other means than the will of the major part of the community is foreign to Locke's thought.[16] Once the legislative is constituted, "the people . . . [have] no power to act so long as the government stands." Locke calls this an "inconvenience . . . thought incapable of a remedy." [17]

Having taken his stand firmly on the side of authority, how can the author of the *Second Treatise of Civil Government* properly be regarded, as he often is, as an exponent of laissez-faire? His "implicit assumption," Professor F. S. C. Northrup writes, is "that the minimum government is the ideal government." [18] The view attributed to Locke is that "to regulate [property] would be the grossest of usurpations, the most flagrant of wrongs." [19] This interpretation is in direct conflict with Locke's own words. In his state of nature, property rests on labor and the invention of money, but "in governments, the laws regulate the right of property, and the possession of land is determined by positive constitutions." [20] When man enters civil society, "he is to part also, with as much of his natural liberty, in providing for himself, as the good, prosperity, and safety of the society shall require; which is not only necessary,

[15] N. C. Phillips, "Political Philosophy and Political Fact: The Evidence of John Locke," in *Liberty and Learning: Essays in Honor of Sir James Hight* (Christchurch: Whitcombe and Tombs, 1950), p. 208.

[16] H. R. G. Greaves; quoted in Phillips, *op. cit.*, p. 212.

[17] Locke, *op. cit.*, p. 432 (par. 157).

[18] F. S. C. Northrop, *Meeting of East and West* (New York: Macmillan, 1946), p. 107. See also pp. 45, 106.

[19] C. E. Vaughan, *Studies in the History of Political Philosophy* (Manchester: Manchester University, 1939), I, 172.

[20] Locke, *op. cit.*, p. 367 (par. 50).

but just, since the other members of the society do the like." [21] Instead of being an extreme exponent of laissez-faire, Locke was a moderate mercantilist quite at peace with the Age of Mercantilism in which he lived.[22]

Locke's constitutionalism boils down to political limitations on government—those imposed at elections, plus the hope that individuals, as well as governments, will be guided by considerations of justice and common sense. "Keeping of faith belongs to men as men," he insists, whether in a state of nature or in civil society. It has been said that Locke was unreasonable "only in his faith in reason." [23]

The Founding Fathers, certainly Madison and Hamilton, were more skeptical. They accepted "momentary passions and immediate interests," rather than "considerations of policy, utility, or justice," [24] as the dominant drives in politics. For them "men are ambitious, vindictive and rapacious"; [25] human nature displayed "infirmities and depravities." [26] Nor did the *Federalist* collaborators look forward, eventually, as did Karl Marx in 1848, to some earthly paradise emerging either from changed economic and social environment or spiritual regeneration. With disdain Hamilton queried:

Have we not already seen enough of the fallacy and extravagance of those idle theories which have amused us with promises of an exemption from the imperfections, the weaknesses, and the evils incident to society in every shape? Is it not time

[21] *Ibid.*, p. 414 (par. 130).
[22] This is the conclusion reached by Professor Jacob Viner in his unpublished manuscript, "John Locke on Property," to which the writer is much indebted.
[23] Phillips, *op. cit.*, p. 208.
[24] Max Beloff, ed., *The Federalist* (New York: Macmillan, 1948), No. 6, p. 22.
[25] *Ibid.*, No. 6, p. 20.   [26] *Ibid.*, No. 37, p. 181.

to awake from the deceitful dream of a golden age, and to adopt as a practical maxim for the direction of our political conduct that we, as well as the other inhabitants of the globe, are yet remote from the happy empire of perfect wisdom and perfect virtue? [27]

Human nature being what it is, man must employ his reason in building institutional fences around human avarice and greed. Ambition must be set against ambition, interest against interest, greed against greed. The art of politics consists in utilizing human nature, in directing it into channels where it will be socially useful or at least harmless.

Madison remarked in *Federalist*, No. 51: "This policy of supplying, by opposite and rival interests, the defect of better motives might be traced through the whole system of human affairs, private as well as public. We see it particularly displayed in all the subordinate distributions of power; where the constant aim is to divide and arrange the several offices in such a manner, as that each may be a check on the other; that the private interest of every individual may be a sentinel over the public rights. These inventions of prudence cannot be less requisite to the distribution of the supreme powers of the state." "You may cover whole skins of parchment with limitations," John Randolph wrote well over a century ago, "but power alone can limit power." [28]

In constitution-making, experience, rather than "the incomparable Mr. Locke," was their guide. The people of America, Madison remarked in *Federalist*, No. 14, "whilst they have paid a decent regard to the opinions of former times and other nations . . . have not suffered a blind

[27] *Ibid.*, No. 6, pp. 24–25.
[28] W. C. Bruce, *John Randolph of Roanoke* (New York: Putnam, 1922), II, 211.

veneration for antiquity, for custom, or for names, to over-
rule the suggestions of their own good sense, the knowledge of their own situation, and the lessons of their own
experience." [29] Painful difficulties, especially during the
so-called "critical period," had suggested an urgent need for
checks on legislative majorities beyond those set at elections. "A succession of powers and persons" will not, John
Adams wrote, lessen the passions of "self-interest, private
avidity, ambition, and avarice. . . . Nor will the apprehension of an approaching election restrain them from
indulgence if they have the power. . . ." [30] "There is,"
Adams insisted, "no possible way of defending the minority
. . . from the tyranny of the majority, but by giving the
former a negative on the latter." [31]

"What," Madison asked in *Federalist*, No. 10, "are so
many of the most important acts of legislation, but so many
judicial determinations, not indeed concerning the rights
of single persons, but concerning the rights of large bodies
of citizens?" In *Federalist*, No. 22, Hamilton agreed that
"the fundamental maxim of republican government . . .
requires that the sense of the majority should prevail." But
the legislature was not an acceptable repository for "all
the most important prerogatives of sovereignty." A political system in which the legislature is supreme would be
"one of the most execrable forms of government that human infatuation ever contrived."

In his famous argument of 1761 against writs of assistance in Massachusetts, James Otis suggested an alternative

---

[29] Beloff, ed., *op. cit.*, No. 6, p. 66.
[30] C. F. Adams, ed., "A Defence of the Constitutions of Government of the United States of America, 1787–8," *Works of John
Adams* (Boston: Little, Brown, 1851), VI, 57.
[31] *Ibid.*, p. 63.

to legislative dominance. "An Act [of Parliament] against the Constitution is void," Otis argued, "an Act against natural Equity is void: and if an Act of Parliament should be made, in the very words of the petition, it would be void. The Executive courts must pass such Acts into disuse." [32] Of Otis' repudiation of Parliamentary sovereignty, John Adams said many years later: "Then and there, the child of Independence was born." [33] Conceived at the same time was America's unique contribution to the theory and practice of free government, that strangely undemocratic, unrepresentative institution for obliging the government to control itself—judicial review.

With us, power had to be divided both within and between nation and states; the powers of the national government as well as those of the states had to be separated, checked, and balanced. To implement this complexus of controls, judicial review was recognized and enforced against national and state legislatures. Madison suggested the peculiarly American approach in *Federalist*, No. 51:

In framing a government, which is to be administered by men over men, the great difficulty lies in this: You must first enable the government to control the governed; and in the next place, oblige it to control itself. A dependence on the people is, no doubt, the primary control on government; but experience has taught mankind the necessity of auxiliary precautions.[34]

Locke's *Second Treatise*, written in a country basically unlike America, could provide no solution. Instead, the Found-

[32] Quoted in E. S. Corwin, *Liberty against Government* (Baton Rouge: Louisiana State University Press, 1948), p. 39. See also Ralph K. Huitt, "The Constitutional Ideas of James Otis," *Kansas Law Review*, 2 (Dec. 1953), 152–173.

[33] Quoted in Corwin, *Liberty against Government*, p. 39.

[34] Beloff, ed., *op. cit.*, No. 51, p. 265.

ing Fathers "reared the fabrics of government," as Madison said, "which have no model on the face of the globe." The Virginian took special pride in the "numerous innovations displayed on the American theatre, in favor of private rights and public happiness." "Posterity," he said, "will be indebted for the possession, and the world for the example." [35]

One must not, however, rule out all Lockian influence. The Founding Fathers, like Locke, stressed the political restraints on government. But whereas he thought of these as the *sole* means of obliging government to control itself, they elevated "dependence on the people" merely to a primary position. During the first one hundred years of our history, controversy raged, as we shall see, on the question of whether judicial control should replace political restraints as our chief reliance against abuse of power.

In 1776 we were firmly committed, as was Locke, to the right of revolution. Madison called this a "transcendent and precious right of the people." [36] "The transcendent law of nature and of nature's God . . . declares that the safety and happiness of society are the objects at which all political institutions aim, and to which all such institutions must be sacrificed." [37] Hamilton considered the right of revolution "that original right of self-defence, which is paramount to all positive forms of government." [38] It is a "fundamental principle of republican government," he wrote, "which admits the right of the people to alter or abolish the established constitution whenever they find it inconsistent with their happiness." [39]

But the *Federalist* collaborators, like Locke, held no brief for a government subject to the continuous and direct pres-

[35] *Ibid.*, No. 14, p. 66.
[37] *Ibid.*, No. 43, p. 225.
[39] *Ibid.*, No. 78, p. 400.
[36] *Ibid.*, No. 40, p. 201.
[38] *Ibid.*, No. 28, p. 135.

sure of the masses. The government is bound by the law which brings it into being: "Until the people have, by some solemn and authoritative act, annulled or changed the established form, it is binding upon themselves collectively, as well as individually; and no presumption, or even knowledge of their sentiments, can warrant their representatives in a departure from it, prior to such an act." [40] If the fundamental law is to be changed, it must be done "by some solemn and authoritative act" of its author, the sovereign people, or by resort to the extraconstitutional right of revolution. Madison took into account the probable consequences of "ambitious" federal encroachments. To combat these, correspondence among the states would be opened, sounding "general alarm," joint plans of resistance concerted—and, "unless the projected innovations should be voluntarily renounced," an "appeal to a trial of force" would be made, such "as was produced by the dread of a foreign yoke." [41] Hamilton depicted revolution as the "characteristic right of freedom" [42] and expressed the hope that "friends of the proposed constitution will never concur with its enemies, in questioning that fundamental principle of republican government." [43]

Constitution makers could do no more than reduce the probability of revolutions. "No form of government can always either avoid or control them," Hamilton wrote in *Federalist*, No. 16. In essay Number 43, Madison agreed that foreclosure of revolution would not be "within the compass of human probability; and that it is a sufficient recommendation of the federal constitution, that it diminishes the risk of a calamity, for which no possible constitution can provide a cure." In this respect the Constitution

[40] *Ibid.*

[41] *Ibid.*, No. 46, pp. 242–243.

[42] *Ibid.*, No. 60, p. 307.

[43] *Ibid.*, No. 78, p. 400.

made a marked advance over the Articles of Confederation. The Articles, "resting on no better foundation than the consent of the several legislatures," had "been exposed to frequent and intricate questions concerning the validity of its powers." In some instances it had "given birth to the enormous doctrine of a right of legislative repeal." The new Constitution, by building "the fabric of American empire" on the "solid basis of *The Consent of the People*," discouraged so "gross a heresy."

"Where the whole power of the government is in the hands of the people, there is the less pretence for the use of violent remedies, in partial or occasional distempers. . . . The natural cure for an ill administration, in a popular or representative constitution, is a change of men." [44]

For the authors of *The Federalist*, as for Locke, freedom and diversity, not repression, reduced the threat of civil disorder, diminished the risk of "calamities for which there is neither preventative nor cure." [45] Political stability results from "comprehending in the society so many separate descriptions of citizens, as will render an unjust combination of a majority of the whole very improbable, if not impracticable." Prudence dictates both political and religious toleration. "In a free government, the security for civil rights must be the same as that for religious rights." [46] "Heresies," Hamilton observed, "can rarely be cured by persecution." [47] The acknowledged right of revolution stands as a perpetual warning against tyranny. Government can ignore it, but, Madison asked, "what degree of madness could ever drive the federal government to such an extremity?" [48]

[44] Beloff, ed., *op. cit.*, No. 22, p. 110, and No. 21, p. 99.
[45] *Ibid.*, No. 26, p. 129.   [46] *Ibid.*, No. 51, p. 267.
[47] *Ibid.*, No. 1, p. 2.
[48] *Ibid.*, No. 46, p. 243. "If the federal government should overpass

We are also committed to the Lockean principle of majority rule. "The majority who rule," Madison said, "are the safest Guardians both of public Good and private rights." [49] For Jefferson, too, "absolute acquiescence in the decisions of the majority" was the "vital principle of republics." [50] But this doctrine was no sooner embodied in the Articles of Confederation and the state constitutions than it was queried on all sides. In Jefferson's own constitution of Virginia, legislative dominance and majority rule prompted him to declare that

one hundred and seventy-three despots would surely be as oppressive as one. An *elective despotism* was not the government we fought for, but one which should not only be founded on free principles, but in which the powers of government should be so divided and balanced among several bodies of magistracy, as that no one could transcend their legal limits, without being effectually checked and restrained by the others.[51]

By 1787 the Americans had advanced well beyond Locke. For them separation of powers was much more than the mark of "well-ordered Commonwealths." It had become an "invaluable precept in the science of politics." [52]

The science of politics, Hamilton remarked in 1787, had

---

the just bounds of its authority," Hamilton observed, "and make a tyrannical use of its powers, the people whose creature it is, must appeal to the standard they have formed, and take such measures to redress the injury done to the constitution, as the exigency may suggest and prudence justify" (*ibid.*, No. 33, p. 156).

[49] James Madison, "Vices of the Political System of the United States," April 1787, *Writings of James Madison* (ed. by Gaillard Hunt; New York: Putnam, 1901), II, 366.

[50] "First Inaugural Address, March 4, 1801," *Writings of Jefferson*, VIII, 4.

[51] "Notes on Virginia," *Writings of Jefferson*, p. 361.

[52] Beloff, ed., *op. cit.*, No. 47, p. 246.

recently "received great improvement." [53] Among other gains, he cited the regular distribution of power into distinct departments, the introduction of legislative balances and checks, the institution of courts composed of judges holding their offices during good behavior—all designed to preclude legislative supremacy and qualify majority rule. The Revolutionary fathers had been ignorant, Dr. Benjamin Rush said, "of the forms and combinations of power in republics." "In our opposition to monarchy," he wrote, "we forgot that the temple of tyranny has two doors. We bolted one of them by proper restraints; but we left the other open, by neglecting to guard against the effects of our own ignorance and licentiousness." [54]

Nowhere were these failures more conspicuous than in the state legislatures where the "injustice" of the laws, especially infringements on the rights of property, had been carried to such a point, Madison complained, as "to bring more into question the fundamental principle of republican Government" [55]—majority rule.[56] Democratic

[53] *Ibid.*, No. 9, p. 36.

[54] Hezekiah Niles, *Principles and Acts of the Revolution* (Baltimore: Niles, 1822), p. 402.

[55] Madison, *Writings*, II, 366.

[56] Madison wrote in 1786 that "there is no maxim in my opinion which is more liable to be misapplied, and which therefore more needs elucidation than the current one that the interest of the majority is the political standard of right and wrong. Taking the word 'interest' as synonymous with 'ultimate happiness,' in which sense it is qualified with every necessary moral ingredient, the proposition is no doubt true. But taking it in the popular sense, as referring to immediate augmentation of property and wealth, nothing can be more false. In the latter sense it would be the interest of the majority in every community to despoil and enslave the minority of individuals; and in a federal community to make a similar sacrifice of the minority of the component States. In fact it is only reestablishing under another name and a more specious form, force

"excesses" had been glaring enough during the critical period, 1783–1787. "Wild and savage licentiousness" promised to be even greater in the years ahead. On the floor of the Philadelphia Convention, Madison, looking to future times, anticipated that "a great majority of the people will not only be without landed, but any other sort of, property." When this occurred, he predicted that the property-less masses will "either combine under the influence of their common situation; in which case, the rights of property and the public liberty will not be secure in their hands; or what is more probable, they will become the tools of opulence and ambition, in which case there will be equal danger on another side." [57] The evils of democracy—"an illuminated Hell," Fisher Ames called it—evoked such general scorn that George Mason suggested moderation lest "we should incautiously run into the opposite extreme." [58] "Notwithstanding the oppressions and injustice experienced among us from democracy, the genius of the people is in favor of it," Mason warned, "and the genius of the people must be consulted." [59] Franklin likewise was moved to state his distaste of everything that might "depress the virtue and spirit of our common people." [60]

The dynamic thread in our political fabric was now obvious. Running through it all are basic conflicts: economic power against political power, interests against numbers, property against persons, minority rights against majority rule.

---

as the measure of right . . ." (letter to James Monroe, Oct. 5, 1786, *Writings of James Madison* [ed. by Gaillard Hunt; New York: Putnam, 1901], II, 273).

[57] Max Farrand ed., *Records of the Federal Convention of 1787* (New Haven: Yale, 1911), II, 203–204 (August 7).

[58] Ibid., I, 49 (May 31).   [59] *Ibid.*, I, 101 (June 4).

[60] *Ibid.*, II, 204 (August 7).

The Founding Fathers were determined to prevent domination of government by legislative majorities. They realized from the start that, without judicial intervention, political majorities would prevail. "Judicial review," Professor Corwin observed, "represents an attempt by the American Democracy to cover its bet." [61] Without it James Harrington's maxim, that "power always follows property," might. be disproved. "This I believe," John Adams said in 1776, "to be as infallible a maxim in politics, as that action and reaction are equal, is in mechanics." [62] " 'Tis . . . certain," James Otis had remarked in 1764, "that the man who owns or controls property has more than a species of private right: he has, in addition, a certain measure of social and political power, though the possessor of it may not have much more wit than a mole or a musquash." [63] Despite the early period of Democratic-Republican rule, responsible political leaders remained under Harrington's spell. By and large his *Oceana* of 1656 influenced American political thought and action perhaps more than Locke's *Second Treatise*.

In an early Supreme Court opinion, Justice Paterson wrote:

The right of acquiring and possessing property, and having it protected, is one of the natural, inherent, and unalienable rights of man. Men have a sense of property: property is necessary to their subsistence, and correspondent to their natural wants and desires; its security was one of the objects, that induced them to unite in society. No man would become a member of a com-

[61] E. S. Corwin, review of B. F. Wright's "Growth of American Constitutional Law," *Harvard Law Review*, 56 (Nov. 1942), 487.

[62] C. F. Adams, ed., *Works of John Adams*, IX, 376.

[63] Quoted from *University of Missouri Studies*, 29, in A. T. Mason, *Free Government in the Making* (New York: Oxford, 1949), p. 96.

munity, in which he could not enjoy the fruits of his honest labour and industry. The preservation of property then is a primary object of the social compact.[64]

And so it was for Federalists and Anti-Federalists alike. But whereas the latter were quite relaxed, being sure that the desire for property was universal and that all men wished only to enjoy it more securely, the former, convinced that democracy is the natural enemy of property, insisted that it be made secure against democratic licentiousness.[65] In the 1780's those who wished to see the dominance of legislative majorities abated, those who felt the need for outside protection of the rights of property and of contract, naturally supported the movement afoot for a new constitution.

But how were the framers to secure such protection? Various measures were proposed, but every motion looking to the imposition of property qualification for suffrage or office-holding failed. The suggestion that the Senate be organized as a barrier for property was also defeated. The difficult and delicate matter of suffrage was ultimately left to the states. As the Constitution came from the hands of the framers, only one brief clause seemed to afford these basic rights protection against state legislative majorities: "No State shall . . . pass any . . . ex post facto law or laws impairing the obligation of contracts. . . ." When this clause came before the Supreme Court,[66] it was given

[64] *Van Horne's Lessee* v. *Dorrance,* 2 Dall. 304 (1795), p. 310.

[65] "For the Federalists the natural right of property was a weapon against democracy; the Constitution . . . was the means by which they hoped to make that weapon efficient. For the Anti-Federalists, the natural right of property was a weapon against governments which ignored the popular will. To them the Constitution appeared to offer opportunities for the creation of such a tyranny" (Richard Schlatter, *Private Property: The History of an Idea* [London, Allen & Unwin, 1951], p. 190).

[66] *Calder* v. *Bull,* 3 Dall. 386 (1798).

a very narrow interpretation. Confining the application of the ex post facto clause to retroactive penal legislation, the Court held that this clause was not "inserted to secure the citizen in his private rights of either property or contracts." This decision, by creating a wide breach in the constitutional protection afforded civil rights, aroused widespread criticism. Even Justice Chase, who delivered the Court's opinion, suggested that legislation adversely affecting private rights might be set aside as violation of natural law:

There are certain *vital* principles in our *free Republican governments* which will determine and over-rule an *apparent and flagrant* abuse of *legislative* power. . . . An act of the legislature (for I cannot call it a *law*) contrary to the *great first principles* of the *social compact*, cannot be considered a *rightful exercise* of *legislative* authority.[67]

Chase's associate, Justice Iredell, repulsed any suggestion that natural law is a judicially enforceable restriction on legislative power. Characterizing such talk as the plaything of "some speculative jurists," he said that if the Constitution itself imposed no limitations, "whatever the legislative power chose to enact, would be lawfully enacted, and the judicial power could never interpose to pronounce it void." [68] Like John Locke in 1690, Iredell believed that legislative supremacy, apart from specific constitutional restrictions, was "an inconvenience incapable of a remedy."

"It is not sufficient to urge," Iredell reasoned, "that the power may be abused, for, such is the nature of all power, —such is the tendency of every human institution. . . . We must be content to limit power where we can, and where we cannot, consistently with its use, we must be content to

[67] *Ibid.*, p. 388. (Emphasis in original.)　　[68] *Ibid.*, p. 398.

repose a salutary confidence." [69] For Justice Iredell, as for Locke, the notion that "keeping of faith belongs to men as men" was a basic tenet.

Within a generation the "salutary confidence" that the people would provide sufficient restraint on government threatened to play hob with Harrington's maxim that political power always follows property. In a single decade Massachusetts, New York, and Virginia held conventions to revise and liberalize their constitutions. Spokesmen for economic interests were vehemently opposed to such changes. For Chancellor James Kent of New York, universal suffrage was an "extreme democratic principle" that had been "regarded with terror, by the wise men of every age." [70] It was "too mighty an excitement for the moral constitution of men to endure." It had a tendency, he said, "to jeopardize the rights of property and the principles of liberty." [71] In Massachusetts, Daniel Webster roused the same fears:

In the nature of things those who have not property, and see their neighbors possess much more than they think them to need, cannot be favorable to laws made for the protection of property. When this class becomes numerous, it grows clamorous. It looks on property as its prey and plunder, and is naturally ready, at all times, for violence and revolution. It would seem, then, to be the part of political wisdom to found government on property. [72]

[69] *Ibid.*, p. 400.
[70] *Proceedings and Debates of the Convention of 1821, Assembled for the Purpose of Amending the Constitution of the State of New-York* (Albany: E. Hosford, 1821), p. 220. Hereafter cited as *New York Proceedings.*
[71] *Ibid.*, p. 221.
[72] *Journal of Debates and Proceedings in the Convention of Delegates Chosen to Revise the Constitution of Massachusetts, 1820–21* (Boston: 1853), p. 312. Hereafter cited as *Mass. Proceedings.*

In Virginia the proposal that existing property restrictions on suffrage be erased moved John Randolph to shout: "It is the first time in my life, that I ever heard of a Government which was to divorce property from power." The effort would prove impossible in any event. "The moment you have separated the two, that very moment property will go in search of power, and power in search of property. . . ." [73]

For all these staunch adherents to the status quo, the fate of free government hung in perilous balance. "There is a tendency in the poor," said Chancellor Kent, "to covet and to share the plunder of the rich: . . . in the majority to tyranize over the minority, and trample down their rights." [74] "Universal suffrage once granted, is granted forever, and never can be recalled." Completely underestimating the genius of reactionaries, Kent concluded: "There is no retrograde step in the rear of democracy." [75]

As Kent in New York and Webster in Massachusetts and Randolph in Virginia grappled with the hard facts of an American society already headed into industrialism, they were taunted by less eminent delegates who harked back to exalted eighteenth-century ideals. The wild forebodings of reactionaries were not only blind to the fundamentals of 1776, but also at odds with the motivations of the common man. "Every member of the convention," P. R. Livingston of New York insisted, is "a friend to property, and to the landed interest." [76] In a country like ours, rich in natural resources and educational opportunities, the Kent-Webster-Randolph theory of social stratification was inapplicable. "Real property," an obscure New York delegate pre-

[73] *Proceedings and Debates of the Virginia Constitutional Convention of 1829–30* (Richmond: Ritchie and Cook, 1830), p. 319.
[74] *New York Proceedings*, p. 221.   [75] *Ibid.*, p. 222.
[76] *Ibid.*, p. 224.

dicted, "will be in the hands of the many" because "the desire of acquiring property is a universal passion." [77]

One cannot read these debates without a sense of the great and continuing paradox that permeates our political thought. Warring against each other were the moral ideals of freedom, the basic axioms Jefferson appealed to in the Declaration, and impassioned insistence that "inevitable" economic inequality must be maintained by specific constitutional safeguards.

The currents of political upsurge, taking shape as "the Jacksonian revolution," made use of various devices—the national nominating convention, the long ballot, rotation in office, subordination of the judiciary—all to bring government closer to the masses and make it more directly responsible to them. Jackson himself as President started a vigorous campaign to destroy government-created embodiments of economic privilege. Representing, as his regime did, both an enlargement of democracy and an expansion of liberated capitalism, it may be that America then came closer to realizing the precepts of the Declaration of Independence than at any time before or since. The country was moving rapidly in the direction of universal male suffrage. Liberty meant more because it was more closely coupled with economic equality. Tools of production were relatively simple and inexpensive, their ownership rather easily obtained and widely diffused. Even if one man were hired to work for another, he could and did look forward, usually not in vain, to independence in his own shop and on his own land. The Great West beckoned, property resources were of vast scope; our government land policy enhanced individual opportunity.

The gains were spiritual as well as economic and political.

[77] *Ibid.*, pp. 242, 243.

"Nothing struck me more forcibly," De Tocqueville wrote in the middle 1830's, "than the general equality of condition. . . ." [78] "There is not one country in the world where man more confidently reaches toward the future, where he feels with so much pride that his intelligence makes him master of the universe, that he can fashion it to his liking." [79] One could then use that familiar tag of later years, "rugged individualism," without risk of ridicule. Yet signs already pointed to a new aristocracy. Increasing population pressure swelled the forces of revolution and counter-revolution. Concentrated wealth and dispersed political power would, it was recognized, put a heavy strain on free government. Webster, casting himself in the role of prophet, remarked that

if the tendency of the laws were to create a rapid accumulation of property in few hands, and to render the great mass of the population dependent and penniless, . . . the popular power must break in upon the rights of property, or else the influence of property must limit and control the exercise of popular power. [80]

De Tocqueville had anticipated the nature of that struggle. "I am of opinion," he observed, "that the manufacturing aristocracy which is growing up under our eyes is one of the harshest which ever existed in the world." [81]

A generation later, John Adams' grandson, Charles Francis Adams confirmed De Tocqueville's forecast. Adams had just returned after serving five years as our

[78] Alexis de Tocqueville, *Democracy in America* (tr. by Henry Reeve; Boston: Allyn, 1882), I, 1.

[79] Quoted in Matthew Josephson, "A Century after Tocqueville," *Virginia Quarterly Review*, 14 (Autumn 1928), 587.

[80] *Mass. Proceedings*, p. 312.

[81] De Tocqueville, *op. cit.*, II, 197.

wartime minister to England. Among the changes the years had wrought, he cited "greatly enlarged grasp of enterprise and increased facility of combination." The corporation was supplanting partnership. Adams spoke of "the most remarkable examples of organized lawlessness, under the forms of law," pointed an accusing finger toward "certain single men at the head of vast combinations of private wealth," and concluded:

These modern potentates have declared war, negotiated peace, reduced courts, legislatures, and sovereign States to an unqualified obedience to their will, disturbed trade, agitated the currency, imposed taxes, and, boldly setting both law and public opinion at defiance, have freely exercised many other attributes of sovereignty. . . . All this they wielded in practical independence of the control both of governments and of individuals; much as petty German despots might have governed their little principalities a century or two ago.[82]

Other thoughtful men, including Edward G. Ryan, Chief Justice of Wisconsin, expressed similar forebodings. Addressing the graduating class at Madison, June 1873, the Chief Justice said:

There is looming up a new and dark power. I cannot dwell upon the signs and shocking omens of its events. The accumulation of individual wealth seems to be greater than it ever has been since the downfall of the Roman Empire. The enterprises of the country are aggregating vast corporate combinations of unexampled capital, boldly marching, not for economic conquests only, but for political power. For the first time really in our politics, money is taking the field as organized power. . . . Already, here at home, one great corporation has trifled with the sovereign power, and insulted the state. There is grave fear that it, and its great rival, have confederated to make partition

[82] *North American Review*, 112 (April 1871), 241–242.

of the state and share it as spoils. . . . The question will arise, and arise in your day, though perhaps not fully in mine, "Which shall rule—wealth, or man; which shall lead—money, or intellect; who shall fill public stations—educated and patriotic free men, or feudal serfs of corporate capital?"

In the transition from agrarianism, the independent small business man had, as Adams and Ryan said, fallen before trusts and monopolies; entrepreneurs had been forced to become workers for someone else; workers themselves had become parts of an industrial machine dependent for mass production on a precise division of labor and upon mass production for profits. More and more workers relied on big companies for their jobs; responsibility for their welfare shifted from themselves to their employers, and ultimately to government. As if by design, industrial absolutism and political democracy had progressed simultaneously. The ground swell of popular agitation that followed extension of the suffrage was traced straight to Jacksonian radicalism. Increasingly the people sought, as Webster had anticipated, to use government as an instrument for protecting and advancing their own welfare against corporate combinations, "boldly marching . . . for political power." Half of his forecast was soon fulfilled. Popular power, in the form of restrictive legislation, began to break in on the rights of property. It remained only for the "influence of property" to find new ways "to limit and control the exercise of popular power."

The New York case of *Wynehamer* v. *New York*,[83] decided in 1856, dramatically posed the issue and discovered a constitutional device of untold potentiality for limiting the resurgent forces of Jacksonian democracy. The defendant, Wynehamer, was indicted and convicted for selling

[83] 13 N.Y. 378–488 (Court of Appeals).

25

liquor contrary to an act passed April 9, 1855, for the prevention of intemperance, pauperism and crime. In setting the prohibition aside as violative of "due process," the Court invoked a constitutional injunction of tremendous consequence—denying government power to deprive a person of "life, liberty or property without due process of law." A three-way split among the Justices indicates the complexity of the issue.

To the lay mind the phrase "due process" suggests procedural limitations—that is, if it limits legislative power at all, it does so in terms not of what can be done, but of how something must be done. A majority in the Wynehamer case had something more sweeping in mind:

In a government like ours, theories of public good or public necessity may be so plausible, or even so truthful, as to command popular majorities. But whether truthful or plausible merely, and by whatever numbers they are assented to, there are some absolute private rights beyond their reach and among these the constitution places the right of property.[84]

One concurring Justice rejected this notion of extra-constitutional limitations on government, but agreed that the prohibition act did take property without due process of law. Even though it complied with "the forms which belong to 'due process of law,' " the legislature had exceeded its powers.[85]

One Justice dissented vigorously, holding that legislative power is supreme except where specifically limited by the Constitution. Echoing Justice Iredell's sentiments, he insisted that judicial review based upon the judges' views of what is reasonable would constitute usurpation, a "veto or dispensing power" that does not "pertain to the judicial

[84] *Ibid.*, p. 387.　　　　　　　[85] *Ibid.*, p. 420.

functions." With Madison, he insisted that "dependence on the people" is the primary control on government:

The remedy for unjust legislation, provided it does not conflict with organic law, is at the ballot box; and I know of no provision of the Constitution nor fundamental principle of government which authorizes the minority, when defeated at the polls, upon the issue involving the propriety of a law, to appeal to the judiciary and invoke its aid to reverse the decision of the majority and nullifying the legislative power.

The courts should approach even doubtful legislation with the greatest restraint, remembering that their primary function is vigilantly and fearlessly to uphold legislative enactments. The judiciary is not the only agency for correcting abuse of power:

The people have a far more certain and reliable security and protection against mere impolitic, over-stringent or uncalled-for legislation than courts can ever afford, in their reserved power of changing . . . the representatives of their legislative sovereignty; and to that final and ultimate tribunal should all such errors and mistakes in legislation be referred for correction.[86]

The Wynehamer decision, foreshadowing "due process" as the constitutional basis for judicial restraint on govern-

[86] *Ibid.*, pp. 474–477 *passim.* Impressive inferential support for the Wynehamer decision appears in an anonymous *American Law Magazine* article of July 1843. Under the title "The Security of Private Property," this paper argued that property needs "every parchment barrier which has been or can be thrown around it." "In a republic, where the legislature . . . is annually elected, and where . . . legislation partakes . . . of the passions and impulses of the moment, it is important to inquire into the extent of the power possessed by the majority to encroach upon the fruits of honest industry, or interfere with the proprietor in his free and undisturbed possession and enjoyment."

ment, did not, however, indicate a dominant trend. Elsewhere, "due process" required no more than a "fairly tried action at law," and several other state courts were deciding similar cases in "precisely the opposite way and invoking the police power in justification." [87] In Thomas M. Cooley's authoritative work of 1868, one finds an even-handed treatment of the issue. In that same year the Fourteenth Amendment, denying, among other things, power in the states to deprive any person of "life, liberty or property without due process of law," added a formidable weapon to the judicial arsenal.

At first the Court seemed reluctant to exploit the Amendment's unlimited possibilities.[88] It refused, as Justice Miller said, to reach any decision that would constitute the judiciary "a perpetual censor upon all legislation of the States." [89] Four Justices, including Chief Justice Chase and headed by Field, dissented at length. Justice Field said that the issues were "of the gravest importance, not merely to the parties . . . but to the whole country." [90] He was convinced that the Fourteenth Amendment was intended "to place the common rights of American citizens under the protection of the National government." [91] Otherwise those privileges and immunities "*which of right belong to the citizens of all free governments*" would be left unprotected.[92] "That only is a free government in the American sense of the term, under which the inalienable right of every citizen to pursue his happiness is unrestrained, except by just, equal, and impartial laws." [93] Though the dissenter did not cite a single authority in support of his broad con-

[87] E. S. Corwin, *Twilight of the Supreme Court* (New Haven: Yale University Press, 1934), p. 70.

[88] 16 Wall. 36 (1873). [89] *Ibid.*, p. 78.

[90] *Ibid.*, p. 89. [91] *Ibid.*, p. 93.

[92] *Ibid.*, p. 97. [93] *Ibid.*, p. 111.

struction of "due process," [94] he denounced the Court's narrow interpretation of the amendment as reducing it to a "vain and idle enactment." [95]

The judicial hands-off position was sustained four years later in *Munn* v. *Illinois*,[96] where a statute fixing rates for grain elevators was challenged. Harking back to fifteenth-century common law principles, Chief Justice Waite reasoned that when a man devotes his property to a use in which the public has an interest, the property ceases to be private; it becomes "affected with a public interest" and hence subject to a greater degree of regulation. Upholding the statute, Chief Justice Waite took the dissenter's line in the Wynehamer case:

For our purposes, we must assume that, if a state of facts could exist that would justify such legislation, it actually did exist when the statute now under consideration was passed. . . . We know that this is a power which may be abused; but that

[94] Ernst Freund, *Standards of American Legislation* (Chicago: University of Chicago Press, 1917), pp. 203–204.

"The evidence," Solicitor General Robert H. Jackson declared, "is just the other way. During the Revolution, and largely at the instigation of the Continental Congress, at least eight of the thirteen States passed laws fixing the price of almost every commodity on the market, from butter and beans to shoes and steel. This was the atmosphere in which the fathers of the Constitution were brought up; this is the way they acted when left to their own devices. Is it likely, then, that when they adopted the fifth amendment they meant to select for outlawry that form of legislation which fixed wages or prices? And if they had no such intention, did the States which ratified the due process clause of the fourteenth amendment understand that they were renouncing the power?" (address before the Public Utilities Section of the American Bar Association, San Francisco, Calif., July 10, 1939, in *Legal Intelligencer*, July 25, 1939, p. 6.)

See, in this connection, Clinton Rossiter, *Seedtime of the Republic* (New York: Harcourt, Brace, 1953), p. 62.

[95] 16 Wall. 36, p. 96.   [96] 94 U.S. 113 (1877).

is no argument against its existence. For protection against abuses by legislatures the people must resort to the polls, not to the courts.[97]

Against this flat refusal to censor state legislation, Justice Field again strongly protested. The decision, he said, was "subversive of the rights of private property." [98] Principles of free government fix absolute limits on legislative power, and these limits could not be altered even by organic law:

There is no magic in the language, though used by a constitutional convention, which can change a private business into a public one. . . . A tailor's or a shoemaker's shop would still retain its private character, even though the assembled wisdom of the State should declare, by organic act or legislative ordinance, that such a place was a public workshop, and that the workmen were public tailors or public shoemakers. One might as well attempt to change the nature of colors, by giving them a new designation.[99]

These major judicial decisions had the effect of exposing property rights to the mercies of legislative majorities, and various forces were soon joined in a movement to expand the scope of judicial power as a safeguard. As one might have anticipated, lawyers, the natural allies of property interests, were in the forefront of the defense. Lawyers had dominated the Philadelphia Convention of 1787. They were conspicuous on the side of property in the state constitutional conventions of the 1820's. The issue of public power versus property rights was now crucial, as the Supreme Court had made it clear that economic interest must look primarily to political controls for protection. Two years after the Munn decision came down the American Bar Associ-

[97] *Ibid.*, pp. 132, 134.   [98] *Ibid.*, p. 136.
[99] *Ibid.*, p. 138.

ation was organized. By 1879 it was embarked on a persistent campaign of education designed to reverse the Court's broad conception of legislative power. In the annual addresses of the president and in the titles of various papers read, it is evident that the Association agreed with Darwin's view of the inevitability of the human struggle and that it accepted Herbert Spencer's evolutionary theories of politics. Extracts from addresses reveal such thoughts as these: "The great curse of the world is too much government"; "If trusts are a defensive weapon of property interests against the communistic trend, they are desirable"; "Monopoly is often a necessity and an advantage," and so on.[100]

In a *Princeton Review* article for March 1878, Judge Thomas M. Cooley went to the heart of the issue:

By far the larger part of all the doubtful legislation which the history of the country presents has taken place since the year 1846, when radical ideas began to be characteristic of State constitutions, and the theory that officers of every department should be made as directly as possible responsible to the people after short terms of service was accepted as a political maxim.[101]

Cooley suggested two safeguards against the rising threat of popular power. One was the Constitution, if properly construed. "If principles are not fixed and permanent, they are not constitutional." [102] The second was "higher law," "natural law." Cooley treated the "laws" of supply and demand as if they were part of the Constitution itself. The principles of free government do not support legislative

[100] Benjamin R. Twiss, *Lawyers and the Constitution* (Princeton: Princeton University Press, 1942), pp. 153, 155.

[101] Thomas M. Cooley, "Limits to State Control of Private Business," *Princeton Review* (March 1878), p. 236.

[102] *Ibid.*, p. 239.

price-fixing even if monopoly exists. "Does . . . the mere fact," he inquired, "that one owns the whole supply of any thing, whether it be of a certain kind of property or of a certain kind of services, confer upon the state the authority to interfere and limit the price he may set upon his wares or his services?" Cooley's defiant answer was that anyone giving an affirmative response "should be expected to show how the power may be harmonized with the general principles of free government." [103] Under Cooley's theory, private monopolists could thus effect regulations of individual rights in ways not open to politically responsible government.

But if these novel doctrines were to be established as the law of the land, lawyers and judges had to recapture what the Jacksonian revolution had repudiated—their exclusive responsibility for interpreting and enforcing the Constitution. Addressing the Bar Association in 1879, President Edward J. Phelps deplored the increasing number of instances in which unhallowed hands had been placed upon that sacred document. The Constitution had, he said, become "more and more a subject to be hawked about the country, debated in the newspapers, discussed from the stump, elucidated by pot house politicians, and dung-hill editors, scholars in the science of government who have never found leisure for the graces of English grammar, or the embellishments of correct spelling." [104] Exclusive interpretation of the Constitution must be regained for that "inner sanctum," that "priestly tribe"—the American Bar.

Thus when society, disrupted by technology and the

[103] *Ibid.*, pp. 267–268. Compare note 94, *supra*.
[104] American Bar Association, *Report of the Second Annual Meeting*, Saratoga Springs, N.Y., Aug. 1879 (Philadelphia: E. C. Markley, 1879), p. 190.

emergence of the corporate form of business organization, sought to safeguard individual liberty and equality of opportunity, when government, through democratic action, attempted to weave again the delicate web of community, the high priests of the law stood defiantly by their icons. For the legal profession, as for Herbert Spencer, the individual's liberty was measured solely by "the paucity of restraint which government imposes on him." Against legislation designed to regulate and control the new potentates, arose an interested clamor for unrestricted competition. Government must not interfere or undertake to regulate free enterprise. To shift from legislating for the few to legislating for the many, to transfer emphasis from the doctrine of pseudo-laissez-faire, under which industrialism flourished, to a social philosophy which took cognizance of human welfare and social justice—all this would, they said, reverse the natural currents that were sweeping the nation on to permanent prosperity. Their supreme confidence arraigned the present and arranged the future.

The Bar Association's campaign was greatly assisted in 1882 by Roscoe Conkling's famous argument in the San Mateo County case.[105] Conkling, who had been a Senate member of the Joint Congressional Committee that drafted the Fourteenth Amendment, then produced for the first time a manuscript Journal of the Committee. From this authoritative source he selected extensive quotations to show that he and his colleagues in drafting the due process clause purposefully used the word "person" as including corporations. "At the time the Fourteenth Amendment was ratified," Conkling told the Justices, "individuals and joint stock companies were appealing for congressional and

[105] *San Mateo County* v. *Southern Pacific R.R.*, 116 U.S. 138 (1885).

administrative protection against invidious and discriminating State and local taxes." [106] The due process clause, the lawyer suggested vaguely, had planted in the Constitution "a monumental truth to stand foursquare to whatever wind might blow."

Conkling's professional and political eminence was impressive, his scholarship less so. Besides his vital role in drafting the amendment for submission to both houses of Congress, he had twice refused appointment—once the Chief Justiceship—to the Supreme Court itself. Yet careful research has revealed that the constitutional lawyer sold the Court a fake bill of goods. Writing in 1938, Howard Jay Graham showed that Conkling's "conspiracy" theory of the Fourteenth Amendment was a fraud, or at least a trick unworthy of a great lawyer. Conkling himself indicated that surmise, not factual knowledge, was the basis of his theory. "Those who devised the Fourteenth Amendment may have builded better than they knew," he commented suggestively. "To some of them, the sunset of life may have given mystical lore." [107] Graham's conclusion is that Conkling "suppressed" pertinent facts and misrepresented others, that he "deliberately misquoted the Journal and even so arranged his excerpts as to give listeners a false impression of the record and of his own relation thereto." [108]

Nevertheless, Conkling's timely disclosures, along with the Bar Association's propaganda campaign and Justice Field's impassioned dissenting opinions, finally yielded a conservative revolution comparable to that of 1787. In 1887 a final element was added—change in judicial personnel.

[106] Quoted from a copy of Conkling's oral argument, possessed by Stanford University, in Howard Jay Graham, "The 'Conspiracy Theory' of the Fourteenth Amendment," *Yale Law Journal*, 47 (Jan. 1938), 371.

[107] Quoted in Graham, *op. cit.*, p. 378.   [108] *Ibid.*, p. 379.

Between 1877 and 1890 seven Justices who had participated in the early cases resigned or died. Field lived on, and in 1888 he was joined by his nephew Justice David J. Brewer and Melville W. Fuller, the latter as Chief Justice. The judicial about-face that soon resulted is the more remarkable in not being clearly foreseen. At the very time the judicial revolution was completed, one commentator, Charles C. Marshall, supplied impressive historical justification for the Court's resistance to use of the Fourteenth Amendment as a barrier against the forces unleashed by the Jacksonian revolution. A lawyer of conservative sympathies, Marshall said that the police power—the power to govern men and things—hitherto exercised by various ruling classes, belonged to the legislature. Property, previously regarded as an absolute right, was legitimately subject to its control. In language reminiscent of Locke, the lawyer wrote:

It is clear that if, according to law, all property affected by a public use or interest, is in its very nature subject to legislative control, then for the legislature to control its use is in no sense to deprive a citizen of such property contrary to the law of the land. What the citizen owns is not absolute property but a *qualified and contingent interest in property.* Control by the legislature is its necessary incident, and such control, when exercised through a statute, is in its very self "due process of law." It is equally clear, for the same reasons, that such legislative control is not the appropriation of private property to public use. When the legislature exercises such control it does not appropriate property, for up to the extent of such control there is no property.[109]

Two great questions, Marshall explained, had vexed the American people: personal liberty and property. The Dred

[109] Charles C. Marshall, "A New Constitutional Amendment," *American Law Review,* 24 (Nov.–Dec. 1890), 912–913.

Scott case opened the first, the Munn decision the second. Each left "a wide section of human rights unprotected by constitutional guaranties."

In a commercial emergency the oracles of law have been approached. Dumb for almost a century on the questions involved because no inquirer had sought the shrine they now give forth a response which startles lawyers and laymen and startles them the more they read and examine. For the first time it is appreciated that there has lain dormant for a century a vigorous principle of the Common Law, an element of Anglo-Saxon government, which in the hands of an aristocracy has often been an instrument of wrong and oppression and which may in the hands of "the people" effect a despoliation of property-owners surpassing the encroachments of the crown at the worst periods of English history.

Marshall accepted the Court's decision in the Munn case as impregnable, both historically and constitutionally. The "storm of criticism emanating from advocates of 'higher law,'" and featured in Field's dissenting opinions, was brushed summarily aside. The theory that "in the absence of constitutional prohibitions" there are barriers implicit in the spirit of our institutions or our form of government was rejected as "contrary to almost the entire weight of judicial authority and legal opinion." Marshall was, nevertheless, sorely concerned: [110]

Our boasted security in property rights falls away for the lack of a constitutional guaranty against this sovereign power thus discovered in our legislatures. It is apparent that against this whim of a temporary majority, inflamed with class-prejudice, envy or revenge, the property of no man is safe. And the danger is even greater in an age teeming with shifting theories of social reform and economic science, which seem to have

[110] *Ibid.*, pp. 930–931 *et passim.*

but one common principle—the subjection of private property to governmental control for the good—or alleged good—of the public.[111]

The Munn decision had revealed a "defect where all was supposed to be perfection." That defect, Marshall insisted, could be "properly remedied only by constitutional amendment." [112] "The possibility of retracing steps," he wrote emphatically, "of reversing or distinguishing, or of otherwise nullifying it through the courts is put quite beyond possibility." [113]

The magazine writer had completely underestimated the inventive genius of Supreme Court Justices. Seven months before his article was printed, what Marshall said had to be done by resort to the formal amending process was already accomplished by judicial decision. By vote of six to three the Justices decided in *Chicago, Milwaukee and St. Paul R.R.* v. *Minnesota*[114] that the question of the reasonableness of rates could not be left by the legislature to a state commission, but must be subject to judicial review.

In a most outspoken dissent, Justices Bradley, Gray, and Lamar charged that the Court "practically over-rules" *Munn* v. *Illinois,* and in so doing had flouted basic principles of free government.[115]

It is complained that the decisions of the board are final and without appeal. So are the decisions of the courts in matters within their jurisdiction. There must be a final tribunal somewhere for deciding every question in the world. Injustice may take place in all tribunals. All human institutions are imperfect —courts as well as commissions and legislatures. . . . It may be that our legislatures are invested with too much power,

---

[111] *Ibid.,* p. 912.　　　　[112] *Ibid.,* p. 931.
[113] *Ibid.,* p. 909.　　　　[114] 134 U.S. 418 (1890).
[115] *Ibid.,* p. 461.

open, as they are, to influences so dangerous to the interests of individuals, corporations and society. But such is the Constitution of our republican form of government; and we are bound to abide by it until it can be corrected in a legitimate way.[116]

A majority of the Court disagreed. "It is from that decision," Judge Charles M. Hough has written, "that I date the flood." [117]

The courageous battle waged by Chief Justice Waite and Justice Miller to keep the Court out of politics had been lost. Nor was this result any cause for surprise. In 1875 Justice Miller had written:

It is vain to contend with judges who have been at the bar the advocates for forty years of railroad companies, and all forms of accumulated capital, when they are called upon to decide cases where such interests are in contest. All their training, all their feelings are from the start in favor of those who need no such influence.

"I am losing interest in such matters," Miller concluded wearily. "I will do my duty but will fight no more." [118]

Just as political democracy was coming into its own, the Court, equating the laissez-faire dogma with the Constitution, protected industrial might against popular power, whether organized in trade unions or in legislative assemblies. In 1949, looking back on this development, Justice Frankfurter commented:

Adam Smith was treated as though his generalizations had been imparted to him on Sinai and not as a thinker who addressed

[116] *Ibid.*, pp. 465, 466.

[117] Charles M. Hough, "Due Process of Law—To-day," *Harvard Law Review*, 32 (Jan. 1919), 228.

[118] Quoted in Charles Fairman, *Mr. Justice Miller and the Constitution, 1862–1890* (Cambridge: Harvard University Press, 1939), pp. 373–374.

himself to the elimination of restrictions which had become fetters upon initiative and enterprise in his day. Basic human rights expressed by the constitutional conception of "liberty" were equated with theories of laissez-faire. The result was that economic views of confined validity were treated by lawyers and judges as though the framers had enshrined them in the Constitution.[119]

As if to demonstrate that they had thoroughly learned the lesson that the American Bar Association had tried to teach, Justices Henry Billings Brown and David J. Brewer interrupted their judicial labors in 1893 to deplore that "ideal state of society where neither riches nor poverty shall exist." "Rich men," Justice Brown said, "are essential even to the well-being of the poor. . . . One has but to consider for a moment the immediate consequences of the abolition of large private fortunes to appreciate the danger which lurks in any radical disturbance of the present social system." [120] Justice Brewer cited "the black flag of anarchism, flaunting destruction of property," and the "red flag of socialism, inviting a redistribution of property." "Power," the Justice noted soberly, "always chafes at but needs restraint." This is true whether the power is in the hands of a monarch or a majority. "Here there is no monarch threatening trespass upon the individual. The danger is from the multitudes— the majority, with whom is the power." Brewer spoke of the move afoot "to minimize the power of Courts" and block "judicial interference." "What, then, should be done?" "My

[119] Concurring in *A.F. of L. v. American Sash and Door Co.*, 335 U.S. 538 (1949), p. 543. Compare Justice Learned Hand's statement in "Chief Justice Stone's Conception of the Judicial Function," *Columbia Law Review*, 46 (1946), 696.

[120] "The Distribution of Property" (address to annual meeting of American Bar Association, Milwaukee, Aug. 1893), *American Bar Association Reports*, XVI, 219.

39

reply is," Brewer commented emphatically, "strengthen the judiciary."

"The argument is," the Justice went on, "that judges are not adapted by their education and training" to settle controversial social and economic issues.

But the great body of judges are as well versed in the affairs of life as any, and they who unravel all the mysteries of accounting between partners, settle the business of the largest corporations and extract all the truth from the mass of sciolistic verbiage that falls from the lips of expert witnesses in patent cases, will find no difficulty in determining what is right and wrong between employer and employees, and whether proposed rates of freight and fare are reasonable as between the public and the owners; while, as for speed, is there any thing quicker than a writ of injunction? [121]

Unless majorities in the legislatures and at the ballot box were thus restrained, Brewer foresaw "the departure from this Western continent of government of the people, by the people and for the people." Even as he urged the Court to expand the range of its authority, Justice Brewer insisted that "there is nothing in this power of the judiciary detracting in the least from the idea of government of and by the people. The courts hold neither purse nor sword. . . . They make no laws, they establish no policy, they never enter into the domain of popular action. They do not govern." [122] Their function is limited "to seeing that popular action does not trespass upon right and justice as it exists in the written constitution and natural law."

The fact remains, nevertheless, that the Court was now

[121] "The Nation's Safeguard" (address to annual meeting, N.Y. State Bar Association, Albany, Jan. 1893), *Report of N.Y. State Bar Association*, XVI, 42–43.
[122] *Ibid.*, p. 46.

in command of authority it had earlier spurned. Virtually a superlegislature, it proceeded to discharge the heavy responsibility of judging delicate matters of "right" and "wrong." Its principal measure for performing this task, "due process," was a poor instrument because it varied according to the user. Justice Iredell's scorn of natural law as a limitation on state legislative power applied equally well to due process. Since this concept provided no fixed standard, all the Court could properly say in raising it as a constitutional bar was that the legislature had passed an act that in the opinion of the judges was inconsistent with abstract principles of justice.

The "retrograde step in the rear of democracy," which Chancellor Kent had lamented as nonexistent, had been found. The "influence of property" had discovered a new way to limit and control the exercise of popular power. Legislative supremacy was not, as Locke believed, "an inconvenience incapable of a remedy." By 1890 judicial authority had been elevated, and economic-industrial oligarchy enthroned. The stage was thus set for one of the longest and most bitterly fought contests in American history—political democracy versus economic oligarchy.

⋆ II ⋆

Freedom and Economic

Oligarchy

THE period 1870–1902 exhibits Greenbackers, Grangers, Populists, Knights of Labor, Anarchists, and the largest Socialist vote ever cast in a presidential election. Though the Supreme Court's outlawing of the income tax in 1895 put a serious crimp in all plans for social betterment, silly prophecies of impending Socialist or Communist overturn were broadcast. "The mere weight of numbers," that dread spectacle that had always terrified American conservatives, was not only asserted but given forceful justification. Edward Bellamy's *Looking Backward*, Henry Demarest Lloyd's *Wealth against Commonwealth*, and Henry George's *Progress and Poverty* now became vital elements in American political thought. Writing in 1902 amid tension and conflict, a New York lawyer, William J. Ghent, considered the shape of things to come.

42

Political collectivism was not indicated as "the next status of society." Other forces were "energetically at work" producing "something in the nature of a Benevolent Feudalism." There would be "morganization of industry," concentration of vast power in the hands of a few men, and great increase in the number of economically dependent classes. "The views and prejudices of men of great wealth" would, Ghent predicted, infiltrate every segment of society —church, school, and press—and to those would be added two even more important classes—the makers and interpreters of the law.[1]

Six years later, what Ghent described as a possibility President Arthur Twining Hadley of Yale proclaimed as embedded in the Constitution itself. The Constitution of the United States, Hadley explained, is a "set of limitations on the political power of the majority in favor of the political power of the property owner." The voter could elect what officers he pleased, but their power was limited by certain rights "confided by the Constitution to the property holders." "Democracy was complete so far as it went, but constitutionally it was bound to stop short of *social democracy*."[2]

Other observers perceived forces at work that made them much less optimistic than Ghent and Hadley. Stating the central issue of the era as that of conflict between "our political liberty and our industrial absolutism," Louis D. Brandeis agreed that the large corporations might develop into "a benevolent absolutism" but it would be "absolutism

[1] W. J. Ghent, "Benevolent Feudalism," *Independent*, 54 (April 3, 1902), 781–782.

[2] Arthur Twining Hadley, "The Constitutional Position of Property in America," *Independent*, 64 (April 16, 1908), 838. (Emphasis in original.)

all the same." [3] Thorstein Veblen noted how the "gradual change of the economic situation had rendered farcical "unmitigated and inalienable freedom of contract." This constitutional dogma so strongly insisted upon by lawyers and judges in cases involving social legislation, had, Veblen declared, begun "to grow obsolete from about the time when it was fairly installed." [4] And in 1905, when Justice Holmes's colleagues on the Supreme Court invoked "liberty of contract" as limiting the power of a state legislature to regulate hours of labor in a bakery, Holmes accused them of writing the doctrines of Herbert Spencer into our fundamental law.[5] With the management of community affairs firmly in the hands of the businessman, what was the prospect for freedom?

Brooks Adams' answer was definitive. The businessman, he said, lacked the moral and administrative capacity to discharge social responsibility. "He might, had he so chosen, have evolved a system of governmental railway regulation," Adams remarked in 1913, "and have administered the system personally, or by his own agents." But Adams denied that he could ever be

brought to see the advantage to himself of rational concession so as to obtain a resultant of forces. He resisted all restraint, especially national restraint, convinced by experience that his one weapon—money—was more effective in obtaining what he wanted in state legislatures than in Congress. Thus, of necessity, he precipitates a conflict, instead of establishing an adjust-

[3] L. D. Brandeis, Testimony before the U.S. Commission on Industrial Relations, Jan. 23, 1915, *Sen. Doc.*, 64th Cong. 1st Sess., XXVI, 7659.

[4] T. Veblen, *The Theory of Business Enterprise* (New York: Scribner's, 1904), p. 274.

[5] *Lochner* v. *New York*, 198 U.S. 45 (1905), p. 75.

ment. He is, therefore, in essence, a revolutionist without being aware of it.[6]

The decade of the 1920's proved the solidity of these dicta. Our stress on material success, our "settled habit of rating the means of livelihood and the amenities of life in pecuniary terms," [7] manifested itself conspicuously at both national and international levels. After Wilson broke down trying to rally America to the League of Nations, the scope of our national and international outlook contracted perilously. Dollar diplomacy ploughed under the ex-President's world-wide dream as our flag followed the dollar into Haiti, Guatemala, and Nicaragua. Both within and without the Western Hemisphere, America had to be left to its own affairs. The United States was nevertheless entangled in world economics and power politics. Futile squabbles with European allies and enemies over war debts, tariffs, loans, and reparations dragged along. Secretary of State Charles Evans Hughes ignored the existence of Soviet Russia, as well as any communications from the League, but astounded the world by pushing through much of his program for disarmament at the Washington Naval Conference of 1922. Another flash of even emptier idealism in 1928 broadcast the Kellogg-Briand Pact, forswearing and outlawing war as an instrument of national policy. A cartoonist of the day depicted the "typical" American family curtly addressing Mars, the god of war, "You're fired." [8] America wanted peace, and its nominal leaders thought that that precious condition, like prosperity, could be attained by wishing for it.

[6] Brooks Adams, *The Theory of Revolutions* (New York: Macmillan, 1913), p. 210.

[7] Veblen, *op. cit.*, p. 268.

[8] Cover design, *Literary Digest*, 71 (Nov. 12, 1921).

In domestic affairs the people were restless, confused, misled—their nominal leaders smug and quiescent. After the 1920 presidential election, in the glow of victory, the guardians of "normalcy" released from Leavenworth federal prison some 263 conscientious objectors incarcerated by the Attorney General. Burleson, Wilson's Postmaster-General, had denied second-class mailing privileges to allegedly Socialist newspapers; Harding's Postmaster-General and political strategist, Will H. Hays, restored them. Hysterical fear of the "red menace" quieted down by 1925 after several rampant years, but economic and political hostility to "radicals" continued. Milwaukee's Socialist Congressman, though elected and re-elected, was never admitted to the House of Representatives.[9] In 1927 Sacco and Vanzetti, foreign born and radical, were executed for murder in Massachusetts on flimsy evidence and by means of legal technicalities accepted by a notoriously prejudiced judge. Twenty-four states enacted criminal-syndicalism or criminal-anarchy laws. The resurrected Ku-Klux Klan anticipated Hitler's religious bigotry, race hate, color and other discriminations and swept up in the southeastern and midwestern states a peak of 6,000,000 members.[10] Synthetic barbarism was organizing toward political power. As De Tocqueville observed of the Switzerland of 1830, there seemed to be more liberty in the laws than in the spirit of the people.

In the Coolidge-Hoover era, and under the dominant philosophy of big business, man's immediate goal was "a full belly and a warm hut." Spurning European culture as effete, 100 per cent Americans were admired yawning in their opera boxes at the Metropolitan. They took "more

[9] Robert K. Murray, *Red Scare: A Study in National Hysteria, 1919–1920* (Minneapolis: University of Minneapolis Press, 1955), pp. 226–230.

[10] S. E. Morison and H. S. Commager, *The Growth of the American Republic*, 4th ed. (New York: Oxford, 1950), II, 556.

pride in the Twentieth Century train than in the annual anthology of American poetry." [11] When Sinclair Lewis defined "babbitry" as the ambition to be "rich, fat, arrogant and superior," business leaders acknowledged the portrait and rushed to acclaim its perfection.[12] God and babbitry had made the U.S.A. "the richest nation in history." [13] This "must have been . . . the intent of the Creator of all things," a prosperity spokesman explained, "in implanting deep in human nature the mighty motive of selfishness, and the constructive assertion of the right of private-property." [14] Even writers, poets, and painters were driven to artistic creation, it was said, by the prospect of material gain. "They had bills to pay and they were moved by the identical economic urge that prompts a businessman to get out of bed in the morning, however cold his room may be." [15] "I have come to the conclusion," a *Nation's Business* author wrote in 1925, "that industry is the fundamental basis of civilization." [16]

And yet our social and political prospects were not unclouded. Despite the screen of stock market propaganda, despite all fairy tales of prosperity, a sense of gnawing uneasiness remained. Impoverishment and wretchedness continued to darken the glow around the plump picture of

[11] William Feather, "A Fourth of July Speech—New Style," *Nation's Business*, 14 (July 1926), 13.

[12] "Dare to Be a Babbitt!" (editorial), *Nation's Business*, 13 (June 1925), 40.

[13] Glen Buck, "The American Ascendency," *Nation's Business*, 15 (March 1927), 16.

[14] Charles N. Fay, *Business in Politics* (Cambridge, Mass.: Cosmos Press, 1926), pp. 111–112. For more of the same, see Feather, "Fourth of July Speech," *op. cit.*

[15] William Feather, "What I've Been Reading," *Nation's Business*, 19 (Feb. 1930), 158.

[16] A. C. Bedford, "What Is a Captain of Industry?" *Nation's Business*, 13 (Nov. 1925), 26.

plenty painted by persons possessing it. "There has been a tendency," Brookings Institute economists cautiously observed, "at least during the last decade or so, for the inequality in the distribution of income to be accentuated." [17] In the golden year 1929 practically 60 per cent of American families were below the minimum subsistence level.[18] When the decade opened, the industrial horizon was darkened by mob outbreaks. Radicalism was held to pervade the ranks of organized labor; false doctrines were said to run wild in college and university faculties. "One great issue confronts the world today," an *American Industries* editorial declared in January 1920.

Strike after strike warns us of a tremendous industrial upheaval threatening the world. When Russia began it, we thought we were safe, but now we are not so sure. Capital and labor are engaged in a great struggle, and tangles of red tape on the one hand and stout "Red" threads on the other tie the whole world together, not for brotherhood, but for strife.[19]

That the innumerable red hunts netted next to no game merely made our conservative Jeremiahs more frantically uneasy. Popular power was still considered hostile to property and industry. Charles N. Fay told the business community with resignation:

Wage-workers will usually constitute the majority of voters in free, civilized countries like ours, . . . and they will be employed by you because they have not initiative enough to be employers themselves. So too, in politics, they will be voters, steered by politicians, because they have not initiative, or time,

[17] Quoted in Frederick Lewis Allen, *The Big Change* (New York: Harper, 1952), p. 144.

[18] *Ibid.*

[19] "An Antidote to Bolshevism" (editorial), *American Industries*, 20 (Jan. 1920), p. 8.

or brains enough to study policies, and make up their minds for themselves, how to vote.[20]

Self-chosen Messiahs suggested that the masses could be prevented from following after political demagogues only if their waking hours were fully used in keeping body and soul together. "Idle hours breed mischief." [21] Therefore emphasis had to be put upon "work—more work and better work, instead of upon leisure." [22] National Association of Manufacturers' President John E. Edgerton reported, October, 1929:

They have for the most part been so busy at their jobs that they have not had time to saturate themselves with false theories of economics, social reform, and of life. They have been protected in their natural growth by absence of excessive leisure and have been fortunate not only in their American-made opportunities to work, but in the necessities which have compelled its reasonable indulgence. . . . Nothing breeds radicalism more quickly than unhappiness, unless it is leisure. . . . As long as people are kept profitably employed, there is little danger from radicalism.[23]

Samuel Vauclain of the Baldwin Locomotive Works gave this idea a sardonic twist, suggesting that the automobile had saved the United States from revolution by giving industrial workers "a glorified rattle" to absorb spare time. "A man who keeps at work to support a car," *Nation's*

[20] Fay, *op. cit.*, p. 164.

[21] J. C. Martien, "The Five-Day Week," *Pocket Bulletin* (official Publication of the National Association of Manufacturers), 27 (Oct. 1926), 3.

[22] J. E. Edgerton, "Industry Has Advanced Further than Religion," *Pocket Bulletin*, 27 (April 1927), 4.

[23] Annual Address of the President, *Proceedings, National Association of Manufacturers* (1929), p. 23.

49

Business rejoiced, "will have little time to give revolutionary impulses to his mental flywheel." [24] Perhaps the automobile had forestalled political revolution. The progressive upsurge which harried corporations in legislative halls and fought them in the courts before 1915 was now dormant. The people were hardly aware of politics at all as they swung pleasureably from one fad to the next. Politics was, in any event, but a frail framework for the economic organization of society.

A yen for politics, Russell H. Conwell had said in his lecture marathon, *Acres of Diamonds,* is *"prima facie* evidence of littleness." [25] This test still held, but the egregious wastes of politics were on the point of being eliminated. "Are we approaching a millennium in which visible government will not be necessary," the editor of *American Industries* mused in May 1925, "and in which the job of running the world will slip away from obstructive politicians and be taken over by men trained in the shop?" [26] "What we need," said Henry Ford, the twentieth-century Hercules of rugged enterprise, "is a strong man in this country to send all these politicians packing."

Production and consumption, harmonized by "efficiency" and governed by inexorable natural laws—these only were worthy of man's attention. This cosmogony had developed a special ideology of its own, the new Koran of profits. There must be no tinkering therewith or with the automatism of unending progress. "Certain fundamental social and economic laws," future Supreme Court Justice George Sutherland declared in an address of 1921, are "beyond the

[24] *Nation's Business,* 14 (March 1926), 99–100.
[25] R. H. Conwell, *Acres of Diamonds* (New York: Harper, 1915), p. 50.
[26] *American Industries,* 25 (May 1925), 21.

right of official control." [27] "Legislation won't prevent it," whatever "it" was, became axiomatic. For those who believed otherwise, rhymed ridicule provided an answer:

> D is for Demagogue
> Who cures every ill
> By use of his
> Patented Law-making Pill.[28]

Content with government which did not govern, the corporation pundits applauded heartily when President Harding in 1921 struck the first keynote of his administration: "We want a period in America with less government in business and more business in government." [29] "Every principle and device," the President said, "which promotes efficiency in private business should be adapted and applied in government affairs." [30]

The central institutions of society were economic. Government aid to business was therefore an act of statesmanship because in the long run, society as a whole would benefit. Government aid to the propertyless masses was but a vain attempt to bring natural economic forces into conformity with the "mere force of numbers." So while industrial leaders rejected regulation and control, they demanded more and higher tariff, and other gratuities, and sought government "interference" to keep down interlopers, especially organized labor. "American business," declared Chamber

[27] Address of George Sutherland, Jan. 21, 1921, before the New York State Bar Association, *Proceedings of the New York State Bar Association*, XLIV, 265.

[28] "The Businessman's Primer," *Nation's Business*, 14 (Jan. 1926), 38.

[29] Quoted in Henry F. Pringle, *The Life and Times of William Howard Taft* (New York: Farrar and Rinehart, 1939), II, 966.

[30] Quoted from an address in *Literary Digest*, 69 (June 4, 1921), 13.

of Commerce President John W. O'Leary, "has learned that government is a valuable partner but a poor master." [31] Business got high tariff protection at home, while abroad economic interests were furthered by the State Department and guarded by Marines; aviation and shipping were sustained by subsidies. Secretary of the Treasury Andrew Mellon, one of the richest men in the world, steadily reduced income taxes, especially in the higher brackets. In 1921, as the wheels of industry were turning more slowly, leaders of industry were quick to see why. "All authorities and members of all parties, groups and schools of thought agree," the New York *Journal of Commerce* asserted, that "internal revenue duties . . . are a chief cause of business depression and disturbance and that they must be revised." [32]

The bounties and other protection industrial magnates required for themselves they righteously denied to labor and agriculture. When farmers, trapped in postwar depression by Hoover's withdrawal of government support for crop prices, tried to get legislative relief, *Iron Age* accused them of "unsporting instinct" in "grumbling over the consequences of the mismanagement of their business of the corngrower." [33] Spokesmen for business regarded organized labor with tyrannous hostility. "The existence and conduct of labor unions, in this country," United States Steel's Judge Elbert H. Gary commented, "are inimical to the best interests of the employees, the employers, and the general public." [34] "My experience is," Samuel Insull com-

[31] *Nation's Business*, 14 (March 1926), 19.

[32] Quoted in *Literary Digest*, 69 (April 2, 1921), 7.

[33] Quoted in *Nation's Business*, 14 (March 1926), 98.

[34] *Literary Digest*, 69 (May 7, 1921), 8. "Labor," S. B. Fay declared, "is organized to hold up the public—not merely an employer here and there—and is as pitiless of public suffering as it is defiant of private right" (*Business in Politics*, p. 118; quoted in James W. Prothro, *The Dollar Decade* [Baton Rouge: Louisiana State Uni-

mented tersely, "that the greatest aid in the efficiency of labor is a long line of men waiting at the gate." [35]

Organization was taboo for labor but excellent and inevitable for industrial management. Under the rubric of "business ethics," trade associations and price agreements flourished, "fair trade" laws were promoted by anxious retailers and government agencies. The Department of Commerce, under Secretary Hoover, encouraged trade associations both as a means of bringing order in business and as an instrument for co-operation between industry and government. Scores of special agents of the Department worked abroad procuring profitable and private information for big business and special interests. Twelve hundred and sixty-eight combinations in manufacturing and mining, involving the merger of four thousand businesses and the disappearance of six thousand, took place in less than ten years. International cartels expanded at a rate before unknown. Though much of this could perhaps be explained and justified in terms of industrial self-government, it did not necessarily mean, as the course of events suggested, that the Sherman Act had outlived its usefulness. "After the middle of the decade," George Soule writes, "court action was seldom resorted to. Of seventy-five antitrust suits started in the fiscal years 1925–1929, thirty-seven were settled by consent decrees, thirteen were ended by pleas of guilty or *nolo contendere*, and five were dropped." [36] "The

---

versity Press, 1955], p. 150). Fay asserted that "the time has come to suppress by law all wholesale organization of labor, for the purpose of fixing wages, or controlling, limiting or preventing work, production or transportation" (*op. cit.*, p. 42; quoted in Prothro, *op. cit.*, p. 152).

[35] John Dos Passos, *U.S.A., The Big Money* (New York: Random House, 1930), p. 527.

[36] George Soule, *Prosperity Decade* (New York: Rinehart, 1947), p. 134.

parties," Walton Hamilton observed, "meet behind closed doors; the negotiations leave no public record; groups who do not participate are left in the dark." [37] Corporate management apparently endorsed these procedures as the commendable effort of business to "cure its own abuses,"— "true self-government," Herbert Hoover called it.[38]

Early in the decade Secretary of Commerce Hoover was heavily publicized as the incarnation of prosperity, the symbol of efficiency, the exponent of economic progress. In all these various aspects he was revered as striking the dominant note of American life, as fulfilling its ideals and interests. He *was* Success itself—a self-made millionaire, a great administrator; he was a humanitarian—he had fed the world's starving; he was superintendent, engineer, promoter and executive manager—the high priest of multi-templed efficiency. Though former President Taft and President Coolidge suspected his universality and distrusted his "progressivism," Hoover was generally considered eminently safe and sane, the leader of the forces of efficiency and profit in the basic war on waste. In the Department of Commerce he at once established a "Committee on the Elimination of Waste in Industry." "We shall find out why 3,000,000 idle men are walking the streets," the *Literary Digest* promptly predicted. "Under Mr. Hoover the engineer is becoming an enormously powerful force for constructive and disinterested public service. Mr. Hoover's labors in this field have only just begun." [39]

By 1928 industrial skill and organization had developed

[37] Walton Hamilton, *Antitrust in Action* (Temporary National Economic Committee, Monograph No. 16, 1940), p. 90; quoted in Soule, *op. cit.,* p. 134.

[38] *New York Times,* Aug. 12, 1928, p. 3, col. 4.

[39] Quoted from *Engineering and Mining Journal* in *Literary Digest,* 69 (April 2, 1921), 23.

so as to fix prosperity as the permanent condition of American society. "We have not yet reached the goal," President-elect Hoover announced, "but, given the chance to go forward with the policies of the last eight years, and we shall soon, with the help of God, be in sight of the day when poverty will be banished from this nation." [40] When economic depression in 1929 blighted this prospect, Hoover's method and goal remained unchanged:

His constant purpose was to rehabilitate the business community so that it might resume control of the nation and preside over a new era of prosperity. . . . In using government to save industry and save banks, while steadfastly denying its right to help people, he sincerely believed that he followed the only course true to the American experience. There was to his mind only one choice: between business rule and bureaucratic tyranny. Only the former was consistent with liberty. [41]

Government itself was identified as "the only tyranny the citizenship of this republic need fear." [42]

Throughout the 1920's, industrial leaders found special satisfaction and encouragement in the political complexion of the national administration. "God is still in His Heaven," N.A.M. President Edgerton commented cheerfully after Harding's death in 1923, "and there is in the White House a

[40] *New York Times*, Aug. 12, 1928, p. 3, col. 4.

[41] Gordon Harrison, *Road to the Right* (New York: Morrow, 1954), p. 275.

[42] "The security of society," Federal District Court Justice Van Orsdel wrote in 1922, "depends upon the extent of the protection afforded the individual citizen under the Constitution against the demands and incursions of the government. The only tyranny the citizenship of this republic need fear is from the government itself. The character and value of government is measured by the security which surrounds the individual in the use and enjoyment of his property" (Justice Van Orsdel in *Children's Hospital* v. *Adkins*, 284 Fed. 613 [Nov. 6, 1922], p. 622).

man whose essential qualities of mind and soul, and whose unswerving attachment to the fundamentals of free government are going to be demanded by an awaking people in the next President of the United States." [43] Edgerton was a good reporter. Coolidge was elected President in 1924. The people demanded a leaderless nation,[44] and they got exactly what they asked for. In succession Harding, Coolidge, and Hoover occupied the White House as spectators, while active business leaders strove to mold the country to their desired pattern. The *Baltimore Sun* had editorialized after the 1920 presidential election: "Personally, we prefer the human Harding to the highbrow Wilson in our presidential chair. Harding, like us, is 'just folks,' and so is his wife." [45] At first the former Ohio journalist, Governor and Senator had felt tremors of inadequacy, but he was finally persuaded that "what the party and the country needed was not a big man—the time for that was past—but a reasonable, careful, common-sense citizen whom the ordinary man would understand as being one of his own kind." [46] Coolidge, who followed the unhappy Harding, "made laissez-faire seem a plan for dynamic action." [47] The philosophy of his regime was equally simple: "The business of America is business." No need for government to do anything. After eight years of Republican rule, the party's 1928 standard

[43] J. E. Edgerton, Annual Address, *Proceedings of the 29th Annual Convention of the National Association of Manufacturers* (1924), p. 118.

[44] William Allen White, *Masks in a Pageant* (New York: Macmillan, 1928), p. 410. See also Irving Stone's chapter, "Calvin Coolidge: A Study in Inertia," in Isabel Leighton, ed., *The Aspirin Age* (New York: Simon and Schuster, 1949), pp. 130–151.

[45] *Baltimore Sun*, March 11, 1921.

[46] Samuel Hopkins Adams, *Incredible Era* (Boston: Houghton Mifflin, 1939), p. 122.

[47] Leighton, ed., *op. cit.*, p. 130.

bearer, Herbert Hoover, counted the nation's blessings statistically—as things acquired—"9,000,000 more homes with electricity . . . 6,000,000 more telephones, 7,000,000 radio sets, and the service of an additional 14,000,000 automobiles." [48] The business of America was business and so remained throughout the decade. [49]

The spirit of the 1920's found its most marked manifestation in "the cramped mind of the clever lawyer, for whom intellectual dignity and freedom had been forbidden by the interests which he served." [50] In his 1924 report Dean Harlan Fiske Stone of the Columbia Law School, himself a devout Republican and later on a Coolidge appointee, deplored the "tendency to make isolated studies of various legal devices without reference to the more significant social functions which they [the lawyers] serve." Dean Stone advocated the study of law as involving "a method of social and economic control," requiring not only "good mental discipline," but also a "thorough-going knowledge of the social functions with which the law deals." [51] Cloistered after 1925 in the nation's highest court, he could not express himself so freely, but privately he voiced a harsh judgment of the American bar.

In declining to express his views for publication, he wrote a magazine editor:

I have no hesitation in saying to you that I think the legal profession, as a whole, presents a very sad spectacle. I fear that it has become so legalized and commercialized in its higher strata

[48] Herbert Hoover, accepting the GOP nomination, *New York Times*, Aug. 12, 1928, p. 2.

[49] Soule, *op. cit.*, pp. 131–132.

[50] Edmund Wilson, *I Thought of Daisy* (New York: Scribner, 1929), p. 61.

[51] *Annual Reports of Columbia University*, 24th series (Columbia University Bulletin of Information, No. 43, July 26, 1924), pp. 51–52.

and has so little professional and public spirit throughout that it is lagging behind the other professions. You rarely find their services enlisted in any case which does not involve substantial professional remuneration and almost never on the unpopular side of a case involving human rights and personal liberty. Sometimes I feel that I would like to be free from the restraints of public position just long enough to say a few very disagreeable, but nonetheless true things about the present condition of our bar.[52]

Within the Supreme Court of the United States a pliant acquiescence in the "natural" scheme of things—that profitable pattern—ordained by business and its lawyer adjuncts for their own benefit, was the order of the day. Nor was this result accidental. William Howard Taft had often gloried in having been able, as President, to appoint six men to the Supreme Bench in four years, the happy consequence being that President Wilson, in twice the time, could appoint only three. In the 1920 presidential campaign composition of the Supreme Court thus became a crucial issue. Taft criticized Wilson severely for his "subservience to labor-union domination," for his appointment of "many persons of socialistic tendency." The former President deplored Wilson's "latitudinarian construction of the constitution," as tending "to weaken the protection it should afford against socialistic raids upon property rights." In Taft's opinion, two of President Wilson's appointees, Louis D. Brandeis and John H. Clarke (he was apparently satisfied with Justice McReynolds), represented "a new school of constitutional construction, which, if allowed to prevail, will greatly impair our own fundamental law." As four of the incumbent Justices were beyond the retiring age of

[52] Harlan F. Stone to Frederick L. Allen, Oct. 5, 1926. On Dec. 3, 1926, Stone expressed these same sentiments in a letter to President Nicholas Murray Butler of Columbia University.

seventy, and as it seemed not unlikely that the next President, like Taft himself, would use the appointing power to further his own political views, there was "no greater domestic issue [in the 1920 election] than the maintenance of the Supreme Court as the bulwark to enforce the guaranty that no man shall be deprived of his property without due process of law." [53]

As Taft had foreseen, the Court's reconstitution followed on the heels of Harding's election. By 1923 four of the nine Justices—Sutherland, Butler, Sanford, and Taft himself as Chief Justice—had been appointed by the Republican President. With Van Devanter, McReynolds, and the infirm McKenna (replaced in March 1925 by Attorney General Stone) these four new judges heightened the rigidities of constitutional interpretation. The genial Chief Justice described by his biographer as "conservative, if not reactionary," [54] thus won his ambition to preside over a court that with three exceptions, Holmes, Brandeis, and Stone, could be counted on to go down the line for big business. Soon after his appointment the Chief Justice announced at a conference of the Justices that he "had been appointed to reverse a few decisions," and with his famous chuckle, "I looked right at old man Holmes when I said it." [55]

The groundwork had already been laid. A generation earlier the "rule of reason" had tamed the Sherman Anti-Trust Act, but the act unquestionably applied to labor unions. A statute intended to be a sword against monopoly had been thus converted into a shield to thwart public regulation and a weapon for industry to wield in its war on organized labor. Exercising the power of a superlegisla-

[53] W. H. Taft, "Mr. Wilson and the Campaign," *Yale Review* (new series), 10 (Oct. 1920), 19–20.

[54] Pringle, *op. cit.*, II, 967.

[55] Quoted by Judge George M. Bourguin, dissenting in *Investors Syndicate* v. *Porter*, 52 F. (2d), 189 at 196 (1931).

ture over both nation and states, the judiciary achieved unprecedented pre-eminence. Up to 1925 the Court had set aside only fifty-three congressional acts as unconstitutional. In the 1920's it handed down twelve, or nearly one-fourth as many of these adverse rulings. Little wonder that in the 1924 presidential campaign Robert M. LaFollette, a life-long Republican and Progressive presidential candidate, could, by making an issue of the judicial veto over congressional legislation, attract four and a half million votes. The public, like former President Taft, was beginning to realize that the permissible scope of social and economic experimentation depended not upon the Constitution, but entirely "upon the Court's own discretion, and on nothing else." [56]

Under Taft's captaincy the Court speedily erected new barriers to protect the rights of property. Constitutional controversy was then especially rife over the common law doctrine that a business to be within the scope of government control must be "affected with a public interest." Chief Justice Waite had introduced this concept into our jurisprudence to validate government regulation of economic affairs. The same concept in Chief Justice Taft's hands was used to restrict power. "Freedom is the general rule, and restraint the exception," he said. A "mere declaration by a legislature that a business is affected with a public interest is not conclusive." It is "always a subject of judicial inquiry." [57] Justice Sutherland, who had been Harding's front-porch adviser during the 1920 presidential campaign, raised still another bar against the power to govern, enforc-

[56] E. S. Corwin, *The Constitution and What It Means Today* (Princeton: Princeton University Press, 1930), p. 125.
[57] *Wolff Packing Co. v. Ct. of Industrial Relations*, 262 U.S. 522 (1923), pp. 534, 536.

ing that differentiation between price-fixing and other aspects of the contractual relation adumbrated by Justice Field. Prices and wages, Sutherland argued, are the very "heart of the contract" and therefore relatively free from government control and regulation.[58]

While "liberty of contract" and other power-paralyzing formulas continued to flourish, effective limitations on state (and congressional) authority were also discovered in the commerce clause. When Pennsylvania attempted to protect immigrants from the frauds of unscrupulous steamship agents, the Supreme Court struck down the licensing statute as a "direct" state interference with foreign commerce. In dissent, Justice Stone queried this judicially created formula. The phrase "direct and indirect," like "business affected with a public interest," was, he said, "too mechanical, too uncertain in its application, and too remote from actualities, to be of value." "We are," he declared, "doing little more than using labels to describe a result rather than any trustworthy formula by which it is reached." [59]

What lay back of this growing obtuseness to government regulation and control, this remarkable expansion of judicial power? Justice Holmes, casting about for an answer, explained: "We fear to grant power and are unwilling to recognize it when it exists." Citing "police power" as an example of the Court's addiction to catch phrases, "to cover and . . . to apologize for the general power of the legislature to make a part of the community uncomfortable by a change," Holmes continued:

I do not believe in such apologies. I think the proper course is to recognize that a state legislature can do whatever it sees fit to do unless it is restrained by some express prohibition in the

[58] *Adkins* v. *Children's Hospital*, 261 U.S. 525 (1923), p. 554.
[59] *Di Santo* v. *Pa.*, 273 U.S. 34 (1927), p. 44.

61

Constitution of the United States or of the State, and that Courts should be careful not to extend such prohibitions beyond their obvious meaning by reading into them conceptions of public policy that the particular Court may happen to entertain.[60]

Arthur Twining Hadley's proposition of 1908 was now fully demonstrated. The fundamental division of powers was, as he said, between the "voters on the one hand and the property owners on the other . . . with the Judiciary as arbiter between them." [61] Under Taft's leadership the Court was no longer simply "one of three equal departments among which the powers of government were distributed." Simeon Baldwin spoke of it as "invested with acknowledged and *supreme* authority." Now "the whole conservative and property philosophy became oriented around 'judicial supremacy.' " [62] This pre-eminence was not, however, unchallenged, and when, in 1929, it became quite evident that he would not be able to fill out the decade, Chief Justice Taft urged like-minded colleagues to hang on at all cost:

I am older and slower and less acute and more confused. However, as long as things continue as they are, and I am able to answer in my place, I must stay on the Court in order to prevent the Bolsheviki from getting control . . . the only hope we have of keeping a consistent declaration of constitutional law is for us to live as long as we can. . . . The truth is that Hoover is a Progressive just as Stone is, and just as Brandeis is and just as Holmes is.[63]

[60] *Tyson* v. *Banton*, 273 U.S. 418 (1927), p. 446.
[61] Hadley, *op. cit.*, p. 838.
[62] Robert H. Jackson, *The Struggle for Judicial Supremacy: A Study of a Crisis in American Power Politics* (New York: Knopf, 1941), p. 72.
[63] Pringle, *op. cit.*, II, 967.

With Van and Mac and Sutherland and you [Justice Butler] and Sanford, there will be five to steady the boat. . . . We must not give up at once.[64]

Taft had accurately appraised the situation. On the crucial issue of the power to govern, the Justices stood six to three. A few well-placed deaths might enable President Hoover,[65] or some other Bolsheviki-oriented successor, to upset the balance disastrously. This opportunity came to Hoover in 1930 with the deaths of Justice Edward T. Sanford and Chief Justice Taft—both from the conservative wing. Then, for the first time in our history, a small group of Senate insurgents, flouting the official theory that judges exercise only judgment and not will, made it clear that personal preference does in fact affect judicial decisions.

This unprecedented display of insurgency began early February 1930, with President Hoover's appointment of Charles Evans Hughes as Chief Justice. A few weeks later, the Senate insurgents successfully protested the President's nomination of Judge John J. Parker as Associate Justice. These appointments, coinciding with economic depression and endemic unemployment, poured new freshets into the swelling flood of reform. While the ill-fated President peered in vain for the corner around which, he said, prosperity was lurking, the Seventy-first Congress mirrored

[64] W. H. Taft to Pierce Butler, Sept. 14, 1929; in Pringle, *op. cit.*, II, 1044.

[65] The source of Taft's fear appears to be Hoover's little book, *American Individualism*, published in 1922 (New York: Doubleday). Equal opportunity, Hoover noted, was threatened at the turn of the century "with a form of autocracy of economic power" (p. 53). "Individualism," he said, "cannot be maintained as the foundation of a society if it looks to only legalistic justice based upon contracts, property, and political equality" (p. 10). This smacked of Wilson's New Freedom, which Taft equated with bolshevism.

63

the public's restless temper and itch for a change. Both Republican insurgents and Democratic liberals were in revolt against the stale sham of normalcy. Upholding its basic tenets was a narrow majority of Supreme Court Justices.

On the surface of things the President's nomination of Mr. Hughes seemed admirable. An eminent lawyer and man of unquestioned integrity, Hughes, as Associate Justice, 1910-1916, had demonstrated qualities of judicial statesmanship. As Secretary of State, he had given dignity, even distinction, to Harding's shabby administration. Yet the nominee himself had been strangely apprehensive when the President broached the appointment. "I don't want a fight over the nomination," he told the President nervously. "If you are convinced that the nomination will be confirmed by the Senate without a scrap, I will accept it. But I don't want any trouble about it." [66] Hoover gave the former Associate Justice every assurance that there would be no trouble, and it looked at first as though the President might be right. Senator George Norris, insurgent Republican and chairman of the Senate Judiciary Committee, promptly told reporters that "favorable action would be taken at the regular meeting of the committee, to be held next Monday." [67] But, oddly enough, the Committee recommended confirmation by a split vote of ten to two, Senator Norris himself being one of the dissenters.

Norris opposed Hughes's confirmation on two grounds: The Senator questioned the propriety of the former Justice's return to the bench after resigning in 1916 to run for the presidency; second, and more importantly, he believed "we

[66] Merlo J. Pusey, *Charles Evans Hughes* (New York: Macmillan, 1951), II, 652.

[67] *New York Times*, Feb. 5, 1930, p. 2, col. 5.

have reached a time in our history when the power and influence of monopoly and organized wealth are reaching into every governmental activity." "Perhaps," the Senator explained, "it is not far amiss to say that no man in public life so exemplifies the influence of powerful combinations in the political and financial world as does Mr. Hughes." [68]

Hughes's confirmation, 52 to 26, with 18 not voting, was almost anticlimatic. But the senatorial inquisition was not finished. To fill the vacancy created by the death of Justice Sanford, President Hoover nominated John J. (known in labor circles as "Yellow Dog") Parker, North Carolina Circuit Court Judge. Though a reputable jurist and an honorable man, Parker proved an easy mark. In 1920 he had said that "the negro as a class does not desire to enter politics." [69] In strict accord with the detested Hitchman precedent,[70] he had upheld the yellow dog contract. For a majority of the Senators this was enough to show that Judge Parker was "obviously incapable of viewing with sympathy the aspirations of those who are aiming for a higher and better place in the world." [71] On May 7 the vote stood 41 to 39 against Parker's confirmation.

Why did the Senators, knowing that Hughes's confirmation was a foregone conclusion, wage this hopeless battle? The insurgents merely wished, as Senator Dill of New Jersey explained,

to place in the Record . . . a warning, . . . to call the attention of the people of this country to the fact that if they would free themselves and have justice at the hands of their Government they must reach the Supreme Court of the United States by putting men on that bench who hold economic theories

[68] *Cong. Rec.*, LXXII, 3373 (1930).   [69] *Ibid.*, p. 8338.
[70] *Hitchman Coal & Coke Co.* v. *Mitchell*, 245 U.S. 229 (1917).
[71] Senator Robert F. Wagner, *Cong. Rec.*, LXXII, 8037.

which are fair and just to all, and not in the interest of the privileged few.[72]

"We all realized from the very beginning that we had no hope of victory," Senator Norris admitted. "Yet we feel justified in having taken up the time of the Senate, . . . to call to the attention of all our liberty-loving citizens the terrible condition that confronts us." The insurgents had made this fight in "a conscientious belief that . . . profit will come perhaps even to the Supreme Court if they will read the debates of the Senate, and if the majority members of that court will even read the dissenting opinions of their brethren, Brandeis, Holmes, and Stone." [73]

This didactic tone makes these debates significant as a prelude to the more dramatic 1936 impasse between the Court and Congress. The senatorial assault was a kind of rehearsal for President Roosevelt's attack of 1937. In 1930, as in 1937, the Court, not Hughes and Parker, was the Senators' real target. "The attack centered on the Court itself." [74] By calling attention to its discretionary authority, the Senators hoped to destroy the "hush-hush" that had heretofore shielded that institution from public scrutiny.[75] The judiciary was under fire because it had, over vigorous minority dissent, moved into "the larger orbit of determining social and economic policies and then imparting to them the force of law." [76]

At long last even professors of constitutional law were alerted to the fact that the business of judging entails lawmaking, even constitution-making. In his 1930 edition of

[72] *Cong. Rec.*, LXXII, 3501.　　[73] *Ibid.*, p. 3573.
[74] *Washington Star*, Feb. 13, 1930.
[75] *Cong. Rec.*, LXXII (pt. 8), 7949.
[76] *Baltimore Sun*, Feb. 13, 1930; reprinted, *Cong. Rec.*, LXXII, 3553.

The Constitution and What It Means Today, Professor Edward S. Corwin asserted: "Judicial review, far from being an instrument for the application of the Constitution, tends to supplant it. In other words, the discretion of the judges tends to supplant it." The identical disclosure came more tersely that same year from the Harvard Law School. "The Supreme Court," said Professor Felix Frankfurter, *"is* the Constitution." [77] "Let us face the fact," Frankfurter commented, "that five Justices of the Supreme Court *are* molders of policy, rather than impersonal vehicles of revealed truth." [78]

Shortly after Hughes's confirmation Professor Frankfurter discussed the Senate debates with Justice Stone and came away impressed with "the statesmanlike interpretation that you placed upon the outbursts in the Senate and in the country." In response, Stone wrote Frankfurter:

There is a very surprising but I think wholesome interest in what the Court is doing, and a disposition to study and discuss it with real intelligence.

What troubles me most about it is that some of the people who ought to be quickest to see this and most prompt to give present tendencies a different trend, seem not to appreciate the situation. I think one aspect of the matter which is not understood is that it [the struggle within the Court] is not a contest between conservatism and radicalism, nearly so much as it is a difference arising from an inadequate understanding of the relation of law to the social and economic forces which control society. . . .

Why don't you write a restrained, considered article dealing with the whole matter. I think it would be helpful.

Did you see in the recent Harpers an article by Judge Pros-

[77] "The United States Supreme Court Molding the Constitution," *Current History*, 32 (May 1930), 240.
[78] "The Supreme Court and the Public," *Forum*, 83 (June 1930), 334.

kauer on the dissenting opinion? I thought it good and very instructive to a lot of people who think law, especially in our Court, is a system of mathematics. Sometimes, though, *I* think if it were applied with scientific precision, that we might come out better than we do now.[79]

In the June 1930 issue of *Forum* magazine, an article by Frankfurter approved the searchlight that the Senators had played upon the Supreme Court.

Surely the men who wield the power of life and death over the political decisions of legislatures and executives should be subjected to the most vigorous scrutiny before being given that power. Public opinion, the President, and the Senate should all have a lively understanding of what the appointment of a Supreme Court justice means. . . .[80]

It is not good, either for the country or the Court, that the part played by the Court in the life of the country should be shrouded in mystery.[81]

In support of his thesis, Frankfurter quoted Justice Brewer's "memorable words" of 1898: "The time is past in the history of the world when any living man or body of men can be set on a pedestal and decorated with a halo." [82]

The lawmakers of 1930 had raised a warning flag, making

[79] H. F. Stone to Felix Frankfurter, April 4, 1930.

In his article, "Dissenting Opinions," Judge Joseph M. Proskauer had concluded: "Even where the theory of the dissent does not ultimately prevail, its expression is no futile gesture. . . . The dissenting judge, if he achieves nothing else, at least whets the reasoning and clarifies the expression of the majority. He accentuates the points of agreement and of difference and thus more accurately defines and delimits the actual holding of the case. . . . And, over and above this, he often points the path by which future generations shall proceed on the never-ending quest for justice" (*Harpers*, 160 [April 1930], pp. 549–555, at pp. 554–555).

[80] Frankfurter, *op. cit.*, 334.   [81] *Ibid.*, 329–330.
[82] *Ibid.*, 334.

it clear that in the years ahead any wanton disregard of the enlightened principle of judicial self-restraint would inevitably make the Court the focus of political controversy and thus jeopardize its power and prestige. "If the system of judicial law that is being written in defiance of state legislation and of congressional legislation is continued," Senator Dill of New Jersey warned, "there is no human power in America that can keep the Supreme Court from becoming a political issue, nation-wide, in the not far distant future." [83]

In this atmosphere of senatorial defiance, Chief Justice Hughes and Justice Owen J. Roberts, whom President Hoover had appointed after the Senate rejected Judge Parker, donned judicial robes. After 1930 their votes became crucial in the harshest of all political issues—the people versus economic oligarchy. Could the Constitution be made to meet the requirements of modern government? Could judicial pre-eminence survive in the fierce struggle for power and political dominance?

[83] *Cong. Rec.*, LXXII, 3642.

★ III ★

Freedom and the New Deal

WITH the crash of 1929, the booming decade collapsed. Despite disaster, the GOP tradition and creed inhibited positive action. Given time and patience, the natural operation of economic forces alone would bring about the revival of prosperity. Such faith was not shaken until 1932, when the country was sunk in the very trough of depression, national income then totaling less than forty billion dollars annually. President Hoover's last-minute intervention in big business, by the device of the Reconstruction Finance Corporation, gave some hint of what had to come—the wholehearted enlistment of a national power able and willing to cope with a national emergency "more serious than war." [1] Government itself had to take "affirmative action to bring about its avowed objectives rather than stand by and hope that general economic laws alone would attain them." [2]

[1] Words of Justice Brandeis in *New State Ice Co.* v. *Liebmann* 285 U.S. 262 (1932), p. 306.
[2] Franklin D. Roosevelt, *Public Papers and Addresses*, 1933 vol., p. 5.

Our Republican leaders [President Roosevelt observed] tell us economic laws—sacred, inviolable, unchangeable—cause panics which no one could prevent. But while they prate of economic laws, men and women are starving. We must lay hold of the fact that economic laws are not made by nature. They are made by human beings.[3]

The New Dealers thus redressed the inadequacies of their own party's tradition by devising a more positive philosophy of popular sovereignty to "benefit the great mass of our farmers, workers and business men." [4] Crushed by the monster it had created, and helpless in the face of disaster, the business fraternity itself turned beseechingly to Washington for instruction, guidance, and leadership. "New conditions impose new requirements upon Government and those who control Government," [5] the Democratic presidential candidate had said in his notable Commonwealth Club speech of September 1932. As President, Mr. Roosevelt's challenge went further: "The power of a few to manage the economic life of the nation must be diffused among the many or be transferred to the public and its democratically responsible government." [6]

In fashioning his innovations, Roosevelt drew on various elements in our complex tradition. Alexander Hamilton had been among the first American statesmen to "lay hold of the fact that economic laws . . . are made by human beings." [7] In 1782 the New Yorker had dismissed laissez-faire as "one of those wild speculative paradoxes, which have grown into credit among us, contrary to the uniform practice and sense of the most enlightened nations." [8] From the

[3] *Ibid.*, I, 657.   [4] *Ibid.*, 1933 vol., p. 5.
[5] *Ibid.*, I, 753.   [6] *Ibid.*, 1938 vol., p. 313.
[7] *Ibid.*, I, 657.
[8] "The Continentalist," *The Works of Alexander Hamilton* (ed. by Henry Cabot Lodge; New York: Putnam, 1903), I, 268.

First Philipic of Demosthenes, Hamilton had learned that "wise men ought to walk at the head of affairs" and "produce the event." [9] President Roosevelt adopted this strategy. Moreover, he boldly invoked the very "instruments of public power" Hamilton had forged. But whereas Hamilton sought to use government on behalf of the rising financial and industrial classes, Roosevelt urged that government must also be swift to enter and protect the underprivileged.

In 1928 Mr. Hoover had spoken confidently of "equality of opportunity," as if it were all but realized.[10] In 1932 Roosevelt said flatly that "a glance at the situation today only too clearly indicates that equality of opportunity as we have known it no longer exists." [11] Roosevelt, like Hoover, wanted to save capitalism, but he tried to do it in a different way. Broadus Mitchell states the contrasting approaches in this fashion:

Hoover, by and large, was content with socializing the "public" losses of corporations, because these would reach to the private losses of individuals. The New Deal went further and was willing to socialize the private losses of unemployed individuals on the ground that, unless aided, these would destroy the public, including corporate, welfare.[12]

[9] "As a general marches at the head of his troops, so ought with politicians, if I dare use the expression, to march at the head of affairs; insomuch that they ought not to wait the *event*, to know what measures to take; but the measures which they have taken, ought to produce the *event*" (quoted in Nathan Schachner, *Alexander Hamilton* [New York: Appleton-Century, 1946], p. 34).

[10] See Hoover's speech accepting the Republican nomination for the presidency, *New York Times*, Aug. 12, 1928, p. 3.

[11] Roosevelt, *op. cit.*, I, 750.

[12] Broadus Mitchell, *Depression Decade* (New York: Rinehart, 1947), pp. 88–89. See also R. G. Tugwell, "The Protagonists: Roosevelt and Hoover," *Antioch Review*, 13 (Sept. 1954), 419–442.

"There are two ideas of government," William Jennings Bryan

Personifying the confidence Hoover vainly preached, and blithely innocent of the complexities before which economists trembled, the President plunged into the task of recovery and reconstruction. In close cadence his special session of Congress enacted "must" legislation with little dissent, adding vast powers to those the President already had. The President himself, surveying the transformation his regime had wrought, jauntily suggested that the seat of government had been transferred from Wall Street to Washington. As Congress responded to his bidding and passively awaited the next command, our politics seemed to some to take on the aspect of monarchy. One man held the center of the stage; one man had power—none seemed able or willing to oppose him. Government drew to itself far-reaching authority, entered fields hitherto left empty or partially occupied by state or local government. Congress began to exercise control over commerce and industry formerly wielded by the private syndromes of wealth. Regulations issuing from the national Capitol displaced innumerable activities of competitive individuals. Even Henry Ford conceded it was "up to the government" to pull the country's banks out of the bog.[13] Washington was "like a hospital," F.D.R. recalled, and "many of the patients came from Wall Street."

And yet the New Deal's first major enactment—the National Industrial Recovery Act—marked no sharp break

---

told the Democratic Convention of 1896. "There are those who believe that, if you will only legislate to make the well-to-do prosperous, their prosperity will leak through on those below. The Democratic idea, however, has been that if you legislate to make the masses prosperous, their prosperity will find its way up through every class which rests upon them" (*Speeches of William Jennings Bryan* [New York: Funk and Wagnalls, 1909], I, 248).

[13] Quoted in Ferdinand Pecora, *Wall Street under Oath* (New York: Simon and Schuster, 1939), p. 256.

with his predecessors's policies. "It is," President Roosevelt remarked in signing NIRA, "a challenge to industry, which has long insisted that, given the right to act in unison, it could do much for the general good which has hitherto been unlawful. From today it has that right." [14] Despite these modest beginnings, thoughtful persons soon began wondering whether freedom could survive even this amount of government regulation. Even if precious American values came through the economic distress, could it endure political control and all its baneful consequences? When, in 1934, the patient seemed likely to survive, legislators and others began to argue with the doctor. Still the titular head of his party, Herbert Hoover became the opposition's major spokesman.

"It seems clear," Supreme Court Justice Harlan Fiske Stone wrote him in March 1934, "that the honeymoon is over and that we may witness the beginning of real political discussion." This was good news to Hoover, as the former President felt sure that New Deal policy meant a long step down the road to "regimentation," "planned economy," "despotism," and so on to ruthless ruin. In the spring of 1934 Hoover developed this surmise in a manuscript and sent it to Justice Stone for comment. These two men were close friends; both were devout Republicans, both distrusted Franklin Roosevelt. Yet their appraisals of the New Deal diverged significantly. Stone's reaction to Hoover's critique was of the "yes" and "no" description:

With the main theses of this paper I fully agree. The principle of individual liberty which has hitherto been regarded as an indispensable factor in our polity should be preserved. It can be preserved only by a system which gives some scope for

[14] Quoted in Arthur Schlesinger, Jr., "His Rendezvous with History," *New Republic*, 114 (April 15, 1946), 551–552.

altruistic, non-compulsory cooperation, and which affords opportunity for rewards for service, through a reasonable maintenance and protection of property rights. I fully agree with the arraignment of the present regime for its reckless disregard of these values. This is the strongest part of the paper. I think even more could be said about present tendencies to depart from traditional forms of democratic government under the Constitution.

Stone deplored the "steady absorption of power by the President, the failure of Congress to perform its legislative duties, the absence of debate in Congress and of open public discussion of public problems, the creation of drastic administrative procedures without legislative definition and without provision for their review by the courts." These, the conservative Republican judge told Hoover, constitute "an even greater menace than the program for whose advancement these sacrifices have been made." Stone also endorsed the former President's emphasis on the value of human liberty, but wondered whether Hoover realized the true dimensions of the problem. The size and power of the modern corporation, sometimes surpassing those of the state governments, and able on occasion to challenge national authority, required positive governmental safeguards to secure individual liberty. Circumstances had transmuted the issue of liberty versus authority into the problem of "responsible use of power"—the power of individuals and groups as well as of official government. Perhaps the basic flaw in Hoover's thinking was his failure to appreciate "the perpetual, and to some extent, irreconcilable conflict between the demands of individual liberty and the necessities of an increasingly complex civilization, in which every individual and every group within the state becomes increasingly interdependent with every other."

"There was," the Justice explained, "undoubtedly much larger scope for individual liberty in the state which Jefferson contemplated than there is in the civilization which we have actually developed in this year of our Lord." The nation then consisted of small, independent communities. Actions of an individual in the next state, or even the next county, had little effect "on Jefferson and his neighbors." "Personally," Stone commented emphatically, "I like the Jeffersonian state better, but I have to recognize that because I live in a highly industrialized modern state, in order to make the system work, I have to suffer restrictions on individual liberty, which Jefferson would probably have regarded as intolerable." The Justice went on to cite illustrations of the way industrial civilization infringed on human freedom, and therefore required more rigid government:

Because certain manufacturers in Detroit have enjoyed freedom to flood the country with automobiles, I have lost freedom in the use and enjoyment of the streets and highways. Because other manufacturers have demanded and secured the benefits of a protective tariff, my freedom as a consumer of foreign goods has been curtailed. The railroad builders and operators, the big business man—and some little ones—the shippers of merchandise in interstate commerce, have all suffered similar restrictions on their freedom of action.

The pertinent question in 1934 was whether America must prove Jefferson's phobia that freedom and urban industrialism are necessarily incompatible. Stone did not think so. Nor was he sure that freedom would be the possession of men in twentieth-century America if government simply abstained from regulating their affairs.

Reform was essential. Restraints, both unnecessary and

unbearable in Jefferson's Garden of Eden, must now be accepted as prerequisites of a system of "ordered liberty." Industrialism had produced a new level of human dependence and interdependence. The connecting lines of interest ran across all boundaries, political and geographic, to tie the nation into a sensitive whole.

Today what the Wall Street banker does may have serious consequences on the fortunes of the cotton planter in Mississippi and the farmer in Iowa. The textile manufacturer of New England is at the mercy of the employer of child labor or underpaid labor in the South. He must yield either to the pressure or abandon his business, with all the consequences to his employees and to his community—unless, perchance, the freedom of action of the employer of child labor is to some extent curtailed in the interest of the larger good.

The depression itself contained persuasive arguments for enlarging the area of government power:

Now, at the end of an era of extraordinary industrial expansion and prosperity, we have been made suddenly aware that we have multiplied and improved the instruments and methods of production beyond our powers of consumption; that the distribution of wealth created by our extraordinary capacity for production is not such as to enable consumption to overtake or even keep pace with production; that our financial system, the creation and use of credit, upon which modern civilization increasingly depends, is maladjusted and honeycombed with grave abuses, and that our foreign trade is shrinking and can be regained, if at all, only after years of effort.

Surely, Stone suggested, the community, through agencies of public control, must take account of any drastic change that places the individual at the mercy of forces beyond his control.

Hoover maintained that the economic crisis was some-how the inevitable consequence of World War I and European in origin. Stone questioned this hypothesis:

It is undoubtedly true that the World War and world dis-orders which have followed it have played a part in this un-happy outcome, but there will be other wars and new clashes of the economic interests of nations. Even without them it seems almost inevitable, without some correction or control of the forces which have produced our present situation, history will in due course repeat itself, but with the difference that the ensuing crisis will be more acute than the present one has been, with even graver political and social consequences.

For the questions he raised, however, Stone had no easy, doctrinaire solution.

The conflict between individual freedom and the private in-terest which it envisages, with the public interest, is never-ending. The line of battle shifts and will inevitably continue to shift as civilization becomes more complex and the interest of the whole becomes increasingly sensitive to the mistakes or misdeeds of the few.

Social problems make unending demands on intelligence. "Some adjustments" must be made "between the demands of individual liberty, and those of the larger social good."

The issues cannot be settled by an appeal to the eighteenth century philosophy of individualism in the abstract, for that philosophy cannot be completely adapted to the twentieth cen-tury state. The demands of the two must, to some extent, be accommodated, but with full realization of the values which that philosophy can contribute to present day society.

Unprecedented social and economic changes raised "major questions" which "statesmanship must attempt to answer."

78

It must ask itself "what reforms are necessary to prevent recurrence of present-time evils, and, second, how can these reforms be effected with the least impairment of individual liberty?"

"Reforms of the first magnitude" were in order. Nor could these be made "without such radical departure from the essential qualities of a free society as is now contemplated." Among other things, the banking and credit systems should be "thoroughly reformed." To prevent recurrence of deep-seated depression, a basic departure from laissez-fair economics was essential. "A possibly more doubtful question, but still one which cannot be summarily dismissed," was whether some method must not be found by which "the flow of production may be more closely related to consumption,[15] and by which industry may be given an opportunity, within reasonable range, to be marked by administrative procedure under law, of stabilizing itself." Such reforms necessarily

[15] On December 17, 1935, Richard B. Scandrett, Jr., wrote Justice Stone that "the great difficulty lies in the stubborn unwillingness of a large number of businessmen to admit and face the basic economic problem which requires the transforming of the potential consuming capacity into an actual purchasing power."

"You are right," Stone replied December 20, 1935. "There is no doubt that the problem of the hour is the reconciliation of the principles of liberty with the type of economic society we have constructed, and that we shall have to find a way of securing a better distribution of income if we are to maintain it. Yet, I can see no recognition of this truth on the part of any important Republican leader. My one feeling is that we have sat asleep at the switch again until the train passed by.

"It is true enough that one of the grave faults of the Roosevelt Administration is its administrative incapacity, its lack of financial foresight, and its reckless disregard of the most elementary principles of justice in dealing with great public problems. This may overturn them if they lose popular favor in the next six months as rapidly as they have in the last six. But the Republicans are doing little to improve their opportunity."

"involve some restraints on freedom of action of the individual."

Mere verbal lamentations over freedom's fate could not make the people forget that Roosevelt had acted to bring about necessary correctives. And Hoover's failure to come to grip with realities led the Justice to question the wisdom of publishing the manuscript:

If published in its present form, at the present time, there is a real risk that it will be misinterpreted and that it will be severely assailed as "stand pat" in its philosophy and outlook. The country is convinced that the time has come for sweeping reforms, and that these are being, and will be, resisted for selfish reasons by those who have an excessive stake in things as they are or have been in the past. People expect that objections will be made to such reforms on the ground that they infringe the principle of freedom of the individual. Even the man in the street is aware that every important reform in the past seventy-five years has been resisted and assailed as an infringement of individual liberty.

Acrimonious debate had attended the establishment of the Interstate Commerce Commission, workmen's compensation, the Sherman and the Clayton Acts. Though "attacked in legislatures, in public prints and in the courts on the ground that they were encroachments upon the American system and a curtailment of the freedom of action of the empire builders who had made America," all were now accepted as an essential part of our constitutional system. Stone anticipated that Mr. Hoover's attack on the New Deal would be placed in "the same category as these earlier pronouncements."

Now the people are disposed to endure the evils of the administration program in the hope that they may bring a better day, freed from the dangers from which we are now suffering.

To accomplish that end they are in the mood to make any necessary sacrifices, but I think they would be overjoyed if someone could point the way to accomplish it without the sacrifices of liberty which they are being called on to make.

Hoover's failure to realize that the New Deal was in response to genuine social wrongs endangered the very freedom he sought most eagerly to protect, provoking Stone to throw out as his final dictum:

If it is thought that . . . reforms are not needed, the time is not yet ripe to assail the program which the administration has sponsored. The time for that will come only when we are more prosperous. It may then succeed, and all programs for any extensive reforms be abandoned, but with, I fear, grave consequences in the future.[16]

As Stone had foreseen, publication of the former President's manuscript, under the title *Challenge to Liberty*,[17] fell on barren soil. Following the 1934 elections the Justice wrote a close friend:

I would like to show you a criticism and prediction which I wrote to one of my Republican brethren with respect to the Republican attitude. It is completely confirmed by what I read in the papers this morning. As I read the returns they do not represent complete satisfaction with the New Deal, so much as they do a realization that our Republican brethren have nothing constructive to offer, and that the people are willing to take their chances with Roosevelt a while longer.[18]

---

[16] Justice Harlan Fiske Stone to Herbert Hoover, March 27, 1934.

[17] New York: Scribner, 1934.

[18] Justice Harlan Fiske Stone to Sterling Carr, Nov. 7, 1934. Hoover's anti-New Deal tract provoked exactly the reaction Stone predicted. "Mr. Hoover," one critic wrote (and many others sounded the same note), "desires freedom for the bankers, for the

After 1932 the business community faced precisely the situation they had long feared most—a great popular leader, backed by the "force of numbers," [19] capable of voicing social discontent and translating it into a bold and comprehensive legislative program. Though the fear of political democracy persists as a monotonous refrain through the literature of our politics, never before had apprehension of it struck the business community with such force. As usual it relied primarily on legal and judicial fortifications. In an address before the Maryland Bar Association, June 1935, Governor Albert C. Ritchie mapped the opposition's strategy:

New forces are loose in the land, and new difficulties confront us. Where else should we look if not to the lawyers for authentic standards by which to test and evaluate these new tendencies and policies. . . . The American bar and the American courts should . . . regard themselves as trustees and guardians of American institutions. Especially should they preserve the Supreme Court as the free and untrammeled agency which it now is, to uphold American institutions against anything which

---

privateers of finance, and for the great captains of industry, and he desires freedom for them to do as they please. He has overlooked the freedom of the man and woman whose toil makes capital possible" (Wayne C. Williams to the editor, *Washington Post*, Oct. 1, 1934).

[19] Words of David J. Brewer, "The Nation's Safeguard" (an address before the New York State Bar Association, Jan. 17, 1893), *Proceedings of the New York State Bar Association*, XVI, 39. Hamilton, James Kent, John Randolph of Roanoke, Abel P. Upshur, and many other American conservatives deplored any possibility of "the control of the few by the many," which Brewer called "despotism." For the most heated pronouncements against the "onslaught of mere numbers," "mere force of numbers," see the *Arguments and Addresses of Joseph Hodges Choate* (collected and ed. by Frederick C. Hicks; St. Paul: West Publishing Co., 1926), pp. 473, 880.

would impair or break them down to the injury of our Republic.[20]

Ritchie's exhortations on the New Deal assumed that, prior to this diabolical interlude, our government had scrupulously refrained from entering the economic sphere. Heretofore only private enterprise shaped our social and economic progress. Suddenly in 1932 we turned our backs on principles that had served us so successfully; we embraced an ultrapaternalistic program of government regulation and control. Selling liberty for mere security, this obnoxious variant of socialism—"creeping socialism"—had started the country down grade to the welfare state and ultimate disaster. A basic change did take place, but it was not the one here suggested.

The New Deal ties in with our past rather strikingly. Laissez-faire was never an exclusive, or even a key principle in American politics. In the heyday of rugged individualism, James Bryce observed somewhat cynically: "Americans talk laissez-faire, but do not practice it." [21] Government support of national economic policy was our practice from the beginning. The protective tariff goes back to the first Congress in 1789. National aid to public works began in our formative years. Internal improvements were fostered by

[20] Albert C. Ritchie, "The American Bar—Trustee of American Institutions" (speech before the annual convention of the Maryland Bar Association at Atlantic City, N.J.), *American Liberty League Document*, No. 48 (June 29, 1935).

[21] "One-half of the capitalists are occupied in preaching *laissez-faire* as regards railroad control, the other half in resisting it in railroad rate matters, in order to have their goods carried more cheaply, and in tariff matters, in order to protect industries threatened with foreign competition" (*The American Commonwealth* [New York: Macmillan, 1921], II, 304). See also Reinhold Niebuhr, "Halfway to What?" *Nation*, 170 (Jan. 14, 1950), 27.

congressional grants on a major scale for toll roads, highways, canals, and railroads. The national government early inaugurated a public-lands policy, giving away vast acreage to veterans and flooding settlers. Later on, when it was seen that individual operators—private enterprisers—were unable to develop large-scale resources of iron, timber, coal, and petroleum, government responded by sanctioning, even encouraging, wide incorporation. The Supreme Court went still further and assured the corporations, through broad interpretation of the Fourteenth Amendment, of legal security and advantage. The kind of society we now have, our transportation networks, the distribution of population, our distinctive American agriculture, the corporate form of business organization—all these are due largely to the exercise of government power—local, state, and federal.

As Lester Ward pointed out in 1895, the charge of paternalism comes with poor grace from the business fraternity. It

is chiefly made by the class that enjoys the largest share of government protection. . . . That government, which fails to protect the weak, is devoting all its energies to protecting the strong. It legalizes and promotes trusts and combinations; subsidizes corporations, and then absolves them from their obligations; sustains stockwatering schemes and all forms of speculation; grants without compensation the most valuable franchises, often in perpetuity; and in innumerable ways creates, defends, and protects a vast array of purely parasitic enterprises, calculated directly to foster the worst forms of municipal corruption. . . . The very possession of wealth is only made possible by government. The safe conduct of all business depends upon the certain protection of law.[22]

[22] "Plutocracy and Paternalism," *Forum*, 20 (Nov. 1895), 305–306, 308 *passim*.

The New Deal built on and continued the positive government tradition, extending its coverage so as to protect the weak as well as the strong. Harold Laski has written:

What is remarkable in the New Deal is the degree in which it is, in fact, simply the completion of a continuous development of discontent with traditional individualism which goes back, in one sense, to Shays' Rebellion, and, in another, at least to the Populism of the period after the Civil War.[23]

Those who joined Grangerism in the seventies and campaigned to regulate the railroads and other public utilities were not radicals bent on enacting socialism. They were not Communists "on the march." [24] They were small businessmen, farmers, day laborers, professional men, and property owners who saw their equality, their liberty, their property —free government itself—menaced by the spread of monopoly and the growth of economic power. The New Deal held that neither freedom nor progress is possible amid conditions of economic anarchy. Our so-called laissez-faire economy had matured into an economic system which, though functioning with considerable success in the past, no longer responded to the much-advertised automatic adjustment. After 1932 the orientation of American political thought became increasingly collectivistic.[25] Economic

[23] Harold J. Laski, *The American Democracy: A Commentary and an Interpretation* (New York: Viking, 1948), p. 69.

[24] See Joseph H. Choate's argument in *Pollock* v. *Farmers' Loan and Trust Company*, 157 U.S. 429 (1895), pp. 532–553. Choate told the court that the income tax was defended "upon principles as communistic, socialistic—what shall I call them—populistic as ever have been addressed to any political assembly in the world" (p. 532).

[25] See Henry Wallace, *New Frontiers* (New York: Reynal, 1934), pp. 22–29, and Thomas Paul Jenkin, *Reactions of Major Groups to Positive Government in the United States, 1930–1940* (Los Angeles: University of California Press, 1945).

rights were added to the roster of our freedoms and government, rather than industrial management or ownership, became the dominant power. The New Deal thus marks that most significant shift from implicit faith in the operation of "natural" economic forces to the belief that social and economic processes can and must be controlled by politically responsible government. Furthermore, government policy built on this theory re-enforces rather than undermines our tradition.

Speaking in 1944 at Fenway Park, Boston, Roosevelt said:

If there ever was a time in which the spiritual strength of our people was put to the test, that time was in the terrible depression of 1929 to 1933. Then our people might have turned to alien ideologies—like communism or fascism. But,—our democratic faith was too sturdy. What the American people demanded in 1933 was not less democracy, but more democracy, and that is what they got.[26]

[26] Robert E. Sherwood, *Roosevelt and Hopkins* (New York: Harper, 1948), p. 43.

"To permit the direction of our public affairs," Theodore Roosevelt wrote Conrad Kohrs, September 9, 1908, "to fall alternately into the hands of revolutionaries and reactionaries, of the extreme radicals of unrest and of the bigoted conservatives who recognize no wrongs to remedy, would merely mean that the Nation had embarked on a feverish course of violent oscillation which would be fraught with great temporary trouble, and would produce no adequate good in the end. The true friend of reform, the true foe of abuses, is the man who steadily perseveres in righting wrongs, in warring against abuses, but whose character and training are such that he never promises what he cannot perform, that he always a little more than makes good what he does promise, and that, while steadily advancing, he never permits himself to be led into foolish excesses which would damage the very cause he champions" (*The Letters of Theodore Roosevelt* [selected and ed. by Elting E. Morison; Cambridge: Harvard University Press, 1952], VI, 1213).

In certain respects the New Deal reverses Emerson's aphorism of antislavery days: "Things are in the saddle and ride mankind." "It is my conception of the New Deal," Rexford Guy Tugwell writes, "that it shall ensure the subjugation of things, and restore to men the freedoms they have earned, together with all the advantages which ought to accrue from our victories over nature." [27]

The New Deal's critics drew heavily upon a single line in our heritage. They played up the dangers of popular power, of unbridled democracy, and tyrannical bureaucracy. They exalted the Hamiltonian axiom of "inevitable economic inequality" as the law of progress. To keep ancient landmarks firmly anchored, they elevated and revered the judiciary, a sanctified body, presumably far removed from politics. They ignored or rejected the vital element in our tradition that sees change as a law of progress, that interprets the Declaration of Independence as setting limitless goals. They did not realize, as Justice Stone's criticism of Mr. Hoover's attack on the New Deal shows, that "the eager and often inconsiderate appeals of reformers and revolutionists are indispensable to counter-balance the inertness and fossilism making so large a part of human institutions." [28]

There is no evidence that purblind opposition deterred the New Deal President. By 1935 he was unmistakably determined to extend and enlarge national authority. To do this, the politically triumphant reformers had to build their

---

"Freedom," Wilson said in 1912, "to-day is something more than being let alone. The purpose of a government of freedom must in these days be positive, not negative merely" (*The New Freedom* [New York: Doubleday, 1913], p. 284).

[27] R. G. Tugwell, *The Battle for Democracy* (New York: Columbia University Press, 1935), pp. 195–196.

[28] Walt Whitman, *Democratic Vistas* (Washington: Redfield, 1871), p. 26.

program on the commerce clause or on the taxing and spending power. Whether the Court would sustain legislative innovations of unprecedented scope turned primarily on the unpredictable votes of Chief Justice Hughes and Justice Roberts. In 1932 they concurred with Justice Sutherland in holding that Oklahoma was powerless, even in the depths of depression, to prevent individuals from entering an already hopelessly crowded ice business.[29] Joining Stone, Brandeis, and Cardozo, they upheld Minnesota's two-year moratorium on mortgage foreclosures.[30] That same year, and again by a vote of five to four, the Court, led by Justice Roberts, sustained a New York State statute fixing minimum and maximum retail milk prices.[31]

Those favoring as well as those opposing the New Deal found comfort in these decisions.[32] Liberals looked fondly on paragraphs of the moratorium opinion in which the Chief Justice spoke of the Court's realization of the public interest as omnipresent. They were encouraged by the Court's recognition of the need for "increased use of the organization of society in order to protect the very bases of individual opportunity." "The question," Hughes said, "is no longer merely that of one party to a contract as against another, but of the use of reasonable means to safeguard the economic structure upon which the good of all depends."[33] F.D.R.'s opponents found consolation in the

[29] *New State Ice Co.* v. *Liebmann*, 285 U.S. 262 (1932).

[30] *Home Building and Loan Association* v. *Blaisdell*, 290 U.S. 398 (1934).

[31] *Nebbia* v. *New York*, 291 U.S. 502 (1934).

[32] For contemporary comment on the Court's ruling, see: *Nation*, 138 (March 14, 1934), 287; *New Republic*, 78 (March 21, 1934), 146–147; *Publishers' Weekly*, 125 (April 7, 1934) 1351–1352; *U.S. Law Review*, 68 (Jan. 1934), 1; *Columbia Law Review*, 34 (March 1934), 401–425; *Southern California Law Review*, 7 (May 1934), 353–371.

[33] 290 U.S. 398, p. 442.

Chief Justice's stress on the emergency (i.e., limited) character of the Minnesota legislation. They could not, however, find that satisfaction in Justice Roberts' opinion sustaining the New York milk law—a price-fixing measure held valid as such and without reference to emergency. Nor could they ignore Justice Roberts' broad-gauge dictum that "the power to promote the general welfare is inherent in government." [34]

Meanwhile, without benefit of constitutional baptism, a far-reaching reorganization of national life had taken place. Commerce, banking, currency, bankruptcy, agriculture, labor—all experienced drastic changes under the impetus of a swift and sprawling recovery program. Few could predict what stand the Justices might take on the larger grist now pouring from the legislative mill. The Minnesota moratorium and the Nebbia milk decisions "held out," as the President said, "a glimmer of hope that the Supreme Court would take a broad view of the Constitution, which would permit its adaptation to the various crises of human affairs." [35] But even in these cases as in many others, our economic fate and judicial fortune depended on the caprice of the odd man on the Supreme Court. So one might still believe that the judiciary would yet prove itself that final bulwark of defense against dangerous popular power.

A major reform measure reached the Court on December 10, 1934, under circumstances that did not augur well for the recovery program. The Panama Refining Company had challenged the validity of executive orders issued under NIRA prohibiting the shipment of "hot oil" (oil production exceeding state allowances) across state lines. Early in the argument, government counsel was forced to admit that the criminal penalties attaching to violation of the relevant

[34] 291 U.S. 502, p. 524.
[35] Roosevelt, *op. cit.*, 1935 vol., p. 6.

code provisions had been inadvertently omitted from the executive order. Counsel for the defendant said that his client had been "arrested, indicted and held in jail for several days . . . for violating a law that did not exist." "Who promulgates these orders and codes that have the force of law?" Justice Brandeis asked impatiently. Completely on the defensive, government counsel confessed that he did not know of "any official or general publication of these executive orders." [36] The die was soon cast. Chief Justice Hughes and seven other Justices held Section 9 (c) of the NIRA invalid as an unconstitutional delegation of legislative power to the Chief Executive.[37]

Four months later, a five-to-four ruling scuttled the recently enacted Railroad Retirement scheme, requiring the carriers to subscribe to a pension plan for superannuated employees.[38] Justice Roberts, switching to the right, brushed the legislation sarcastically aside as based on "the contentment and satisfaction theory" of social progress. Congressional effort to compel railroads to pension off older workers must fail, he ruled, for want of any relation between the pensioning system and the efficiency or safety of the national rail network.

Justice Roberts' reactionary stand plainly signified the New Deal's doom. The fatal blow was struck on May 27, 1935, "Black Monday," when NIRA (symbolized by the Blue Eagle) was guillotined out of the recovery program.[39] As the decision was unanimous, liberal prospects were

[36] *Washington Post*, Dec. 11, 1934; quoted in E. S. Corwin, *Constitutional Revolution Ltd.* (Claremont: Claremont Colleges, 1941), p. 40.

[37] *Panama Refining Company* v. *Ryan*, 293 U.S. 388 (1935).

[38] *Railroad Retirement Board* v. *Alton Railroad Company*, 295 U.S. 330 (1935).

[39] *Schechter Corporation* v. *United States*, 295 U.S. 495 (1935).

sorely blighted. Only a small glimmer of hope could be gleaned from the concurrence of Justices Stone and Cardozo. The concurring Justices agreed that there ought to be national power adequate to control our national economy —that "the law is not indifferent to considerations of degree"—but they could not then bring themselves to the point of obliterating "the distinction between what is national and what is local in the activities of commerce." [40]

A breach among the Justices, barely perceptible in the NIRA case, opened widely less than a year later in the Court's didactic ruling that a processing tax designed to finance a scheme for the control of agriculture could not be upheld as a tax. Justice Roberts, who spoke for the Court, was joined by the Chief Justice in this six-to-three decision. "It is an established principle," the majority opinion concluded, "that the attainment of a prohibited end may not be accomplished under the pretext of the exertion of powers which are granted." [41] Since Congress' powers did not extend directly to the control of agriculture, that subject matter could not be reached indirectly under the taxing and spending powers.

The Court's decision provoked sharp reaction from dissenters and commentators alike. The majority opinion, Justice Stone declared in dissent, reverses "the time-honored principle of constitutional interpretation that the granted power includes all those which are incident to it. . . ." Justice Roberts, he charged, subjected a grant of power "to limitations which do not find their origin in any express provision of the Constitution and to which other expressly delegated powers are not subject." [42] "What we face now,"

[40] *Ibid.*, p. 554.
[41] *United States* v. *Butler*, 297 U.S. 1 (1936), p. 68.
[42] *Ibid.*, pp. 83–84 *passim.*

Dean Lloyd K. Garrison said, "is the question, not how governmental functions shall be shared, but whether in substance we shall govern at all." [43]

In the Court's drive to limit government power at all levels, two more blows were struck. In the Guffey Coal case of May 18, 1936, the Justices voted five to four that Congress had failed to salvage NIRA remedies for the notoriously distressed bituminous coal industry.[44] By that same narrow margin, three weeks later, they found that the pains New York State had taken to frame a valid minimum wage law for women were all in vain.[45] Now even the most conservative journals feared the consequences of judicial obtuseness. The rationale of the minimum wage decision, that chaos and chaos alone is constitutional, the magazine *America* warned, "plays into the hands of radical change." [46]

William Allen White, himself a veteran and stalwart Republican, called the decision "tragic."[47] Congressional Republican wheelhorse Hamilton Fish was "frankly shocked" by this "new Dred Scott decision." [48] Even the Republican Party, usually a paragon of deference to judical supremacy, expressed the belief that minimum wage legislation could be enacted "within the Constitution as it now stands." [49]

In general, however, the response of the opposition was one of loud jubilation. In face of the stark fact that nine

[43] Garrison, "The Constitution and the Future," *New Republic*, 85 (Jan. 29, 1936), 328.

[44] *Carter* v. *Carter Coal Co.*, 298 U.S. 238 (1936).

[45] *Morehead* v. *Tipaldo*, 298 *U.S.* 587 (1936).

[46] "The Minimum Wage Decision," *America*, 55 (June 13, 1936), 217.

[47] Quoted *Cong. Rec.*, 74th Cong., 2d Sess., June 5, 1936, LXXX, 9040.

[48] *Ibid.*   [49] *New York Times*, June 12, 1936, p. 14.

Justices, at times only five or six, had made government impotent, Herbert Hoover thanked "Almighty God for the Constitution and the Supreme Court." [50] Chief Justice Hughes, addressing the American Law Institute in May 1936, remarked triumphantly: "I am happy to report that the Supreme Court is still functioning." Members and guests of the Institute applauded the announcement so that the Chief Justice had "to pause for more than two minutes." [51] It remained for the American Liberty League to corral the opposition.

This ill-fated organization was the outgrowth of the Association against the Prohibition Amendment. The parent body was not made up, as one might suspect, of topers; it included on its rolls the great financial interests that resented shifting tax burdens from the shoulders of beer drinkers to their own. After 1933, with the Eighteenth Amendment repealed, the Association's objective was to scuttle the Sixteenth Amendment, authorizing Congress, following the Supreme Court's disabling decision of 1895, to levy a tax on incomes. August 2, 1933, Captain William H. Stayton, "nationally known as the father of the Repeal Amendment," denounced the income tax amendment as "the source of nearly all our calamities and woes" and "as an instrument to redistribute wealth, to communize the nation, and to confiscate the property of one man and dole

[50] Herbert Hoover, "Crisis to Free Men," *American Ideals versus the New Deal* (New York: Scribner, 1936), p. 5.

[51] *New York Times*, May 8, 1936, p. 2, col. 2. Harold Ickes called this "undoubtedly a political speech" and cited in evidence the heading in the *Chicago Daily News* report: "Chief Justice Hughes Appeals: Protect Courts from Tyranny." Ickes therefore urged that a speech be made "demonstrating that the Supreme Court is in politics, with particular reference to the political activities of the Chief Justice himself" (*The Secret Diary of Harold Ickes* [New York: Simon and Schuster, 1954], II, 136).

it out to others." But by 1934 a far more serious threat loomed on the political horizon—F.D.R. and his crusading New Dealers. A shift in objectives followed. So what was formerly an association for the repeal of the Eighteenth Amendment became the American Liberty League.

Even prior to formal dissolution on December 30, 1933, the board of directors had passed on December 6 a resolution

suggesting that the individual members of the Executive Committee of the Association against the Prohibition Amendment continue to meet from time to time and have in view the formation of a group, based on our old membership in the Association, which would in the event of danger to the Federal Constitution stand ready to defend the faith of the fathers.

Four days earlier Captain Strayton addressed a letter to the Association's members saying:

At a recent meeting of a group of the former members of the Executive committee of the Association against the Prohibition Amendment, it was the opinion of all those present that governmental conditions and tendencies call for the formation of a patriotic organization to advocate the restoration and preservation of the fundamental principles of the Constitution. . . . Some of us believe that the prosperity, liberty and happiness of the people of our country,—and perhaps the very continuation of our old form of government—depend upon the activities of such an organization to represent the people and not the office-holders.

Accordingly, the League's purposes were, among others, "to defend and uphold the Constitution of the United States," "to teach the necessity of respect for rights of persons and property," "to encourage and protect individual and group initiative and enterprise, to foster the right to work, earn, save and acquire property, and to preserve the ownership and lawful use of property when acquired."

Mr. Stayton knew that only the most appealing battle cry—"the Constitution"—was a match for the forces to be put down. He wrote the members, August 24, 1934:

I do not believe that many issues could command more support or evoke more enthusiasm among our people than the simple issue of "the Constitution." The public ignorance concerning it is dense . . . , but, nevertheless, there is a mighty—though vague—affection for it. The people, I believe, need merely to be led and instructed, and this affection will become almost worship and can be converted into an irresistible movement. It is for this reason that,—against my own wishes and beliefs—I have, in these letters, urged that we should not, for the present, advocate the repeal of even the XVIth Amendment. I think our first appeal should be to the effect that "The Constitution is perfect; we do not seek to change it, or to add to or subtract from it; we seek to rescue it from those who misunderstand it, misuse and mistreat it. To correct these evils amendments may be required later, but we hope not."

And we should remember that he who takes the "Constitution" for his battle cry, has as his allies, the Fathers of old. It will be of inestimable aid to quote Washington, Franklin, Hamilton, Adams, Jefferson, Madison, Monroe and other mighty men of the past, and to recall the Supreme Court's stirring opinions handed down by Marshall and his fellow Justices.

We shall not have to say,—for it will be universally recalled —that these men gave of their spirit, their love and their very lives for this Constitution.

The thrill of the Gettysburg address is largely the "Constituion."

When Lincoln said "We here highly resolve that these dead shall not have died in vain," he moved American hearts as they have rarely been moved. That very appeal, those very words, is our "Issue" if we devote our Organization solely to the "Constitution"—its restoration and preservation.

The League's Vice-President, Raoul E. Desvernine, spelled out the underlying theory.[52] "The Constitution," he wrote in his book *Democratic Despotism*, is "our emperor, our king." Property is "the arch upon which civilized government rests." Property is at "the very foundations of American tradition." Ignoring these maxims, the New Dealers had misconceived the basic tenets of our politics:

We find latent in their conception of law that law emanates solely from the will of the majority of the people, and can, therefore, be modified at any time to meet majority wishes. This doctrine is absolutely totalitarian, and is contrary to our basic conceptions of the source of law. . . . Our political system is predicated on the doctrine that there are some immutable laws of nature and certain other divinely sanctioned rights, which the Constitution and our tradition recognized as being above and beyond the power of the majority, or of any other group of individuals or officials of the Government.

Thus far, they have met with an insurmountable obstacle in the . . . Judiciary. Fearing that this is a barrier they cannot jump, they now propose either to remove it as a barrier or so to impair it, that it will not block their progress. They make a variety of proposals to deprive the Supreme Court of its power to declare legislation and executive acts unconstitutional.[53]

The entire legislative program—the securities and exchange regulation, the social security measures, the Tennessee Valley Authority, old age benefits, and unemploy-

[52] The full story is told by James C. Pitney in "American Liberty League," on file at the Firestone Library, Princeton. See also Frederick Rudolph, "The Liberty League, 1934–1940," *American Historical Review*, 56 (Oct. 1950), 19–33.

[53] From *Democratic Despotism* by Raoul Desvernine. Copyright 1936 by Dodd, Mead & Co., Inc., pp. 6, 22, 27–28, 175–177 *passim*.

ment compensation—all overwhelmingly approved by the American people in 1932, 1934, and 1936 was in danger of being lost, as Assistant Attorney General Robert H. Jackson commented, in "a maze of constitutional metaphors." [54] "A dead hand was being laid" upon the entire legislative program—"to stay it all," the President said. "It was the hand of the Supreme Court of the United States." [55]

The enormity of the situation is evident from the correspondence between Justice Stone and Harvard Law School Professor Felix Frankfurter. Commenting on a series of restrictive decisions, February 17, 1936 Stone wrote:

It just seems as though, in some of these cases, the writer and those who united with him didn't care what was said, as long as the opinion seemed plausible on its face, if not compared with any other. The worst of it is that the one [Hughes] that you find most difficult to understand is the one chiefly responsible.

Professor Frankfurter was especially "troubled," "puzzled" that Chief Justice Hughes did not agree with Justice Stone's dissent in *Great Northern R. Co.* v. *Weeks* (297 U.S. 135, 1935). Later on Justice Stone reverted to the fact that "there never has been a time in the history of the Court when there has been so little intelligible, recognizable pattern in its judicial performance as in the last few years." Writing Frankfurter, Feb. 25, 1936, he said:

I can hardly see the use of writing judicial opinions unless they are to embody methods of analysis and of exposition which will serve the profession as a guide to the decision of future

[54] *Reorganization of the Federal Judiciary*, Hearings before the Committee on the Judiciary (U.S. Senate), 75th Cong., 1st Sess., pt. 1 (1937), p. 44.
[55] Roosevelt, *op. cit.*, 1937 vol., Introduction, p.l.

cases. If they are no better than an excursion ticket, good for this day and trip only, they do not serve even as protective coloration for the writer of the opinion, and would much better be left unsaid.

The basic cleavage between judicial oligarchy and popular power could no longer be concealed or circumvented. In one short term the Court had woven a tight constitutional web to bind government at all levels. The implacable four—Butler, McReynolds, Van Devanter, and Sutherland—were firmly convinced that government, state and national, should give up any attempt to control economic affairs. Hughes and Roberts swung unpredictably from side to side, sometimes opposing each other. But in the two most power-crippling decisions in our history[56] they were solidly with the irreconcilables. What would the President do? There was no doubt in his mind where the trouble lay. Like the Federalists in 1801, the Old Guard, he believed, had taken refuge in the judiciary. "They steal," Mr. Roosevelt said, "the livery of great national constitutional ideals to serve discredited special interest." [57]

Throughout the 1936 presidential campaign democratic orators muted the discord between the Court and New Deal, giving no hint that President Roosevelt would, if re-elected,

[56] *U.S.* v. *Butler*, 297 U.S. 1 (1936), and *Colgate* v. *Harvey*, 296 U.S. 404 (1935). To illustrate his point that the Court followed no "intelligible, recognizable pattern," Justice Stone suggested that Frankfurter compare *Tax Commissioner* v. *Jackson*, 283 U.S. 537, with *Mayflower Farms* v. *Ten Eyck*, 297 U.S. 266; *Zahn* v. *Board of Public Works*, 274 U.S. 325, with *Colgate* v. *Harvey*, 296 U.S. 404; *Los Angeles Gas Co.* v. *Railroad Commission*, 289 U.S. 287, 304, 305, with the decision in *West* v. *Chesapeake and Potomac Telephone Co.*, 295 U.S. 662, and *United States* v. *Shreveport Grain and Elevator Co.*, 287 U.S. 77, 82, 83, with *Crooks* v. *Harrelson*, 282 U.S. 555, 560.

[57] Roosevelt, *op. cit.*, 1936 vol., p. 14.

wage an all-out war on the judiciary. As to the politically feasible remedy, the Democratic platform of 1936 could only say:

If these problems [social and economic] cannot be effectively solved by legislation within the Constitution, we shall seek such clarifying amendment as [we] . . . shall find necessary, in order adequately to regulate commerce, protect public health and safety and safeguard economic security. Thus we propose to maintain the letter and spirit of the Constitution.[58]

Even after his overwhelming electoral triumph, Roosevelt could not be sure that the Court would give ground. Did not the traditional theory of the judicial function insist that the Justices are, and must be, immune to election returns? In no mood to take chances, the newly elected Chief Executive sent to Congress, on February 5, 1937, his blunt proposal of a drastic shake-up in the judiciary. The President's solution was to give a Supreme Court Justice past seventy, six months in which to retire. If he failed to do so he could continue in office, but the Chief Executive would appoint an additional Justice—presumably younger and better able to carry the heavy load. As there were six Justices in this category, the President would have at once six appointments to make.

The President tendered the bitter cup to the elderly jurists on the elevated ground that they slowed efficient dispatch of judicial business. "Can it be said," he reasoned, "that full justice is achieved when a court is forced by the sheer necessity of keeping up with its business to decline, without even an explanation, to hear 87 per cent of the cases presented to it by private litigants?" [59]

[58] "Democratic Platform of 1936," *New York Times*, June 26, 1936, p. 13.
[59] Roosevelt, *op. cit.*, 1937 vol., p. 53.

From the very start the daring proposal, dubbed "Court Packing," ran into noisy opposition. Supreme Court Justices were straightway pictured as demigods far above the sweaty crowd, weighing public policy in the delicate scales of the Immutable Law. "Consitutionality" was intoned as if it were a tangible fact, an esoteric treasure, as undeviating and precise as the orbits of the spheres. It was the Constitution, organic and deific, that prevented the power to govern, not the currently dominant judicial view of what was right and what was wrong.

President Roosevelt's views were less rigid. "Our Constitution is so simple and practical," the smiling Chief Executive commented, shortly after the Court had tossed out NIRA and AAA, "that it is possible always to meet extraordinary needs by changes in emphasis and arrangement without loss of essential form." [60] But this was a vain hope so long as the old men refused to retire, presumably lest the President be given an opportunity to appoint a successor. On March 1, 1937, Harry Hopkins said:

It is a plain fact at the present time that unless the complexion of the Supreme Court can be changed, two or three elderly judges living in cloistered seclusion and thinking in terms of a bygone day can block nearly all the efforts of a popularly elected President and a popularly elected Congress to correct these ills. . . . Those who oppose this plan are not afraid *for* democracy. They are afraid *of* democracy.[61]

In the President's original proposal there was no hint of a desire to change the decisions of the Court or to subordinate the views of the Justices to those of the Executive and Congress. He wished only to clear a crowded docket. In his message of March 4, however, he moved closer to the

[60] Sherwood, *op. cit.*, p. 89.   [61] *Ibid.*, p. 108.

real issue, likening the judiciary to an unruly horse on the government gang plough, unwilling to pull with its teammates, the Executive and Congress.[62] As he saw it now, the crucial question was not whether the Court had kept up with the calendar, but whether it had kept up with the country. In a nationwide Fireside Chat on March 9, the President threw off the cloak of sophistry and frankly explained:

When the Congress has sought to stabilize national agriculture, to improve the conditions of labor, to safeguard business against unfair competition, to protect our national resources, and in many other ways, to serve our clearly national needs, the majority of the Court has been assuming the power to pass on the wisdom of these acts of the Congress—and to approve or disapprove the public policy written into these laws. . . . We have, therefore, reached the point as a nation where we must take action to save the Constitution from the Court and the Court from itself. We must find a way to take an appeal from the Supreme Court to the Constitution itself. We want a Supreme Court which will do justice under the Constitution—not over it. In our courts we want a government of laws and not of men.[63]

To support the charge that "the Court has been acting not as a judicial body, but as a policy-making body," the President did not invoke the authority of starry-eyed New Dealers; rather he drew his most devastating ammunition from the "most distinguished justices of the present Supreme Court." Proceeding to illustrate, he commented:

That is not only my accusation. . . . In the case holding the A.A.A. unconstitutional, Justice Stone said of the majority

[62] *Public Papers and Addresses,* 1937 vol., p. 116.
[63] *Ibid.,* pp. 125–126.

opinion that it was a "tortured construction of the Constitution." And two other Justices agreed with him.

In the case holding the New York minimum Wage Law unconstitutional, Justice Stone said that the majority were actually reading into the Constitution their own "personal economic predilections." . . . And two other Justices agreed with him.

In the face of these dissenting opinions, there is no basis for the claim made by some members of the Court that something in the Constitution had compelled them regretfully to thwart the will of the people.[64]

Just as the President built his case against the Court on impeccable authority and tradition, so the majority of the Judiciary Committee, in reporting against the plan, was likewise inspired by tradition and authority. In its adverse report, the Senate Judiciary Committee said:

If the Court of last resort is to be made to respond to a prevalent sentiment of a current hour, politically imposed, that Court must ultimately become subservient to the pressure of public opinion of the hour, which might at the moment embrace mob passion abhorrent to a more calm, lasting consideration.

True it is that courts, like Congresses, should take account of the advancing strides of civilization. True it is that law, being a progressive science, must be pronounced progressively and liberally; but the milestones of liberal progress are made to be noted and counted with caution rather than merely be encountered and passed. Progress is not a mad mob march; rather, it is a steady, invincible stride.[65]

Alexander Hamilton might well have written these words. With us democracy is not to be equated with majority

[64] *Ibid.*

[65] Adverse of the Senate Judiciary Committee, *Senate Reports*, 75th Cong., 1st Sess. (1937), No. 711, pp. 19–23 *passim.*

rule. Reliance on political responsibility declared and enforced at the ballot box and in legislative halls—the very essence of democracy in most free societies—is not enough for us. This, moreover, was the design and purpose of a "written Constitution and uncontrolled judiciary."

Our law reports are filled with decisions scattered throughout those long years [the Judiciary Committee reported], reassuring the citizen of his constitutional rights, restraining States, restraining the Congress, restraining the Executive, restraining majorities, and preserving the noblest in rights of individuals.[66]

The historic Court-packing episode thus underscores the most characteristic aspect of our tradition—its ambiguity, its richness, its complexity. It high-lights what may be our major contribution to the theory and practice of government—rejection of any and all absolutes, whether under the auspices of majorities or minorities, of interests or of numbers. In this struggle, as we shall see, both sides won, both lost. The inconclusiveness of the outcome is itself significant.

For five months an orgy of debate raged. Clergymen, educators, businessmen, lawyers, and citizens scurried to Washington, bearing witness in torrents of words for and against the plan. The newspapers, even those out of sympathy with the six recalcitrant Justices, vigorously protested. Through the years, and despite increasing evidence that judicial interpretation, not fundamental law, had entrenched economic privilege, the American people had come to regard the Court as the symbol of their freedom. Tarnished though the symbol was, it, like the English monarchy, made for national stability and poise in crisis. Like its Eng-

66 *Ibid.*

lish counterpart, it commanded loyalty of citizenry, providing an impregnable barrier against dictatorship and radicalism. "The President wants to control the Supreme Court" became the war cry. If this Court plan were accepted, the press averred that "not a thing would stand between the ambitions of an unscrupulous man . . . becoming absolute dictator of this country." [67]

Roosevelt's false assertion that the Court lagged behind its docket lent credence to such charges, enabling his enemies, as Secretary of Interior Ickes put it, to play "a bad hand perfectly while we have played a good hand badly." [68] The President himself confessed that his initial approach had been a big blunder. [69] Throughout the furor, that select group which knew most about the situation, the Justices themselves, kept silent. No one doubted where they stood, or that they held the trump card in this political game. The problem was to get them into the fray without offending their professional dignity and their alleged remoteness from political controversy. Leader of the opposition, Senator Burton K. Wheeler, hesitated to approach members of the Court on a purely political mission. He recalls his misgivings about an appointment with Justice Brandeis, known as the most fastidious stickler for proprieties on the Bench. The interview had hardly begun, however, before Wheeler realized that his anxiety was groundless.

[67] "Arouse and Beware," *American Agriculturist*, Feb. 27, 1937, p. 1.

[68] Ickes, *op. cit.*, II, 145.

[69] "I made one major mistake when I first presented the plan," F.D.R. later commented. "I did not place enough emphasis upon the real mischief—the kind of decisions which, as a studied and continued policy, had been coming down from the Supreme Court. I soon corrected that mistake—in the speeches which I later made about the plan" (*op. cit.*, 1937 vol., p. lxv).

"Why don't you confer with the Chief Justice?" Brandeis eagerly suggested. The Senator demurred, explaining that he did not know Hughes. "Well," Brandeis said reassuringly, "the Chief Justice knows you and knows what you are doing." [70] That jurist's leadership was at stake, and he knew it.

When the President's proposal was announced, Secretary Ickes wrote in his diary:

What a blow this will be to the prestige of Chief Justice Hughes, who has had a chance during the last four years to make a high place for himself as one of the great Chief Justices in American history but who has not shown either the strength or the adroitness to control his court and make it an instrument for social and political progress! [71]

Only Brandeis' protest had kept Hughes from appearing before the Judiciary Committee "for the purpose of giving the facts as to the work of the Court." [72] Now with Brandeis' endorsement he plunged into the struggle with alacrity. Though the Senator did not reach him until Saturday, March 20, the Chief Justice was able to prepare a long and closely reasoned document for presentation to the Judiciary Committee the following Monday, March 22. "The baby is born," Hughes said with a broad smile, as he put the letter into Wheeler's hand late Sunday afternoon.[73]

The Chief Justice's literary *coup* of March 21 not only scotched the allegation that the Justices were not abreast of their docket, but also conveyed the erroneous impres-

[70] Interview with Senator Burton K. Wheeler, Feb. 25, 1944.
[71] Ickes, *op. cit.*, II, 66–67.
[72] Merlo J. Pusey, *Charles Evans Hughes* (New York: Macmillan, 1951), II, 754.
[73] *Ibid.*, p. 755.

sion that the Court approved his letter. Ignoring the customary disavowal of authority to speak for members of a body not consulted, Hughes said he was "confident that it is in accord with the views of the Justices," though he admitted "on account of the shortness of time I have not been able to consult with members of the Court generally." [74]

If the Chief Justice had consulted all his colleagues, they would have been divided. In that case, there might have been no letter, or at least a very different one. Later on Justice Stone tried to set the matter in perspective:

In the interest of accuracy, and to avoid the perpetuation of a mistaken impression, may I say that . . . the Justices other than those named in the letter did not join in the expression of the opinion (that the Constitution does not authorize two or more Supreme Courts or two or more parts of a Supreme Court functioning in effect as separate courts). The fact is that I did not then, and do not now approve of such an extra-official expression on a constitutional question by the Court or its members. Justice Cardozo, with whom I discussed the matter, was of the same view.

I first learned of the Chief Justice's letter when a copy of it was printed in the newspapers shortly after its date. I was not consulted in connection with its preparation. Justice Cardozo told me that he was not. I have never formed any opinion on the constitutional point in question or discussed it with any members of the Court. There was no reason of which I am aware why all the members of the Court should not have been consulted in connection with the preparation of a document

[74] *Reorganization of the Federal Judiciary*, pt. 3, pp. 491–492. "The whole thing," Secretary Ickes recorded, "has the appearance of a unanimous Supreme Court opposing the President's proposal" (*op. cit.*, II, 104).

which purported to state "the views of the Justices," or for expressing the views of Justices who for any reason could not be consulted. Although the Court was then in recess, all its members were in the city. They could have been brought together for a conference on an hour's telephone notice, or less. Throughout the recess Justices Sutherland, Cardozo and myself were in our homes, which are within five minutes' walk of the residence of the Chief Justice.[75]

Hughes's literary maneuvers struck hard at the President's proposal. But the most telling blow was still to be dealt. As the President bore down upon the Justices, the really big issue facing them and the country remained unresolved. What would be the fate of the Wagner Labor Relations Act? Would the Justices now turn their backs on recent rulings so as to permit the national government to substitute law for naked force in labor relations? Several cases had been argued February 10 and 11, 1937. Industrial peace—or war—seemed to hang in the balance when, on April 12, 1937, Chief Justice Hughes put forward a broad and encompassing definition of commerce and conceded to Congress the power to protect the life lines of national economy from private industrial warfare. Arguments of the sort that had proved effective in NIRA and Guffey Coal cases now availed nothing. "These cases," Hughes commented summarily, "are not controlling here." [76]

The Chief Justice's colleagues naturally supposed that the man who took a position apparently so completely at odds with his earlier pronouncements must have seen a new light. "Every consideration brought forward to uphold

[75] H. F. Stone to Felix Frankfurter, Dec. 29, 1939.
[76] *National Labor Relations Board* v. *Jones-Laughlin Steel Corporation*, 301 U.S. 1 (1937), p. 41.

the Act before us was applicable to support the Acts held unconstitutional in cases decided within two years," [77] Justice McReynolds growled in dissent. Though Hughes denied to his dying day that he had changed his position, President Roosevelt firmly believed that this "clear-cut victory [for his program] on the bench . . . did more than anything else to bring about the defeat of the plan in the halls of Congress." Before a single judge resigned, before any appointments were made, "the Court began to interpret the Constitution instead of torturing it." [78]

Chief Justice Hughes, head of a body supposedly immune from politics, had played a leading role in the most hotly contested political issue since the Civil War. What is more, he scored a victory, as the late Justice Jackson put it, "over the master liberal politician of our day." [79] Not everyone, however, admired his leadership of a strategic retreat. "I would have had more respect for the Court," Harold Ickes commented in his diary, "if it had gone down fighting and snarling after the manner of Justice McReynolds." [80] "I believe," Ickes recorded, "Hughes can be and ought to be 'debunked.' " [81] Though the language Federal Circuit Court Judge Charles E. Clarke used to describe Hughes's judicial statesmanship is less drastic, it is not uncritical. The Chief

[77] *Ibid.*, p. 77.

[78] Roosevelt, *op. cit.*, 1937 vol., p. lxvi, *et passim.*

[79] Robert H. Jackson, *The Struggle for Judicial Supremacy: A Study of a Crisis in American Power Politics* (New York: Knopf, 1941), p. 196.

"Either the Court would change or there would be a new Court. Observers generally credit Mr. Chief Justice Hughes with the political skill which accomplished the change" (T. Arnold, *The Folklore of Capitalism* [New Haven: Yale University Press, 1937], p. 339).

[80] Ickes, *op. cit.*, II, 107.   [81] *Ibid.*, II, 137.

Justice seemed to think of his function, Judge Clark writes, as "a holding operation, to keep the Court as it was, to 'save' it from the attack of the democratic leader elected by the people." "As a Justice," Judge Clark observed, "he went to rather extreme lengths to distinguish away, rather than overrule, outworn cases. . . . To attempt to control or shape the future of the Court, or to direct it into strange waters, would have been foreign to his nature." [82] Hughes's forte, Thomas Reed Powell observed, was his ability to pose polar opposites without admitting that they were opposites.[83]

Why did Hughes and Roberts shift their positions? Why did they deny the power to govern in 1935 and 1936 and then uphold that power in 1937? Political considerations alone could have hardly dictated their course. For an explanation, one must go back to 1930 and to Justice Stone's disinclination to credit considerations of conservatism and radicalism as marking the basic line dividing the

[82] Charles E. Clark, review of *Charles Evans Hughes*, by Merlo J. Pusey, *Notre Dame Lawyer*, 27 (Spring 1952), 484, 486.

Samuel Hendel gives this appraisal: "When the pressure for innovation became great, and the risks to the nation and to the Court itself apparent, reluctantly at first, but increasingly he went along with change. Having sedulously sought to protect the precedents of the Court, sometimes at the risk of offending logic, he witnessed and often participated in the shattering of one precedent after another. He stood thus as a kind of heroic and, in a sense, tragic figure, torn between the old and the new, seeking at first to stem the tide but then relentlessly caught up and moving with it" (*Charles Evans Hughes and the Supreme Court* [New York: Columbia University Press, 1951], p. 279). See, in this connection, Irving Brant, "How Liberal Is Justice Hughes?" *New Republic* (July 21, 1937), pp. 295–298, and (1937), pp. 329–332.

[83] T. R. Powell, "Charles Evans Hughes," *Political Science Quarterly*, 67 (1952), p. 172.

Justices. Judicial differences arose, Stone said, from "an inadequate understanding of the relation of law and the economic forces which control society." It took the presidential election of 1936, the organization of the C.I.O., a wave of sit-down strikes, and finally President Roosevelt's proposal to enlarge the Supreme Court, to instill in the Chief Justice what Stone and other dissenters had long tried in vain to teach him—that the majority's recalcitrance imperiled the values they thought they were safeguarding.[84] In 1937 Hughes finally realized anew what he had seen and known over thirty years earlier, as counsel for the Armstrong Insurance Committee investigations, that liberty can be and is infringed by economic forces as well as by government and that government must intervene to safeguard the individual against these forces. He then saw too that such intervention made inevitable "the continual expansion of federal power with consequent contractions of state power." "Hughes had the acumen," the *Nation* commented June 14, 1941, "to recognize the inevitable."

Experience taught the late Justice Roberts the same lesson:

Looking back [he wrote in 1951], it is difficult to see how the Court could have resisted the popular urge for uniform standards throughout the country—for what in effect was a unified economy. . . . An insistence by the Court on holding federal power to what seemed its appropriate orbit when the Constitution was adopted might have resulted in even more radical changes in our dual structure than those which have been grad-

[84] "The earnestness and the extent of popular demand," Professor F. D. G. Ribble observed, "may well have been a factor in determining this adjustment. Those who believe that judges legislate . . . will have no difficulty with the idea that in legislating they may take into some account the scale of values of the people for whom their task is performed" ("Charles Evans Hughes," *Columbia Law Review*, 41 [Nov. 1941], 1199–1200).

ually accomplished through the extension of the limited jurisdiction conferred on the federal government.[85]

By thrusting themselves into the vortex of political controversy to jettison a faltering economic oligarchy, the
judges had forced an advance in their own civic education.
At the same time the Court made clear to others what it
had long sought anxiously to conceal—that judicial decisions are, in fact, born of the travail of economic and political
conflict.

Americans learned that judges are human, and that the judicial
power need be no more sacred in our scheme than any other
power. . . . They dared look upon the judicial Medusa-head,
and lo' they were not turned to stone. . . . It was then that
the symbol of divine right began to crumble.[86]

Economic interests learned a very special lesson. After
1937 they knew that the judiciary was no longer a safe
bastion against government regulation of our social and
economic life. Dependence on the people had been re-
established as the primary control on government.

[85] Owen J. Roberts, *The Court and the Constitution* (Cambridge:
Harvard University Press, 1951), pp. 61–62. By this same token
John Maynard Keynes saw F.D.R. as the savior, not the destroyer,
of the existing order. "You have made yourself," Keynes told the
President, "the trustee for those in every country who seek to mend
the evils of our condition by reasoned experiment within the
framework of the existing social system. If you fail, rational change
will be gravely prejudiced throughout the world, leaving ortho-
doxy and revolution to fight it out. But if you succeed, new and
bolder methods will be tried everywhere, and we may date the
first chapter of a new economic era from your accession to office"
(open letter to *New York Times*, Dec. 31, 1933; quoted in R. F.
Harrod, *The Life of John Maynard Keynes* [London: Macmillan,
1951], p. 447).
[86] Max Lerner, *Ideas for the Ice Age* (New York: Viking, 1941),
p. 259–60.

* IV *

The Supreme Court

in Search of a Role

NINETEEN THIRTY-SIX was the crucial year. By that time the Supreme Court, as we have seen, had come to think of itself as "the only agency of government that must be assumed to have capacity to govern." [1] In an opinion of unusual vehemence, Justice Stone then urged his colleagues to consider the wisdom of judicial humility.

Justice Roberts, speaking for six of his colleagues, including the Chief Justice, had raised the specter of "legislative power, without restriction or limitation," "vested in a parliament . . . subject to no restrictions except the discretion of its members." [2] But, Stone countered, consider the status of the Supreme Court's power. "Courts are concerned only with the power to enact statutes, not with their wisdom." [3] The Executive and Congress are, moreover,

[1] *United States* v. *Butler,* 297 U.S. 1 (1936), p. 87.
[2] *Ibid.,* p. 63.   [3] *Ibid.,* p. 78.

limited by "the ballot and the processes of democratic government," and "subject to judicial restraint." "The only check upon our own exercise of power is our own sense of self-restraint." [4] Even when Courts keep within the narrow province assigned to them by the Constitution, they should be deferential to legislative findings of fact, out of which controverted statutes arise, and ever mindful of the awesome nature of judicial authority. Precisely because it is unfettered, Stone reasoned, judicial responsibility should be discharged with a finer conscience. Nor did the fact that governmental power, especially that of the purse, is fraught with frightening possibilities of abuse alter the Court's function. Justice Robert's inference that such power, unless judicially limited, might be put to undesirable and constitutionally prohibited ends Stone dismissed as hardly rising to "the dignity of argument." [5]

Such suppositions are addressed to the mind accustomed to believe that it is the business of courts to sit in judgment on the wisdom of legislative action. . . . Congress and the courts both unhappily may falter or be mistaken in the performance of their constitutional duty. But interpretation of our great charter of government which proceeds on any assumption that the responsibility for the preservation of our institutions is the exclusive concern of any one of the three branches of government, or that it alone can save them from destruction, is far more likely, in the long run, "to obliterate the constituent members" of "an indestructible union of indestructible states" than the frank recognition that language, even of a constitution, may mean what it says. . . .[6]

Stone's dissent evoked widespread comment. "Never before," Columbia University Professor Howard L. McBain

---

[4] *Ibid.*, p. 79. [5] *Ibid.*, p. 87.
[6] *Ibid.*, pp. 87–88.

wrote in a popular article featuring the Justice's blast, "has a dissenting minority gone quite so far toward calling into question the motives of the majority and clearly implying that they have abused their judicial prerogative." [7]

The Justice was quick to take notice.

I thought your article in yesterday's *New York Times* very interesting and able, but perhaps I should enter one disclaimer. I do not question the motives of my brethren, and did not intend to do so in the vigorous language which I used in my dissenting opinion. I do question a method of thinking which is perhaps the greatest stumbling-block to the right administration of judicial review of legislation.

Continuing, Stone explained his position at length:

The *common untrained mind* is accustomed to think that legislation which it regards as bad or unwise must necessarily be unconstitutional. Where there is a choice of interpretations of a constitutional provision, such a habit of thought is very likely to make a choice of the interpretation which would lessen the possibility of enacting a bad law. The difficulty with this method is that lessening the power to enact bad laws likewise lessens the power to enact good ones, and the judgment of what is good or bad, which is essentially a legislative function, is likely to be affected by the passions and prejudices of the moment. Such an approach to constitutional construction tends to increase the dead areas in the Constitution, the lacunae in which no power exists, neither state nor national, to deal with the problems of government.[8]

There was nothing personal in these intracourt battles. Justice Stone queried his associates' conception of their role in the governmental process, not their motives. "The

[7] *New York Times Magazine*, Jan. 19, 1936, p. 2, col. 2.
[8] H. F. Stone to H. L. McBain, Jan. 21, 1936. (Emphasis added.)

fact that we have intellectual differences," he said, "has not yet made us uncivilized." [9] "If judges can be brought to understand what I conceive to be the true nature of the judicial function I can think of no institution likely to be of more enduring value." [10]

Two days later McBain expressed regret for having drawn from Stone's words "a deduction as to motives which you did not intend." On second thought, however, the educator stood by his guns. The implications had been spelled out only after very careful thought, and they still seemed "not unreasonable." "Frankly I do question the motives of your colleagues," McBain reiterated. "Their motives are so inextricably interwoven with their thought processes as to reveal themselves without their even being conscious of the revelation."

Stone seemed unprepared to continue his disclaimer. On January 28, 1936, he admitted what his original letter to Professor McBain made all too clear—that even judges can be, and often are, prisoners of their own experience. "In the long run, I do not suppose it makes much difference whether unfortunate interpretations of the Constitution are purposeful, or only the product of muddy thinking and the subconscious force of unrecognized prejudices."

Dissenting again a few months later, Stone reaffirmed his indictment. In the second Minimum Wage case of 1936 [11] he assailed the majority's deification of the private-wage bargain and cited the judges' "personal economic predilections," as the only possible explanation for their decision. As in Justice Holmes's classic New York Bake Shop dis-

[9] H. F. Stone to De Witt Clark, Feb. 21, 1936.
[10] H. F. Stone to H. L. McBain, *loc. cit.*
[11] *Morehead* v. *Tipaldo*, 298 U.S. 587 (1936), p. 633.

sent of 1905, he scathingly denounced substitution of political-economic preference for the Constitution. The Fourteenth Amendment had

no more embedded in the Constitution our preference for some
particular set of economic beliefs, than it has adopted, in the
name of liberty, the system of theology which we may happen to approve.

It is not for the courts to resolve doubts whether the remedy
by wage regulation is as efficacious as many believe, or is better
than some other, or is better even than the blind operation of
uncontrolled economic forces. The legislature must be free to
choose unless government is to be rendered impotent. . . . We
should . . . leave the selection and the method [for solution
of public issues where] the Constitution has left them, to the
legislative branch of the Government. . . .[12]

Justice Sutherland, champion of the old court, much an-
noyed by Stone's telltale revelations, used an early opportunity to challenge his theory. Sutherland agreed that
rational doubts should be resolved in favor of controverted
legislation. "But," he asked, "whose doubts, and by whom
resolved?" The Constitution places on judges the duty "to
say the final word as to the validity of a statute assailed as
unconstitutional." So long as the Court holds that authority,
"its exercise cannot be avoided without betrayal of the
trust." A judge should not be governed by doubts of colleagues, even when they numbered four. The oath he takes

[12] *Ibid.*, p. 636. Empoyees and employers, Sutherland held in
Adkins v. *Children's Hospital*, 261 U.S. 525, have an equal right to
obtain from each other the best terms they can as the result of
private bargaining. That was the "freedom of contract" protected
by the Constitution. Stone, dissenting in 1936, said that a wage "is
not always the resultant of free bargaining." It may be "forced
upon employees by their economic necessities and upon employers
by the most ruthless of their competitors" (*ibid.*, p. 635).

is individual, not composite: "he discharges a duty imposed on *him*." In the end, judicial responsibility is purely personal; a judge cannot subordinate his conviction to that of others and "keep faith with his oath or retain his judicial and moral independence." [13]

As a piece of enigmatic writing, what Sutherland says about the judicial function is hard to match. After insisting on the absolute and unfettered right, nay, duty, of the judge to exercise his own personal discretion, he falls back on semantics, on a psychologically tenuous distinction between "will" and "judgment." Further to confuse the issue, he returns to the theme that the only checks on the judge are his "oath," "his own conscientious and informed convictions," his "duty to make up his own mind and adjudge accordingly." This seems but another way of saying that the check, if any, is self-restraint. At this point one might dismiss the distinction between "will" and "judgment" as of no consequence, were it not that Sutherland returns to it again, insisting with Thomas M. Cooley that " 'Courts *declare the law as written.*' " [14]

Four judges plus one are right, without that one, wrong. "If the Constitution . . . stands in the way of desirable legislation," Sutherland observes, "the blame must rest upon that instrument, and not upon the court for enforcing it according to its terms." [15]

[13] *West Coast Hotel* v. *Parrish*, 300 U.S. 379 (1937), pp. 401–402.
[14] *Ibid.*, pp. 402, 404.
[15] *Ibid.*, p. 404. It was Justice Roberts' statement of the judicial function in *U.S.* v. *Butler*, a theory very similar to Sutherland's, that may have aroused Stone to speak out so vehemently in dissent. Said Roberts: "When an act of Congress is appropriately challenged in the courts as not conforming to the constitutional mandate the judicial branch of the government has only one duty,—to lay the article of the Constitution which is invoked beside the statute which is challenged and to decide whether the latter squares

There is a grim sort of courage in Sutherland's obvious reference to Justice Stone's betrayals. "Burn me if you will," he seems to say. "I can do no other." Justice Stone's remarks in his AAA dissent offended the proprieties. They were "ill considered and mischievous" [16] in lifting the veil from mystery, revealing behind judicial pageantry nine human beings, all participants in the governing process and no nearer the source of ultimate wisdom than are others. Such stage play, considered by some an immemorial necessity, protected judges, strengthened their prestige, enabling them, by recourse to "*the* law," "*the* Constitution," to "beautify," in Justice Holmes's language, "what may be disagreeable to the sufferers." [17] When judges upset "desirable legislation," blame must rest on the document of 1787, not upon the Court. The great vice of Stone's disclosure, his notion that judges might exercise "self-restraint," and could by their own will construe the Constitution so as to uphold "desirable legislation," was that it ignored the Constitution and endangered the standing of the Court itself. Once the veneer that coats the surface of the Court's doings wears thin, once the public recognizes the personal nature of judicial power, it will get rough handling, making it impossible for an impartial and independent judiciary (and for constitutional lawyers) to function at all. Stone

---

with the former. All the Court does, or can do, is to announce its considered judgment upon the question. The only power it has, if such it may be called, is the power of judgment. This Court neither approves nor condemns any legislative policy" (*U.S.* v. *Butler*, 297 U.S. 1 [1936], pp. 62–63).

[16] With undisguised reference to the words Stone used in his dissenting opinion of 1936, Sutherland commented: "The suggestion that the only check upon the exercise of the judicial power . . . is the Judge's own faculty of self-restraint, is both ill considered and mischievous" (300 U.S. 379 [1936], p. 402).

[17] Dissenting in *Tyson* v. *Banton*, 273 U.S. 418 (1927), p. 446.

had done the Court an incalculable disservice in letting the judicial cat out of the legalistic bag.

Sutherland's complaint recalls Hans Christian Andersen's fable of the royal robes which could be seen only by the loyal, the pure, and the righteous. Stone was the urchin who blurted out the facts.

In 1937 the Court perforce chose to follow Stone rather than Sutherland. Soon the pre-eminent role which the old bench insisted on playing in economic affairs had vanished beyond recognition.[18] "As the tide set in towards regulation, the judiciary . . . put up a furious fight against regulation. In a glorious twilight, the Supreme Court made a gallant

[18] "While substantive due process in the economic field has not been expressly rejected in principle," Wallace Mendelson observes, "it has not been used to invalidate any state or national act since 1937" ("Justices Black and Frankfurter: Supreme Court Majority and Minority Trends," *Journal of Politics*, 12 [1950], 67).

"It would be erroneous," Samuel Handel writes, "to think that . . . the Court has abandoned its supervisory role. They [recent developments] mean simply that the Court is presently disposed to accord considerable discretion, short of finality, to legislative determinations of reasonableness and justice divorced from additional hampering restrictions imposed by special doctrine" (*Charles Evans Hughes and the Supreme Court* [New York: King's Crown Press, 1951], p. 136). In some states, "due process" persists as a substantative limitation on legislative power. See Monrad G. Paulsen, "The Persistence of Substantive Due Process in the States," *Minnesota Law Review*, 34 (1950), 91–118.

In *Lincoln Federal Labor Union* v. *Northwestern Iron and Metal Co.*, 335 U.S. 525 (1949), Justice Black said that "due process" as a substantive limitation, which he described as "the Allgeyer-Lochner-Adair-Coppage" line of reasoning, was rejected "at least as early as 1934 when the Nebbia Case was decided." Since then the Court had "consciously returned closer and closer to the earlier constitutional principle" that the states may regulate injurious practices, so long as specific constitutional provisions or federal laws are not thereby violated. "Under this constitutional doctrine,"

last stand against New Deal measures—and then quietly surrendered judicial supremacy." "The result," Walton Hamilton observes, "was inevitable; for in function, tradition, process, the courts are poorly equipped for the task of continuous oversight." [19] At the very moment popular control over the Justices was vindicated, the public be-

---

Black observed, "the due process clause is no longer to be so broadly construed that the Congress and state legislatures are put in a strait jacket when they attempt to suppress business and industrial conditions which they regard as offensive to the public welfare" (pp. 536–537).

In 1944 (*Federal Power Commission* v. *Hope National Gas Co.*, 320 U.S. 591) when Justice Frankfurter commented that "Congressional acquiescence to date in the doctrine of Chicago, Milwaukee, and St. Paul Railroad v. Minn. . . . may fairly be claimed," Justices Black and Murphy wrote a concurrence taking strong exception to Frankfurter's view. "That was the case," they said of the Chicago, Milwaukee decision, "in which the majority of this Court was finally induced to expand the meaning of 'due process' so as to give courts power to block efforts of the state and national governments to regulate economic affairs. . . .

"We feel compelled to say that we do not understand that Congress voluntarily has acquiesced in a constitutional principle of government that courts, rather than legislative bodies, possess final authority over regulation of economic matters. Even this Court has not always fully embraced that principle, and we wish to repeat that we have never acquiesced in it, and do not now" (pp. 619–620).

It was not only laissez-faire that had passed into judicial limbo. There was objection after 1937 to the enthronement of any economic theory. "It is equally immaterial that such state action may run counter to the economic wisdom either of Adam Smith or of J. Maynard Keynes, or may be ultimately mischievous even from the point of view of avowed state policy" (*Osborn* v. *Ozlin*, 310 U.S. 53 [1939], p. 62). To the same effect the Court declared in 1946: "It may commend itself to a State to encourage a pastoral instead of an industrial society. That is its concern and its privilege" (*Freeman* v. *Hewit*, 329 U.S. 249 [1946], p. 252).

[19] Statement before the Joint Committee on the Organization of Congress, May 29, 1945, 79th Cong., 1st Sess., p. 701.

came aware of the arbitrary personal element in judicial decisions. Simultaneously, the Court's strength and its weakness were fully exposed to the public gaze. The veiled mystery of the judicial process had at last been made all too clear—in fact destroyed. That the Supreme Court does actually operate within the ambit of political considerations became quite well known.

The sharp rejoinders in dissenting opinions sketch the enormity of the 1937 judicial revolution as the dissenters saw it. The Constitution "is gone," [20] Justice McReynolds shrieked. "If the provisions of the Constitution be not upheld when they pinch as well as when they comfort," Justice Sutherland commented stoically, "they [the constitutional pinchers] may as well be abandoned." [21] McReynolds and Sutherland were quite right. *Their* Constitution was gone —*their* Constitution being that of about 1895, not the Constitution of 1787; *their* Constitution regarded and construed, as Justice Sutherland said, in his West Coast Hotel dissent, as of changeless meaning. And just as McReynolds' and Sutherland's Constitution was grounded in the theory of laissez-faire, in the view that liberty is possible only in a society relatively immune from government control, just so the Constitution of Chief Justice Hughes (revised version) and Justice Stone recognized that liberty means freedom within a social organization. It was now understood that freedom can be interfered with by forces other than government, that liberty is as much dependent upon legislative implementation of, say, the right to bargain collectively, as

[20] Justice McReynolds dissenting in the Gold Clause cases (294 U.S. 240 [1935] as reported in the *New York Times*, Feb. 19, 1935, p. 1, col. 7, continued on p. 16, cols. 5 and 6.
[21] *Home Building Loan Assoc.* v. *Blaisdell*, 290 U.S. 398 (1934), p. 483.

upon judicial protection of employers against the arbitrary power of government.[22]

The sudden retreat of Hughes and Roberts not only shocked the conservative minority, so recently the majority, but disturbed conservative legal-political thought generally. Ultraconservatives really were afraid for the future because the new concept of public power suggested to them "a ramp, with no convenient landings for a logical mind, slightly out of breath, perhaps, to rest on. . . ."[23] Justice McReynold's fatalistic complaint in his Jones-Laughlin dissent is quite understandable: "Almost anything —marriage, birth, death—may in some fashion affect commerce."[24] Moreover, it soon became evident that "political momentum," the force that terrified Herbert Spencer, was a factor in the calculus of judicial as well as legislative action. In rapid succession many old landmarks were effaced. Brickbats, as well as plaudits, greeted the drastic consequences of judicial self-restraint. President Frank J. Hogan of the American Bar Association, brooding over the judicial catastrophe, expounded its meaning:

The plain result of all this is that no lawyer can safely advise his client what the law is; no business man, no farmer, can know whether or not he is breaking the law, for if he follows established principles he is likely to be doing exactly that. What was a constitutional principle yesterday may be a discarded doctrine tomorrow, and this, all this, in what has so often been proudly proclaimed to be a government of laws and not of men. "Shifts

[22] Chief Justice Hughes expressed this view in *West Coast Hotel* v. *Parrish*, 300 U.S. 379 (1936), p. 391, and in *National Labor Relations Board* v. *Jones-Laughlin Steel Corp.*, 301 U.S. 1 (1937), p. 33.

[23] Charles P. Curtis, *Lions under the Throne* (Boston: Houghton Mifflin, 1947), p. 175.

[24] *National Labor Relations Board* v. *Jones-Laughlin Steel Corp.*, 301 U.S. 1 (1937).

in constitutional doctrines" is but a phrase which describes the abolition of *stare decisis;* the replacing of stability by instability, the substitution of uncertainty for certainty, and of plenary power for limitations upon power; the transfer from States and local communities to a centralized government at Washington of "most if not all activities of the Nation." If these be consummations devoutly to be wished, then we have the fulfillment of the wish.

The conclusion to be drawn from all of this is that reliance against the exercise of arbitrary power must be placed by the people henceforth in the legislative rather than in the judicial department of the National Government. . . . The guards have been let down, many of the limits have been obliterated. . . . Freed is the Congress, by the action of the Supreme Court, from all but a very few constitutional fetters on its exercise of power. Legislative independence and legislative wisdom are America's almost sole reliance for the continuance of that security of the blessings of liberty for which the Constitution was framed and the Government of the United States of America created.[25]

The American Bar Association's president was unduly pessimistic; his prophesies misinterpreted the events of 1937. The Court-packing plan itself left judicial power intact. The judiciary retreated; it did not surrender. One may also recall that for Madison "dependence on the people" was always the "primary control on government" [26]— judicial pre-eminence a comparatively recent development.

[25] An address by Frank J. Hogan, "Shifts in Constitutional Doctrines," in *Legal Intelligencer,* July 22, 1939, p. 8. Also in *Reports of the American Bar Association,* 64 (1939), 498–500.

[26] Making "the judiciary paramount to the legislature," Madison wrote in 1788, "was never intended and can never be proper" (quoted by Edward S. Corwin in *Reorganization of the Federal Judiciary,* Hearings before the Committee on the Judiciary [U.S. Senate], 75th Cong., 1st Sess. [1937], p. 172). For Hamilton, too, the primary control on government was political—change of rep-

Hogan exaggerates the role the Court must play in a free society. Chief Justice Marshall had been quite content to rely on the "wisdom and discretion of Congress," along with the usual political restraints for "obliging government to control itself." Chief Justice Waite had most emphatically told aggrieved litigants seeking judicial protection against the alleged wrongs of state legislators to resort to the ballot box rather than the courts. Justice Bradley vainly voiced these same sentiments in the Chicago, Milwaukee, St. Paul R.R. case of 1890. The same plaintive note had become a resounding refrain in the dissenting opinions of Justices Holmes and Stone. But no one expressed his faith in democratic processes more forcefully than did John Marshall himself:

The wisdom and the discretion of Congress, their identity with the people, and the influence which their constituents possess at elections, are, in this, as in many other instances, . . . the *sole* restraints on which they have relied, to secure them from its abuse. They are the restraints on which the people must often rely *solely*, in all representative governments.[27]

Someone has compared the judicial bowing out to political expediency in 1937 to the British king's strategy in 1832. Just as William IV relinquished his power in order to keep his place, so the justices yielded to President Roosevelt's Court-packing threat. The parallel is suggestive. The Court, like the king, did not abdicate. It merely surrendered the power it had itself previously annexed so as to give force and effect to the not very ambient laissez-faire dogma. When Stone in 1936 proclaimed the wisdom of

resentatives by popular election. See Beloff, ed., *op. cit.*, No. 60, p. 307.
[27] *Gibbons* v. *Ogden*, 9 Wheaton 1 (1824), p. 197. (Italics added.)

judicial self-restraint, he did not hint at, or even imply, self-abnegation, much less suicide. That the Court still has a role, and an important one, to play in public affairs is illustrated by major decisions: The Flag Salute cases of 1940 and 1943 and the Arizona Train Limit case of 1945 may suffice to underscore it. In all these cases, the Justices explored and disputed the role courts should play in the governing process.

At the very moment the Court abandoned guardianship of economic interests, it seemed ready to shoulder a special responsibility for speech, thought, and religion. Having surrendered the heavy responsibility of passing on the wisdom of social and economic policy, it was soon faced with the question of whether judicial "self-restraint" is equally applicable to the review of legislation infringing those freedoms that had come to be thought of as "implicit in the concept of ordered liberty." [28] Is the Court under any peculiar responsibility to scrutinize legislative infringements of those rights which constitute the "basis of all our civil and political institutions?" In its broader aspect, the question confronting the Justices was the perennial one— whether the judiciary should, or can be, the primary guardian of any constitutional values, or must it always remain auxiliary to the usual political restraints?

"It is the paradox of the period, if paradox it be," Herbert Wechsler wrote, "that new areas of constitutional protection were emerging even as the power to govern was being sustained. And Justice Stone's part in this branch of the development was . . . commanding." [29] Just as Stone had led the battle for judicial self-restraint in cases involv-

[28] *Palko* v. *Conn.*, 302 U.S. 319 (1937), p. 325.
[29] Herbert Wechsler, "Stone and the Constitution," *Columbia Law Review*, 46 (1946), 793.

ing social and economic legislation, so it was he who, with the "casualness of a footnote"[30] (to use Justice Frankfurter's somewhat derogatory language) suggested a formulation that ultimately flowered into the so-called doctrine of "preferred freedoms."

In the otherwise obscure case of *United States* v. *Carolene Products Company*,[31] decided in 1938, Stone wrote these lines into the body of his opinion for the Court:

Regulatory legislation affecting ordinary commercial transaction is not to be pronounced unconstitutional unless in the light of the facts made known or generally assumed it is of such a character as to preclude the assumption that it rests upon some rational basis within the knowledge and experience of the legislators.[32]

He would not go so far as to say that no economic legislation would ever violate constitutional restraints, but he did suggest confining the Court's role strictly. Attached to this proposition was the famous footnote 4:

It is unnecessary to consider now whether legislation which restricts those political processes which can ordinarily be ex-

[30] *Dennis* v. *U.S.*, 341 U.S. 494 (1951), p. 526. In *Jones* v. *Opelika* (316 U.S. 584 [1942], p. 608) Stone declared that the First Amendment put speech, press, and religion in a "preferred position." He thus encouraged a "mischievous" trend. "Not without justification," Justice Frankfurter observed, a belief was thus engendered that "there is a constitutional principle, expressed by those attractive but imprecise words" (341 U.S. 494 [1951], p. 527). In *Kovacs* v. *Cooper* (336 U.S. 77 [1949], pp. 90–91) Frankfurter denied that a majority of the Court had subscribed to the doctrine of preferred freedoms. But Justice Rutledge was quick to demonstrate "the conclusion opposite to that which he draws" (*ibid.*, at 106). Frankfurter himself has insisted that the judiciary should guard with "a jealous eye" the right of free discussion (*A.F.L.* v. *Swing*, 312 U.S. 321 [1940], p. 325).

[31] 304 U.S. 144 (1938).   [32] *Ibid.*, pp. 151–154, note 4.

pected to bring about repeal of undesirable legislation, is to be subjected to more exacting judicial inquiry under the general prohibitions of the Fourteenth Amendment than are most other types of legislation. . . .

Nor need we inquire whether similar considerations enter into the review of statutes directed at particular religious . . . or national . . . or racial minorities . . . whether prejudice against discrete and insular minorities may be a special condition, which tends seriously to curtail the operation of those political processes ordinarily to be relied upon to protect minorities, and which may call for a correspondingly more searching judicial inquiry.

This highly controversial, history-making formulation, was the work of Justice Stone's law clerk Louis Lusky, now a practicing lawyer in Louisville, Ky. It is perhaps the most striking example of Justice Stone's custom of allowing his law clerks to include in footnotes, as sort of trial balloons, suggestive and potentially fruitful ideas.

There are three paragraphs in the footnote. The first, written by Chief Justice Hughes, says: "There may be narrower scope for operation of the presumption of constitutionality when legislation appears on its face to be within a specific prohibition of the Constitution, such as those of the first ten amendments, which are deemed equally specific when held to be embraced within the Fourteenth. . . ." In his article featuring the footnote, Lusky completely ignores this paragraph.

"My guess is," Lusky's former law partner George Braden observes, "that Chief Justice Hughes added the paragraph to protect some theory he had which he thought the citations to his opinions demonstrated." "The first paragraph appears to be unnecessary, if not actually inconsistent with the remainder of the footnote." What Hughes says either obviates the necessity for speaking, as the second paragraph does, of restrictions on political processes, if the First and Fifteenth Amendments cover political processes, or is not exhaustive if non-specific prohibitions must be relied on to protect political processes. Likewise the third paragraph on minorities is potentially more extensive than any specific prohibition contained in the Constitution.[33]

One may conclude that judicial review and political restraints are supplementary, or, at least, interrelated, doctrines. If the political processes cannot be depended upon to provide a corrective for legislation restricting, say, the right to vote, freedom of speech and assembly, or statutes directed against discrete and insular minorities, the courts are under special obligation to scrutinize the infringements. Stone's basic thought was this:

I am first of all a man of reason. I believe in reason and its power in the market place of discourse. I am also a democrat. I believe that our governments are to be run by the governed. Therefore I shall use my great power as a Supreme Court Justice sparingly, but I shall use it when it is necessary to preserve the democratic process or to protect those injured by unreason under circumstances where political processes cannot be relied on to protect them.[34]

[33] The Carolene Products Co. footnote should be read in connection with Stone's equally significant footnote in *South Carolina Highway Dept.* v. *Barnwell Brothers*, 303 U.S. 177 (1938), pp. 184–185, note 2, and *Helvering* v. *Gerhardt*, 304 U.S. 405 (1938), p. 416. For a brilliant exposition of the underlying theory of the footnote and its relation to national security, see Lusky, "Minority Rights and the Public Interest," *Yale Law Journal*, 52 (1942), 1–42. See also George Braden, "The Search for Objectivity in Constitutional Law," *Yale Law Journal*, 57 (1948), pp. 571–594, and especially note 28, p. 580.

[34] Braden, *op. cit.*, pp. 580–581. Braden suggests that Stone was "addressing himself to a problem arising out of the use of the pre-

Though the groundwork had been laid in the earlier opinions of Justice Holmes,[35] Justice Brandeis,[36] and Chief Justice Hughes,[37] the Court did not immediately assume special guardianship of the so-called preferred freedoms. In the leading case of *Minersville School District* v.

---

sumption of constitutionality as a means of forestalling the Due Process Clause attacks on economic legislation. His problem was to make the presumption stick in economic cases without being plagued by it in civil liberties and similar cases. Accordingly, he suggested by typical judicial indirection that legislation restricting political processes and legislation directed at 'discrete and insular' minorities should not have a favorable presumption of constitutionality to protect the legislation against attack. His expressed reason for the latter half of this was that political processes 'can ordinarily be expected to bring about repeal of undesirable legislation,' but that minorities such as racial and religious groups are subject to prejudice 'which tends seriously to curtail the operation of those political processes ordinarily to be relied upon to protect minorities' " (pp. 579–581).

[35] According to Professor Frankfurter, Holmes "attributed very different legal significance to those liberties of the individual which history has attested as the indispensable conditions of a free society" and "was far more ready to find legislative invasion in this field than in the area of debatable economic reform" (*Mr. Justice Holmes and the Supreme Court* [Cambridge: Harvard University Press, 1938], p. 51). Frankfurter's own views seemed first to diverge from and then to coincide with those of Holmes. Frankfurter himself observed: "There is truth behind the familiar contrast between rights of property and rights of man. But certainly in some of its aspects property is a function of personality. . . . Especially in a civilization like ours, where the economic independence of society is so pervasive, a sharp division between property rights and human rights largely falsifies reality. . . . But the various interests of human personality are not of equal worth. There is a hierarchy of values" (*ibid.*, p. 49).

[36] See especially *Whitney* v. *Calif.*, 274 U.S. 357 (1927), pp. 375–377.

[37] See *Stromberg* v. *Calif.*, 283 U.S. 359 (1931) and *Near* v. *Minn.*, 283 U.S. 697 (1931). Hughes's opinions stimulated a rash of articles. See Harry Shulman, "The Supreme Court's Attitude toward Liberty of Contract and Freedom of Speech," *Yale Law Journal*, 42

Gobitis,[38] the Justices voted to uphold power in the state to require the flag salute of school children in violation of the religious scruples of Jehovah's Witnesses. By the time this case reached the Justices, April 21, 1940, this issue had been before them three times. In each instance, they disposed of the matter in *per curiam* opinion, for want of a substantial federal question. As late as April 17, 1939, Justice Stone joined his colleagues in denying appeal from the Supreme Court of California, upholding the flag salute. When, less than a year later, it became evident that he would dissent in the Gobitis case, Justice Frankfurter was astonished and dismayed. In a five-page letter Frankfurter elaborated the consideration he had given this "tragic issue," all the more delicate for him in that it involved a "clash of rights, not the clash of wrongs. . . . For resolving such clash we have no calculus," he commented. "We are not exercising an independent judgment; we are sitting in judgment upon the judgment of the legislature."

Frankfurter assured Stone that "nothing has weighed as much on my conscience, since I have come on this Court, as has this case. . . . All my bias and predisposition are in favor of giving the fullest elbow room to every variety of religious, political and economic view." Frankfurter's stand was the more soul-wrenching in that it entered

a domain where constitutional power is on one side and my private notions of liberty and toleration and good sense are on the other. . . . I want to avoid the mistake comparable to that

---

(1931), 262; "Presumption of Constitutionality," note in *Columbia Law Review*, 31 (1931), 1136; Louis A. Warsoff, "The Weight of the Presumption of Constitutionality under the Fourteenth Amendment," *Boston University Law Review*, 18 (1938), 319; Walton Hamilton, "The Jurist's Art," *Columbia Law Review*, 31 (1931), 1085.

[38] 310 U.S. 586 (1940).

made by those whom we criticized when dealing with the control of property. . . . My intention . . . was to use this opinion as a vehicle for preaching the true democratic faith of not relying on the Court for the impossible task of assuring a vigorous, mature, self-protecting and tolerant democracy by bringing the responsibility for a combination of firmness and toleration directly home where it belongs—to the people and their representatives themselves.

In all this, Frankfurter thought he was but following Stone's pointed admonitions about judicial self-restraint. "I have tried in this opinion really to act on what will, as a matter of history, be a lodestar for due regard between legislative and judicial powers, to wit, your dissent in the *Butler* case."

Nor was this the only case in which Stone had stated the guiding rule Frankfurter thought he was following:

I am aware of the important distinction which you so skillfully adumbrated in your footnote 4 (particularly the second paragraph of it) in the Carolene Products Co. case. I agree with that distinction; I regard it as basic. I have taken over that distinction in its central aspect in the present opinion . . . by insisting on the importance of keeping open all those channels of free expression by which undesirable legislation may be removed, and keeping unobstructed all forms of protest against what one deems invasions of conscience, however much the invasion may be justified on the score of the deepest interests of national wellbeing.

"We are not," Frankfurter emphasized, "the primary resolver of the clash." The Court's spokesman was concerned lest we "exercise our judicial power unduly, and as though we ourselves were legislators by holding with too tight a rein the organs of popular government." [39]

[39] Justice Felix Frankfurter to Chief Justice Harlan F. Stone, May 27, 1940. (Emphasis added.) The full text of the letter is included herein as an Appendix, pages 217–220.

It was most embarrassing to be confronted by an antagonist who, as Stone said, quotes "my favorite author against me." But, he retorted, any "vulgar intrusion of law in the domain of conscience," as in this case, imposes on the Court a larger responsibility than in legislation dealing with the control of property. "I am truly sorry not to go along with you. The case is peculiarly one of the relative weight of imponderables and I cannot overcome the feeling that the Constitution tips the scales in favor of religion." [40]

For Justice Frankfurter the great lesson of the controversy over the Supreme Court fight was that judges may not interpose personal valuations in any sphere of judicial competence. To him judicial review itself appears tainted, undemocratic, "inherently oligarchic." [41] For him the "precise issue" before the Court in the Gobitis case "is whether the legislatures of the various states and the authorities in a thousand counties and school districts of this country are barred from determining the appropriateness of various means to evoke that unifying sentiment without which there can ultimately be no liberties, civil or religious." Judicial intervention in this area would amount to no less than "the pronouncement of pedagogical and psychological dogma in a field where courts possess no marked and certainly no controlling competence." [42]

Invoking, as he believed, the essence of Stone's Carolene Products Co. footnote, Frankfurter reasoned:

Except where the transgression of constitutional liberty is too plain for argument, personal freedom is best maintained—so

[40] For this pencil-written, undated note, I am indebted to Mr. Justice Frankfurter.

[41] *A.F. of L.* v. *American Sash and Door Co.*, 335 U.S. 538 (1949), p. 555.

[42] 310 U.S. 586, pp. 597–598.

long as the remedial channels of the democratic process remain open and unobstructed—when it is ingrained in a people's habits and not enforced against popular policy by the coercion of adjudicated law.[43]

At the end Frankfurter threw down the very caveat Stone had hurled at his colleagues in 1936. "To the legislature no less than to courts is committed the guardianship of deeply-cherished liberties." [44]

Stone dissented alone. The Minersville School Board had struck at the heart of liberty; its patent destruction of religious freedom could not survive "searching judicial scrutiny," and no niceties of judicial self-restraint should keep the court from saying so. If a modest estimate of its own power were to yield wholesome results, the Court must be cautious, lest it rush to the other extreme. The flag salute requirement could not stand, even though it were thought to enhance the interest of national unity.

Where there are competing demands of the interests of government and of liberty under the Constitution and where the performance of governmental functions is brought into conflict with specific constitutional restrictions, there must, when that is possible, be reasonable accommodation between them so as to preserve the essentials of both. . . . It is the function of courts to determine whether such accommodation is really possible. . . .[45]

Far from being free to wash its hands of such questions by deferring to legislative judgment or by making the usual presumption of constitutionality, the Supreme Court had a positive duty, enjoined by the Constitution itself:

[43] *Ibid.*, p. 599.   [44] *Ibid.*, p. 600.
[45] *Ibid.*, p. 603.

The framers were not unaware that under the system which they created most governmental curtailments of personal liberty would have the support of a legislative judgment that the public interest would be better served by its curtailment than by its constitutional protection.[46]

Frankfurter had not, as he supposed, taken over the "central aspect" of the distinction drawn in the Carolene Products Co. footnote. Quite the contrary. Citing this case, Stone wrote:

We have previously pointed to the importance of a searching judicial inquiry into the legislative judgment in situations where prejudice against discrete and insular minorities may tend to curtail the operation of those political processes ordinarily to be relied on to protect minorities. . . . And until now we have not hesitated similarly to scrutinize legislation restricting the civil liberty of racial and religious minorities although no political process was affected.

Nor should the Court "refrain from passing upon the legislative judgment" simply because "the remedial channels of the democratic process remain open and unobstructed." This seemed to him "no more than the surrender of the constitutional protection of the liberty of small minorities to the popular will." [47] In reply to Frankfurter's argument that liberty is best maintained when it is ingrained in a people's habits and not enforced against popular policy by adjudicated law, Stone concluded:

The Constitution expresses more than the conviction of the people that democratic processes must be preserved at all costs. It is also an expression of faith and a command that freedom of mind and spirit must be preserved, which government must

[46] *Ibid.*, pp. 604–605.   [47] *Ibid.*, p. 606.

obey, if it is to adhere to that justice and moderation without which no free government can exist.[48]

It would be difficult to cite a better example of how reasonable and honest men can differ as to basic constitutional principles and as to the role of the Court in bringing about their enforcement.[49] "Though we read the scales differently in weighing these 'imponderables,' " Frankfurter wrote Stone after the decision came down, "I cannot but feel confident that our scales are the same. In any event, . . . we care not differently for the only things that give dignity to man—the things of the spirit." [50]

The Justices stood eight to one. Three years later the flag salute issue was again before them. Then the late Justice Jackson, speaking for the Court, adopted Stone's dissenting views and went even further in elevating the Court's role as guardian of the so-called "preferred freedoms":

If there is any fixed star in our constitutional constellation, it is that no official, high or petty, can prescribe what shall be orthodox in politics, nationalism, religion, or other matters. . . .[51] The very purpose of the Bill of Rights was to withdraw certain subjects from the vicissitudes of political controversy, to place them beyond the reach of majorities and officials

[48] *Ibid.*, pp. 606–607.
[49] "One who is not able to agree with Mr. Justice Frankfurter's conclusions must nevertheless recognize that in profoundness of thought, in power and in clarity, this opinion has seldom been surpassed" (John R. Green, "The Supreme Court, the Bill of Rights and the States," *University of Pennsylvania Law Review*, 97 [1949], 608, 623).
[50] Felix Frankfurter to Harlan F. Stone, handwritten note, undated.
[51] *West Virginia State Board of Education* v. *Barnette*, 319 U.S. 624 (1943), p. 642.

and to establish them as legal principles to be applied by the courts.[52]

These rights and privileges "may not be submitted to vote; they depend on the outcome of no election." Jackson summarily brushed aside Frankfurter's suggestion that judges, having no marked competence in this area, must stay out:

We act in these matters not by authority of our competence but by force of our commissions. We cannot, because of modest estimates of our competence in such specialties as public education, withhold the judgment that history authenticates as the function of this Court when liberty is infringed.[53]

[52] *Ibid.*, p. 638.

[53] *Ibid.*, p. 640. Justice Jackson wrote in this case one of the strongest statements of the "preferred freedoms" doctrine: "Much of the vagueness of the due process clause disappears when the specific prohibitions of the First [Amendment] become its standard. The right of a State to regulate, for example, a public utility may well include, so far as the due process test is concerned, power to impose all of the restrictions which a legislature may have a 'rational basis' for adopting. But freedoms of speech and of press, of assembly, and of worship may not be infringed on such slender grounds. They are susceptible of restriction only to prevent grave and immediate danger to interests which the State may lawfully protect" (319 U.S. 624, p. 639).

Justice Stone sometimes found himself at odds with the "preferred freedoms'" position of Black, Douglas, and Rutledge, as in *U.S.* v. *Ballard*, 322 U.S. 79 (1944), *Marsh* v. *Ala.*, 326 U.S. 501 (1945), and *Thomas* v. *Collins*, 323 U.S. 516 (1945). Judge Learned Hand went so far as to disasssociate Stone from the doctrine completely ("Chief Justice Stone's Conception of the Judicial Function," *Columbia Law Review*, 46 [1946], 696, 698). The core of truth in Hand's view seems to be that what Stone asserted was the need for "more exacting judicial scrutiny" in cases involving legislative infringement of civil liberties—not presumption of the unconstitutionality of such legislation. Such a presumption is appropriate only where legislation "on its face" violates First Amendment freedoms. See Stone's opinion in *Jones* v. *Opelika*, 316 U.S. 584 (1942).

136

Civil rights was not the only area in which the Justices differed as to the role the Court should play in a free society. What measures may a state adopt to safeguard the health, safety, and welfare of its citizens without infringing the power of Congress to regulate commerce? May a state, in the interest of public safety, limit train lengths to seventy cars, for example, without burdening interstate commerce? Who has the authority to resolve this conflict?

From the time he ascended the bench, Justice Black, a former United States Senator from Alabama, had been inclined to narrow the scope of judicial power in cases of this sort. Except where the local statute discriminates against interstate commerce, relief from state regulation must come from Congress, not the Court. In the Arizona Train Limit case of 1945,[54] Black stated his views with characteristic vigor. Justice Stone disagreed. For him judicial review supplemented political restraints. He interposed the judicial veto not only in behalf of helpless minorities, as in the Gobitis case, but also to protect national commerce and to achieve a free market against state encroachments.

It had been accepted constitutional doctrine at least since 1845, Stone argued, that the commerce clause standing alone gave the Court some power to invalidate local legislation obstructing commerce. If train lengths were to be regulated at all, the rule adopted plainly demanded "national uniformity." This Congress alone could prescribe. In the absence of congressional action, the Court had a clear duty to undertake the delicate task of accommodating conflicting national and local interests. "Where Congress has not acted, this Court, and not the state legislature, is under the commerce clause the final arbiter of the competing demands of state and national interests." [55] "In applying this rule,"

---

[54] *Southern Pacific Co.* v. *Arizona*, 325 U.S. 761 (1945).
[55] *Ibid.*, p. 769.

Stone added in a footnote, "the Court has often recognized that to the extent that the burden of state regulation falls on interests outside the state, it is unlikely to be alleviated by the operation of those political restraints normally exerted when interests within the state are affected." [56] It would seem to follow that the scope of the judicial function in constitutional cases is determined in part, at least, by the operation of political processes and restraint. Where these cannot be relied upon, the Court is obligated to safeguard interests that might otherwise go unprotected. The Court, in a word, must provide a corrective in constitutional cases when the political processes cannot be depended upon to supply it.

Black, like Frankfurter in the Flag Salute case, cast aside Stone's views as violating the wise principles of judicial self-restraint. The New Deal Justice insisted that

the determination of whether it is in the interest of society for the length of trains to be governmentally regulated is a matter of public policy. Someone must fix that policy—either the Congress, or the state, or the courts. A century and a half of constitutional history and government admonishes this Court to leave that choice to the elected legislative representatives of the people themselves, where it properly belongs both on democratic principles and the requirements of efficient government.[57]

In the absence of conflicting congressional action, the Arizona law must be left undisturbed. The majority's contrary decision, Black charged, was a "result of the belief

[56] *Ibid.*, p. 767, note 2. For a perceptive analysis of Stone's doctrine of political restraints vis-à-vis the scope of the judicial function, see Noel T. Dowling, "The Methods of Mr. Justice Stone in Constitutional Cases," *Columbia Law Review*, 41 (Nov. 1941), pp. 1171–1181.

[57] 325 U.S. 761, p. 789.

. . . that both the legislature of Arizona and the Congress made wrong policy decisions in permitting a law to stand which limits the length of railroad trains." [58] Stone's Court, like Hughes's a decade earlier, had, in Justice Black's view, transcended its proper role. "Representatives elected by the people to make their laws, rather than judges appointed to interpret those laws, can best determine the policies which govern the people. That at least is the basic principle on which our democratic society rests." [59]

For Black the mounting dominance of the judiciary under Stone's leadership had now come full circle. It remained for him to hurl back the very charge that Stone himself had brought in 1936 against the recalcitrant Four Horsemen. "I thought . . . and still believe," Black said of Stone's ruling in the Arizona Train Limit case, that "the Court was assuming the role of a 'super-legislature' in determining matters of governmental policy." [60] Black anticipated that the Court might press the commerce power to such a point as to leave a "no man's land immune from any effective regulation whatever." There was danger lest the commerce clause, like due process, lend itself to "inordinate expansion of this Court's power at the expense of legislative power." Said Black: "The judicially directed march of due process philosophy as an emancipator of business from regulation appeared arrested a few years ago. That appearance was illusory. That philosophy continues its march." [61]

This charge seems extravagant. Stone, like Madison, believed that dependence on the people constitutes the primary control on government. In each of the two cases just considered, in which he claimed for the judiciary power beyond that acceptable to Frankfurter and Black, the

[58] *Ibid.*, p. 792.   [59] *Ibid.*, pp. 794–795.
[60] *Morgan* v. *Virginia*, 328 U.S. 373 (1946), p. 387.
[61] *Hood* v. *DuMond*, 336 U.S. 525 (1949), p. 562.

political processes were an uncertain reliance for repeal of undesirable legislation.[62] His rule was the more arduous one: "As between the competing demands of different constitutional provisions, there must of necessity be some reasonable accommodation, so as to preserve the essentials of both. That is where the judicial function comes in." [63]

Many other examples might be cited illustrating Supreme Court Justices in dispute about their essential role. In practice they have not vacated the power arena; they have not left the field wide open for legislative action. Legislative independence and wisdom are not, as American Bar President Hogan gloomily predicted in 1939, "America's almost sole reliance" for the blessings of liberty secured by the Constitution. On occasion, the Supreme Court is still a refuge for minorities, vexed and harried by interested and overbearing state legislative majorities, still a defense against vulgar intrusions of ignorance and bigotry in the area of conscience and belief. The Court still protects "interstate movement of goods from local burdens and repressions." We can still count on the Justices to enforce the restrictive reflexes of federalism and thus prevent the centralization which Hamilton strove to achieve.

In retrospect, the year 1936 looms up as a watershed, a great divide. In the old Court, Justice Stone had pleaded for a more comprehensive, responsible view of the judicial function, for informed recognition of the social and economic roots of constitutional issues, for explorations going "beyond the examination of precedents and legal formulas." [64] Finally, in two momentous dissents, he exploded.

[62] See Dowling, *op. cit.*, pp. 1171–1181.

[63] H. F. Stone to Justice Wiley Rutledge, Jan. 24, 1944.

[64] H. F. Stone, "Fifty Years' Work of the United States Supreme Court," *American Bar Association Journal*, 14 (1928), 428, 435.

Only the Justices' "personal economic predilections," he blurted out in words understandable to expert and layman alike, prevented the Constitution from functioning as "a continuously operative charter of government." Judges should be controlled by a more informed "sense of self-restraint."

After the Court's surrender in 1937, the Justices faced alternative uses of their fearful power. At their peril, they could continue Sutherland's concept of the "rigid and changeless Constitution, apparently to be applied in the same way, no matter how much the subject to which it is applied, may change." They could relinquish the power they had previously usurped and refuse to censor legislation they did not approve. Or they could travel Stone's road of judicial self-restraint. The inclusiveness of the 1937 retreat is shown by the acrimonious debate that has since ensued between the Justices as to the meaning of their surrender. In case after case they have re-examined the function of the judiciary as an instrument of government, trying to determine where the Justices might appropriately interpose a check and where they should stay out. Three distinct concepts have emerged: *The Court as "resolver of the clash"* between, say, the demands of free speech and religion and considerations of national security, between the claims of the part against those of the whole, as in the Arizona Train Limit case. *The Court as avowed defender of civil liberties*, on the basic theory that thought, speech, and religious belief constitute the matrix, the "indispensable condition of nearly every other form of freedom." *The Court as a circumspect participant in the governing process*, lest it "prevent the full play of the democratic process." Fiercely rejecting the doctrine of preferred freedoms, Justice Frankfurter holds that the Constitution does not give the Court a greater veto power when dealing with one phase of liberty than with another. "Judicial restraint is equally necessary whenever an exercise of political or legislative power is challenged." "Courts are not representative bodies. They are not designed to be a good reflex of a democratic society," he contends. "Their judgment is best informed, and therefore most dependable, within narrow limits." [65]

Though each of the above concepts has its adherents and defenders, the allegiance thereto has not always been constant, or consistent. "Even for those who know how and are not afraid to handle matters of degree in fact," Herman Pritchett has observed, "the task is difficult. Consensus is harder to achieve, . . . the old sense of certainty is gone, and judicial decisions take on the experiential quality of life itself." [66] Professor Dowling has pointed out how reconsideration of the scope of judicial power brought out "greater recognition of the play of opinion and estimates of the wisdom of legislative action, of evaluation of interests and appraisal of their need for protection, than the Court is

[65] *Dennis* v. *U.S.*, 341 U.S. 494 (1951), p. 525. Justice Frankfurter's conception of judicial review is not always so modest. In *West Virginia* v. *Sims*, 341 U.S. 22 (1951), which dealt with the power of the state to withdraw unilaterally from an interstate compact agreement, he points to a totally new area for the Court to appropriate. "To determine the nature and scope of obligations, as between States [he wrote] whether they arise through the legislative means of compact or the 'federal common law' governing interstate controversies . . . is the function and duty of the Supreme Court of the Nation." Justice Frankfurter claimed for the Supreme Court freedom to examine determinations of law by state courts, and even determinations of its own Constitution, where an interstate compact brings into issue the rights of other states and of the United States (p. 28).

[66] C. Herman Pritchett, *The Roosevelt Court, 1937–1947* (New York: Macmillan, 1948), p. 269.

wont to admit." [67] Disregard for continuity has itself been a source of concern lest it give "fair ground," as Justice Frankfurter put it, "for the belief that law is the expression of chance, . . . of unexpected changes in the Court's composition and the contingencies in the choice of successors." [68] Apparently Justice Black feels that it is too late to keep intact the ideal or delusion that our government, thanks to judicial review, is a government of laws and not men. In the Dennis case of 1950 he, dissenting, frankly expressed the hope that "in calmer times, when present pressures, passions and fears subside, this or some later Court will restore the First Amendment liberties to the high preferred place where they belong in a free society." [69] Black thus rouses the very feelings that Frankfurter is most anxious to dispel—that judicial decisions do, in fact, reflect "time and circumstances."

A case decided in 1945[70] showed how effectively the struggle of 1937 and its aftermath had punctured the myth that the judge wills nothing, how completely "protective coloration" (to use Justice Stone's revealing phrase) had vanished from the judicial murals. With the assent of seven participating colleagues, Stone had upheld congres-

[67] Dowling, *op. cit.*, p. 1164.

[68] *U.S. v. Rabinowitz*, 339 U.S. 56 (1950), p. 86. As a professor at the Harvard Law School, Frankfurter deplored any effort to portray Supreme Court Justices as "impersonal vehicles of revealed truth." He then urged recognition of them as "moulders of policy" (*Forum*, June 1930, p. 334). As a Supreme Court Justice, he holds that "it is hostile to a democratic system to involve the judiciary in the politics of the people" (*Colegrove v. Green*, 328 U.S. 549 [1946], pp. 553–554).

[69] 341 U.S. 494, p. 581.

[70] *Fernandez v. Weiner*, 326 U.S. 340 (1945); *United States of America v. Rompel*, 326 U.S. 367 (1945).

sional power to tax community property as the sole property of one spouse. The Court's decision naturally enraged the formerly favored taxpayers of California, Texas, and Louisiana. Such uninformed criticism nettled the Court's spokesman, Chief Justice Stone, almost to the point of driving him to take refuge in the discredited mechanistic theory of constitutional interpretation upheld by Justices Roberts and Sutherland.

Until I began to receive letters from disgruntled Californians and Texans about the opinion [he lashed out somewhat irreverently in a letter to an old friend], I never realized how many kinds of an SOB there are. Most of the writers do not seem to understand that Congress specifically imposed the tax in question, and that Congress has very great powers of taxation. They seem to think that in some way the Court invented the tax and put it on them. I don't blame them for not liking the tax and I am sorry it fell to my lot to say that Congress could impose it. But one must do his duty in this job as well as in any other.[71]

Justice Stone, primarily responsible for crystallizing the issue of the Court's role, did not shrink from the heavy demands of the judicial process. No one was more keenly aware than he of "the difficulties into which the would-be omniscient judge may fall." Unlike a majority of the old Court, he did not spurn the task of reconciling "the conflicting demands of laissez-faire with the exertion of regulatory power by government." He was sensitive to "complexity of the strands in the web of freedoms which the judge must disentangle." [72] "The dividing line," he said, "must be a shifting one as society becomes more complex."

[71] H. F. Stone to Sterling Carr, Jan. 3, 1946.
[72] Paul Freund, *On Understanding the Supreme Court* (Boston: Little, Brown, 1949), p. 28.

The judge must balance his own values against those of his colleagues; he must try to estimate which among these is most likely to win support in the "sober second thought of the community"—the solid foundation of all law. In the old Court, as on the reconstituted Bench, he insisted that when two interests are in conflict the Court must determine whether accommodation is possible between them so as "to preserve the essentials of both." [73]

Initially the new Court's more cautious attitude augured well for the triumph of restraint. Stone's labors, however, were not at an end. In his battles with the New Deal justices, insistence on "self-restraint" became primarily a warning that statutory policy, like constitutional logic must not be pressed too far. With the shift of emphasis from constitutional to statutory construction, legislative interpretation became an arena of equally bitter conflict. The battle for judicial self-restraint had not been won. The judge must still restrain himself lest he enact his own preferences into law. In 1945, Chief Justice Stone reminded a liberal critic:

My more conservative brethren in the old days did that and read them into the Constitution as well. What they did placed in jeopardy a great and useful institution of government. The

[73] Stone did not advocate an objective theory of judicial review. "A man who said 'the only check upon our own exercise of power is our own sense of self-restraint' could hardly believe in a self-executing objective standard of constitutionality. It is perhaps unfair to set forth his thesis as an example of the effort to catch the will-o'-the-wisp of objectivity, but it does seem appropriate to present it as an early attempt to do the next best thing—i.e., to make an open declaration of personal beliefs. Chief Justice Stone, may not have stricken out the 'personal' in 'personal predilection'; he did evolve a well considered philosophy of self-limitation and present it for public criticism as such" (George D. Braden, "The Search for Objectivity in Constitutional Law," *Yale Law Journal*, 57 [1948], 582).

pendulum has now swung to the other extreme, and history is repeating itself. The Court is now in as much danger of becoming a legislative and Constitution-making body, enacting into law its own predilections, as it was then.[74]

Writing in 1954, the late Justice Robert H. Jackson concurred in this judgment:

The question that the present times put into the minds of thoughtful people is to what extent Supreme Court interpretations of the Constitution will or can preserve the free government of which the Court is a part. A cult of libertarian judicial activists now assails the Court almost as bitterly for renouncing power as the earlier "liberals" once did for assuming too much power. This cult appears to believe that the Court can find in a 4,000-word eighteenth-century document or its nineteenth-century Amendments, or can plausibly supply, some clear bulwark against all dangers and evils that today beset us internally.[75]

As his career neared its end, Chief Justice Stone, like Justice Jackson, saw no chance of teaching self-restraint to judges cognizant of their unshackled power and willing, even eager, to use it ruthlessly. This outcome was perhaps inevitable, for the 1937 struggle had produced no permanent reconciliation; and, as Walton Hamilton has said, "Courts are poorly equipped for the task of continuous oversight."

"Do you recognize," Senator O'Mahoney asked Attorney General Cummings in the Senate Judiciary Committee hearings on the Court-packing plan, "that this bill does not

[74] H. F. Stone to Irving Brant, Aug. 25, 1945.

[75] Robert H. Jackson, *The Supreme Court in the American System of Government* (Cambridge: Harvard University Press, 1955), pp. 58–59.

afford a permanent remedy for the conditions of which you complain?"

"Oh, Senator," the Attorney General replied reflectively, "there is no such thing as permanence in life." [76]

[76] *Reorganization of the Federal Judiciary*, Hearings before the Committee on the Judiciary (U.S. Senate), 75th Cong., 1st Sess., pt. 1 (1937), p. 17.

★ V ★

Welfare Capitalism:

Opportunity and Delusion

WHEN, in 1937, President Roosevelt made his daring attack on the judiciary, that widely advertised Maginot line caved in. Thereafter "the Constitution" ceased to be an effective fortress against government regulation of our economic life. The presidential elections of 1932, 1934, and 1936 had vindicated Brandeis' insight of 1905 that "our country is, after all, not a country of dollars, but of ballots." [1] "Sovereign powers" were no longer "for sale." The conditions Brooks Adams portrayed in 1913 had passed.

If an election be lost [Adams had commented], and the legislature, which has been chosen by the majority, cannot be pacified by money, but passes some act which promises to be annoying, the first instinct of the capitalist is to retain counsel,

---

[1] "The Opportunity in the Law," an address delivered May 4, 1905, before the Harvard Ethical Society; reprinted in *Business—A Profession* (Boston: Small, Maynard, 1914), p. 338.

148

not to advise him touching his duty under the law, but to devise a method by which he may elude it, or, if he cannot elude
it, by which he may have it annulled as unconstitutional by the
courts. . . . Capital finds the judicial veto useful as a means
of at least temporarily evading the law, while the bar . . .
quite honestly believes that the universe will obey the judicial
decree.

No delusion [Adams observed in a remarkable forecast of
1937's face-losing judicial retreat] could be profounder and
none, perhaps, more dangerous.[2]

In the face of tremendous election returns and judicial
quiescence, it was not enough for the opposition to lobby
the formal organs of government.[3] The people—Hamilton's
"pure, original foundation of all legitimate authority"—
had to be brought in line with the ideology of business. As
"the people" in 1936 had carried forty-six states, this was
quite an undertaking. Nevertheless, economic privilege
would try to do again what it had often succeeded in doing
before—fashion a "retrograde step in the rear of democracy." Could a counterrevolution similar to that of 1789,
of 1890, now be successfully launched against the renais-
sance of popular government?

[2] Brooks Adams, *The Theory of Revolutions* (New York: Macmillan, 1913), pp. 209, 213–214, 219.

[3] Writing in 1943, the late Justice Jackson announced in a
majority opinion that "The laissez-faire concept or principle of
non-interference has withered at least as to economic affairs, and
social advancements are increasingly sought through closer integra-
tion of society and through expanded and strengthened governmental controls" (*West Virginia State Board of Education* v.
Barnette, 319 U.S. 624 [1942], p. 640). Since 1937 the Justices have
been especially wary in cases involving government regulation of
economic affairs, lest they slide "from the narrow confines of law
into the more spacious domain of policy" (*Phelps Dodge Corp.* v.
N.L.R.B., 313 U.S. 177 [1941], p. 194).

Shortly after the presidential election of 1936, Colby M. Chester suggested a new approach. "Public misunderstanding of industry," Mr. Chester told the National Association of Manufacturers, December 9, 1936, "can ruin the Nation." [4] Echoing an old theme, another N.A.M. spokesman noted the following year that "the hazard facing industrialists is the newly realized political power of the masses. Unless their thinking is directed toward sane and established measures, we are definitely headed for adversity." [5] It was agreed, as Chester suggested, that "the story of how all the people's prosperity is affected by industrial processes should be told, and told and retold to the public, to every group, in every form, constantly, persistently, in a well organized fashion." [6] In the vastly changed context of political dominance and majority rule, the familiar rags to riches legend, so popular at the turn of the century, would not be enough. Nor would Adam Smith's more sophisticated dogma suffice. "It is no longer adequate," Bronson Batchelor explained. "It neither meets the needs of the times nor commands the public's respect." The ideology of business must be "completely modernized." [7] Substantial works were needed, books and articles dealing "adequately and enthusiastically with the roots of American liberty from a historical, philo-

[4] Colby M. Chester, "Forward with Industry," opening address of the President of the National Association of Manufacturers, 41st Convention, Dec 9, 1936, p. 13.

[5] H. O. Patten, speaking for the Board of Directors of the N.A.M., in *Violations of Free Speech and the Rights of Labor*, Report of the Committee on Education and Labor, U.S. Senate, 75th and 76th Cong. (1937–1939), No. 6, pt. 16, p. 7693.

[6] Chester, *op. cit.*

[7] Bronson Batchelor, *Profitable Public Relations* (New York: Harper, 1938), p. 84.

sophical and religious viewpoint." [8] Business was not long in finding its voice.[9]

The revamped reactionary strategy had been forshadowed in 1934 when the National Association of Manufacturers began to step up its public relations program. In that year only $36,000 was appropriated for public education, for "practical patriotism." In 1937 the public relations budget rose to $793,000, or from 7 per cent to 55 per cent of N.A.M.'s budget.[10] "Educational" literature was easily available at reduced rates to public school teachers and university professors. The radio was utilized, the highways plastered, with the popular slogans "Prosperity Dwells Where Harmony Reigns," "What Helps Industry Helps You," and so on. During the war years corporate enterprise boldly entered the seemingly sterile domain of political theory. Unable to sell clients' products, commercial advertisers cast themselves in the elevated role of political philosphers. A facile exegesis of free enterprise was neatly fitted into the news comment of radio broadcasters, into the addresses and books of businessmen, into the public comment of educators.

But nowhere was the new technique so skillfully exhibited as in newspaper and magazine advertising. The Chesapeake

[8] H. W. Prentis, Jr., "Preserving the Roots of American Liberty," an address before the joint dinner of the Association of American Colleges and the American Association of Junior Colleges in Baltimore, Maryland, Jan. 2, 1942, p. 17. See also Clarence Randall, *A Creed for Free Enterprise* (Boston: Little, Brown, 1952), p. 4.

[9] See S. H. Walker and Paul Sklar, *Business Finds Its Voice: Management's Effort to Sell the Business Ideal to the Public* (New York: Harper, 1938).

[10] Ralph A. Brady, *Business as a System of Power* (New York: Columbia University Press, 1943), ch. 6.

& Ohio Railroad carried an elaborate interpretation of Jefferson's famous euphemism, "Pursuit of Happiness," and pressed its campaign further in a full-page, heart-gripping spread entitled "Missing in Action." Clad in pajamas, a dejected little boy is pictured groping his way up faintly lighted stairs. The telegram his mother prayed would never come had just been delivered.

Poor little guy [opines the commercial artist-philosopher]. We—all of us—wish there were something we could do. . . . Why shouldn't it be this?

We can resolve that the plans your father had for you shall remain within your reach, that you shall have the chance to grow and learn, that your opportunities will be bounded only by your get-up-and-go, that you will progress and prosper in direct relation to your own ability—in a land of freedom and opportunity. Those are the things your dad valued, the things for which he gave his life. Though some may strive to change all that—provide you with the "benefits" of an all-powerful government, the advantages of regimentation, the "blessings" of bureaucracy—we can resolve that they won't succeed.

Writing in 1943, Merle Thorpe, editor of *Nation's Business*, specifically raised the question whether American democracy at the end of the war would throw off political controls of our lives and livelihoods, or whether the people would accept them as a permanent part of our social and economic structure. Giving back a resounding, "No," Mr. Thorpe inveighed against those "timid souls" who hold that "our frontiers are gone"—that "we have reached a rocking-chair maturity"—that "private enterprise carries within itself the seed of its own destruction." These weaklings would replace the system of private enterprise "with government authority to regiment every citizen with licenses, permits, directives and allocations." "Today's men of faith," the editor concluded, "foresee a resurgence of private enterprise, if the people through their representatives permit a program of full production by freeing the individual of handicaps and restrictions." [11]

The National Association of Manufacturers' highly successful campaign to end OPA encouraged the belief that few obstacles impeded the road back to normalcy. The N.A.M. pleaded in a widely circulated statement of 1946:

Remove price controls on manufactured goods and production. Goods will then pour into the market, and, within a reasonable time prices will adjust themselves naturally—as they always have—in line with the real worth of things. Competition has never failed to produce this result. . . . This is the way you can get the goods you want at prices you can afford to pay.

Spokesmen for business were determined that the alarming government objectives, collectively labeled "welfare state," would not become fixed in the American pattern. No longer limited to government care of the sick, the aged, and the needy, "welfare" now meant government responsibility for security, prosperity, and abundance. Its methods are insurance, subsidies, and taxes. Its beneficiaries are everyone—for industrial workers, job security; for farmers, guaranteed prices; for government workers, higher pay; for pensioners, bigger checks; for veterans, windfalls and benefits without number; for foreign governments, billions in cash contributions; for the businessman, government contracts beyond any peacetime record. "The conclusion can hardly be escaped," the late Russell Davenport commented in 1949, "that the welfare state is of necessity the

[11] Merle Thorpe, "Freedom Is Not Free" (editorial), *Nation's Business*, 31 (Nov. 1943), 21.

prelude to a total state." Nevertheless, this incredibly ambitious program appeared to be so generally accepted as to make candidates in the 1948 presidential campaign wary of opposing it. The business fraternity itself sensed in the "welfare" concept a toughness that suggested maturity and permanence.

How could so-called government of laws and not of men be restored? How could "cramping, crippling, . . . ignorant bureaucracy," supported by "an under-educated or a wrongly educated public opinion" be stopped? [12] By 1950 at least one hundred million dollars of industry's advertising budget and an unknown but hefty share of its employee-relationship expenditures, had been devoted to public education. This "intensive sales job," this slanted probing into our ideological past, had become "very much an industry in itself," "absorbing more and more of the energies expended by top men of management." Suddenly, in 1950, it was discovered that all these expenditures of effort and money were not "worth a damn." [13]

Frank Abrams of New Jersey's Standard Oil remarked soberly:

It always seems rather sad to me that we of the industrial and business world deceive ourselves that we can "make friends and influence people" through such things as paid newspaper advertising, pamphlets and billboards. Some of that may help under certain conditions. But when it becomes the main chan-

[12] Grove Patterson, "The Shield of Democracy," an address before the Convention of the Association of National Advertisers, White Sulphur Springs, Oct. 24, 1940, pp. 13–14; reprinted by the Bureau of Advertising of the American Newspaper Publishers Association.

[13] William Holley Whyte, "Is Anybody Listening?" *Fortune*, 42 (Sept. 1950), 78.

nel of our effort, I think it is almost an insult to the intelligence
of the average reader. . . . "Free enterprise, it's wonderful,"
we say, and then we congratulate each other on what a swell
"ad" we have written. . . .[14]

In trying to sell the free enterprise dogma, the experts
ran into the difficulty that hampers anyone who attempts to
portray the imponderables of our creed. Not only were
spokesmen for business plagued by uncertainty as to what
they were trying to communicate, but they were further
handicapped in not being willing to say frankly that they
were "worried over what has been happening at the polls."
What the businessman is after, a *Fortune* magazine writer
observed in 1950, "is a Republican victory." [15]

In 1948 Harry S. Truman blighted that prospect. "The
conclusion emerges clearly from the election," the editors of
Business Week observed. "Business management must learn
to live with the fact that this country is farther left, more
New Dealish, than either the professional analysts or most
businessmen had been prepared to believe." [16] Now even
industrialists themselves agreed that the ruthlessness implicit
in Herbert Spencer's creed—"that he who grabbed the most
and gave least was the noblest citizen" [17]—was outmoded.
The demand for welfare was no longer what it used to be

[14] Frank W. Abrams, "The Businessman's View," in Committee
for Economic Development, *How Can a Better Understanding of
Our Economic System Be Fostered?* (New York: Committee for
Economic Development, 1950), p. 12.

[15] Whyte, *op. cit.*, p. 79.

[16] *Business Week*, Nov. 6, 1948, p. 124. See also *Time*, Nov. 15,
1948, and Nov. 29, 1948, p. 22, and "The Missed Election" (editorial), *Life*, Nov. 15, 1948, p. 50.

[17] Robert Wood Johnson, *Or Forfeit Freedom* (New York:
Doubleday, 1947), p. 28.

—"the irresponsible clamor of the mob for bread and circuses." Welfare must now be recognized as "a justifiable demand, consonant with the necessities of social evolution," and in keeping with our political tradition.

But whose responsibility is it to formulate and administer the welfare program? Certainly not government's, for that ultimately would spell not a glorious welfare society but an inglorious welfare state. This ignominious prelude to statism, to totalitarianism, to despotism, must be avoided. So in the late 1940's certain publicists, industrial leaders, and university officials began alerting business to a fresh responsibility, to a unique venture in twentieth-century capitalism. Davenport called it "the greatest opportunity on earth," and peculiarly the concern of free enterprise.[18]

Similarly Harvard's Business School Dean, Donald K. David, pointed ominously at "the danger of drifting." (Herbert Spencer used the term "political momentum.") Differentiating between welfare society, which he approved, and welfare state, which he deplored, the Harvard educator demonstrated how easy it is to drift into the lethal arms of the welfare state. To foil the octopus of welfare, businessmen must be vigilant and aggressive. "Responsibility for this program," Dean David said, "is going to be placed in the hands of the businessman, because we have, whether some people like it or not, an industrial civilization; and the businessman, whether he likes it or not, has to assume new responsibilities." [19] The opportunity thus envisaged for American businessmen loomed as "the most exciting aspect of this

[18] Russell W. Davenport, "The Greatest Opportunity on Earth," *Fortune*, 40 (Oct. 1949), 65 ff. In 1952 Davenport and the editors of *Fortune* elaborated this thesis in *U.S.A.: The Permanent Revolution* (New York: Prentice-Hall, 1951).

[19] Donald K. David, "The Danger of Drifting," *Harvard Business School Review*, 28 (Jan. 1950), 32.

challenging moment in history." [20] Taking up the cry, New
York's Attorney General Jacob Javits declares that the
modern Republican objective should be "to get the private
economy—business—to undertake the principal role in
attaining the aims and aspirations of the people for peace, the
further development of free institutions and higher standards of living." [21]

These innovators seem as confident now as lawyers and
judges had been in the 1890's, as Taft and Sutherland were
in the 1920's. There is, however, an important difference. Formerly the Supreme Court could be counted on to
interpose Spencer's verities against positive government.
Now the Justices refused to enforce laissez-faire or any
other economic dogma. Much of the welfare program had
already been brought within the four corners of the Constitution. And since the welfare obsession could not be
scuttled by recourse to "the Constitution," free enterprise
itself must replace government in providing the requisite
social services. In other words, if we were to have a welfare
society, it must be firmly grounded in our free enterprise
tradition; it must be accomplished under the auspcies of
competent and efficient business leadership, not under the
arbitrary power of wasteful, bureaucratic government.

In a handsome brochure of 1949, Robert Wood Johnson,
formerly president of Johnson & Johnson, manufacturers
of surgical supplies, told how the change-over can be accomplished. Too often, he explains, labor and management
have turned to government instead of solving industrial
puzzles for themselves. But unfortunately "our government

[20] Donald K. David, "Developing Administrative Concepts," in
Edward C. Bursk, *Getting Things Done in Business* (Cambridge:
Harvard University Press, 1953), p. 49.
[21] *New York Times*, Feb. 13, 1955, p. 67, col. 5.

and all other governments—are 'inherently incompetent.' This is true for the simple reason that good action and good thinking in any successful and happy society cannot be legislated; it must be self-willed." The American way is for management and labor to get together and work out solutions under the guidance of "Christian principles." "The answers are in the grass roots and will not be found in Washington," Johnson asserts. "The place for the solution of our difficulties is in our own back yard. We must do the job ourselves—each in his own business and each in his own town, county and state." In short, the alternative to the welfare state is "welfare capitalism." For Mr. Johnson this is merely "the application of the Golden Rule" to business.[22] Under its auspices, repeal of "the law of Scarcity" [23] was plainly in sight.

Though Russell Davenport was anxious to blight the burgeoning welfare state, he did not fully share Johnson's faith in "Golden Rule" band-aids as the cure for our social and political maladies. Welfare capitalism has more earthy rootage; it actually pays dividends.[24] Davenport therefore begged businessmen not to resign themselves to "an apparently irresistible wave." Like Mr. Johnson, he insisted that the "way out is not primarily the task of politicians, or even of the people at large. It is primarily the task of the enterprisers, the businessmen." "The people who are *best* able to implement such [economic] rights, in all their manifold

[22] "Welfare Capitalism versus Welfare State," an address before the Atlantic Chamber of Commerce, Atlanta, Ga., Sept. 28, 1949, pp. 5, 11, 15.

[23] Johnson, *Or Forfeit Freedom*, p. 32.

[24] This is not to suggest that Mr. Johnson ignores the material gains of welfare capitalism. To allow business "a period of substantial profits which can be retained and used to build for the future," he writes, "will pay in reduced costs . . . pride and a better life for everyone concerned, from top manager to boiler tender and neighbors across the street" (*ibid.*, pp. 96–97).

aspects, are the people actually engaged in the economic process, namely the owners, managers, and workers. . . . They, not the government, are the actual guardians of the Right to Life." The true solution is "conscious and concerted voluntary action, to transfer the primary responsibility, and therefore the initiative, from government to private hands." [25]

The Johnson-Davenport substitution of welfare capitalism for the welfare state is no isolated phenomenon. More sophisticated variants of a new order appear in the works of Adolf Berle, Jr.,[26] David Lilienthal,[27] and others.[28] In all these writings one notes important shifts of emphasis. Formerly there was talk of natural rights and the sanctity of property. Today the economic, social, and spiritual advanatages of business, especially big business, are emphasized. The corporation is applauded for its growing sense of trusteeship. A heightened social consciousness among captains of industry now enables them to place considerations of the general economic interests on a par with their own larger profits. The antagonism between economic

[25] Davenport, "The Greatest Opportunity on Earth," pp. 66–68 *passim.* (Emphases in original.)

[26] See Adolf Berle, Jr., *The Emerging Common Law of Free Enterprise: Antidote to the Omnipotent State?* Address before the Brandeis Lawyers Society, Dec. 13, 1949 (Publications of Brandeis Lawyers Society, 1951), and *The Twentieth Century Capitalist Revolution* (New York: Harcourt, Brace, 1954).

[27] David Lilienthal, *Big Business: A New Era* (New York: Harper, 1952).

[28] For the most outspoken statement of the new order, see John K. Jessup, "A Political Role for the Corporation," *Fortune,* 44 (Aug. 1952), 112. See also "Basic Elements of a Free Dynamic Society," Round table discussion, *Harvard Business Review,* 29, 30 (Nov. 1951–Feb. 1952), 55–68, 87–104; Sheldon Glueck, *The Welfare State and the National Welfare: A Symposium on Some of the Threatening Tendencies of Our Times* (Cambridge: Addison-Wesley Press, 1952).

oligarchy and political democracy, so troublesome to Brandeis at the turn of the century, has been replaced by the concept of co-operation and co-existence. The "harmony of interests" doctrine has given way to the spectacle of new and powerful countervailing forces that provide self-regulation in the economic community, safeguarding the interests of all.[29]

In 1932 Mr. Berle had predicted the coming of an "economic organism, now typified by the corporation, not only on an equal plane with the state, but possibly even superseding it as the dominant form of social organization." [30] In 1949 he anticipated that

rules of law and social standards may so govern the internal as well as external functioning of the corporation that a democratic, non-governmental economic system may emerge, capable alike of planning and stabilizing an economy and also of escaping the dangers which come from merging political and economic power. . . .

It is my belief that such rules of law and social standards are already appearing, and already are beginning to govern the corporate enterprise. . . . [Berle sees] coming into being what may be called the "intra-corporate common law" which does not regulate operations but rather sets up standards by which corporations are judged.[31]

---

[29] John K. Galbraith propounds this thesis in his book, *American Capitalism: The Concept of Countervailing Power* (Boston: Houghton, 1952). See Chapters 9 and 10. "Given the existence of private market power in the economy, the growth of countervailing power strengthens the capacity of the economy for autonomous self-regulation and thereby lessens the amount of over-all government control or planning that is required or sought" (p. 155).

[30] Adolf Berle, Jr., and Gardiner Means, *The Modern Corporation and Private Property* (New York: Macmillan, 1932), p. 357.

[31] Address before the Brandeis Lawyers Society, pp. 7–8.

In *Modern Corporation and Private Property* of 1932, Berle and Means had been concerned about "bigness" and the long-run effects of the separation of ownership from control of corporate enterprise.[32] But David Lilienthal wrote in 1953:

Today the degree of actual control and "absolutism" that remains in the hands of the directors and officers of the largest American corporations has changed almost beyond recognition. . . . What is important as a practical matter is that the meaning and content of "corporate economic power" has changed completely; it has been so watered down that it is hardly recognizable as "economic power." It certainly is not that "new form of absolutism" of which Berle wrote in 1932.[33]

That the corporation continues to grow in monster proportions is not denied, but with this growth has come an

[32] "A society in which production is governed by blind economic forces is being replaced [Berle and Means observe] by one in which production is carried on under the ultimate control of a handful of individuals. The economic power in the hands of the few persons who control a giant corporation is a tremendous force which can harm or benefit a multitude of individuals, affect whole districts, shift the currents of trade, bring ruin to one community and prosperity to another. The organizations which they control have passed far beyond the realm of private enterprise—they have become more nearly social institutions" (*The Modern Corporation and Private Property*, p. 46; used by permission of Macmillan).

Berle and Means quote Adam Smith with approval: " 'The directors of such companies, . . . being the managers rather of other people's money than of their own, it cannot well be expected that they should watch over it with the same anxious vigilance with which the partners in a private copartnery frequently watch over their own. Like the stewards of a rich man, they are apt to consider attention to small matters as not for their master's honour, and very easily give themselves a dispensation from having it. Negligence and profusion, therefore, must always prevail, more or less, in the management of the affairs of such a company' " (p. 346).

[33] Lilienthal, *op. cit.*, pp. 25–26.

awareness of its responsibility for the happy functioning of the economic system, a responsibility enforced by an "emerging common law." With this has come a realization on the part of the corporation of the duty to supply goods, services, and employment. "Intra-corporate common law," rather than stringent government regulation, exacts a standard of conduct. Both Berle and Lilienthal are struck by the postwar action of General Motors in holding to the list price when the normal functioning of supply and demand would have driven the price of automobiles far higher. Quite unwittingly, without deliberate plan or purpose, our great industrial corporation had become the "conscience-carrier of twentieth century American society." [34] "In tangible fact," Berle wrote, "two, and only two, great methods of productive organization have emerged: socialist collectivism, operated by government commissariats, and private collectivisms, operated by great corporations of the American type." [35] "Non-statist socialism," an economic body with a social conscience, was not a deliberate choice but, Berle commented cryptically, "we seem to like it." [36]

It follows, Berle concluded, that

the really great corporation managements have reached a position for the first time in their history in which they . . . must consider the kind of a community in which they have faith, and which they will serve, and which they intend to help to construct and maintain. In a word, they must consider at least in its more elementary phases, the ancient problem of the "good life." . . . If private business and business men do not assume

[34] Adolf Berle, Jr., *Twentieth Century Capitalist Revolution* (New York: Harcourt, Brace, 1954), p. 182.
[35] Address before the Brandeis Lawyers Society, p. 7.
[36] *Ibid.*

community responsibilities, government must step in and American life will become increasingly statist.[37]

Despite implications in the "American corporate system" for "both splendor and terror," Berle looks to the future with confidence. On all sides he finds an encouraging stress on performance and results. It is result and not dogma that interests people, he says. "Who cares whether the telephone is owned by the state or by the local telephone company provided the service is good and the price is a dime?" [38] "In private-enterprise logic, the stuggle was . . . for greatest profits. . . . Today, the general economic interest is of at least equal concern." [39]

Mr. Lilienthal likewise sees corporate management as "enterprising, increasingly productive," as valuing "productivity for the general welfare and the national defense." If it is allowed to develop, he is convinced that big business will bring with it luxuries and opportunities beyond our fondest dreams. "A world of great machines, . . . a new awareness of beauty, a new spirit of brotherliness," is at hand.[40] The "bigness" Brandeis roundly denounced forty years ago as a "curse" [41] Lilienthal welcomes as a savior. "Size is our greatest single functional asset. . . . Bigness . . . can bring closer to reality the American dream: individual freedom, social justice, material well-being, world moral leadership." [42] The former TVA chairman claims that in the modern business corporation we have "an expression of the heroic size of man himself." "We have the material

[37] Berle, *Twentieth Century Capitalist Revolution*, pp. 166–167.
[38] Address before the Brandeis Lawyers Society, p. 18.
[39] *Ibid.*, p. 20. [40] Lilienthal, *op. cit.*, p. 204.
[41] See *Other People's Money and How the Bankers Use It* (New York: Stokes, 1914), ch. 8.
[42] Lilienthal, *op. cit.*, p. 33.

foundation of a society which can further the highest values known to men, values we describe as 'spiritual.' " [43]

What prospect is there that the industrialist will be able to cope with the task envisaged by and for him? Does welfare capitalism represent, as its proponents imply, a new approach? Or is it a thinly disguised reassertion of the businessman's beaverlike persistence to maintain status quo— a fresh drive, perhaps, to win "the universalization of those saving principles of American democracy—the right of those who own property to control it?" [44] May this not be the belated fulfillment, in all its glory, of the benevolent order William J. Ghent envisaged in 1902? Is this proposal, in any event, in harmony with our political heritage?

It is hard to withhold the conclusion that welfare capitalism represents essentially the defensive, negative strategy of earlier years. Pride in capitalism, the vaunted social consciousness of twentieth-century corporate management, its efficiency in terms of the individual, societal, and national welfare—all this minimizes the necessity of government regulation and control. A half century ago William J. Ghent sketched in broad outline our industrial development as we see it today, including the "moralizing" effects of the New Deal. Ghent then foresaw a vast increase in "economically dependent classes," but the exactions of economic oligarchy would be "qualified and restricted."

The forecaster commented significantly:

Democracy tends to restrain it, and ethics to moralize it. . . . Our [economic] nobility will thus temper their exactions to an

[43] Lilienthal, *op. cit.*, pp. 204, 190.

[44] Annual address of President John E. Edgerton, Oct. 14, 1929, *Proceedings of the Thirty-fourth Annual Meeting of the National Association of Manufacturers, New York City*, p. 16.

endurable limit; and they will distribute benefits to a degree that makes a tolerant, if not a satisfied people. They may even make a working principle of Bentham's maxim, and after, of course, appropriating the first and choicest fruits of industry to themselves, may seek to promote "the greatest happiness of the greatest number." For therein will lie their greater security.[45]

The Spencerian dialectic is, of course, outmoded. Welfare capitalism, like previous "retrograde steps," must work within the existing milieu. The fantastic growth of concentrated economic power must now be justified and oriented within the welfare state culture. Politics can no longer be derided in the unvarnished language that the Reverend Dr. Conwell used in the late nineteenth century. But big government, unlike big business, can still be castigated as the destroyer of liberty, as a breeder of bureaucracy, as the prime example of inefficiency and waste.[46] As in the 1920's, government is considered a good partner but a poor master. Welfare capitalism requires, as Davenport says, "a positive commitment to the capitalist system," a willingness "to pass as much responsibility as possible over

[45] W. J. Ghent, "Benevolent Feudalism," *Independent*, 54 (April 3, 1902), 783–784.

[46] The derogatory attitude toward politics still prevails. "To too many Republicans for their party's good," Albert Clark observes, " 'politics' is a nasty word. . . . The G.O.P.'s basic attitude . . . often seems to be that it's something to be avoided when possible. Often it appears that Republicans look on politics as something they have to practice just a few weeks in election years. In between times, it's strictly for the birds—and Democrats" (Albert Clark, "Ponderous Pachyderm: Why the Elephant Gets Outmaneuvered by the Donkey," *Wall Street Journal*, Oct. 27, 1954, p. 8). President Eisenhower struck this note at the end of the 1954 election campaign. After making his radio-TV appeal, he turned to Press Secretary Hagerty and remarked: "By golly, sometimes you sure get tired of all this clackety clack" (quoted in *Wall Street Journal*, Nov. 2, 1954, p. 1, col. 3).

to private hands, through tax incentives and other devices."

In its various manifestations, welfare capitalism demonstrates that industrial leaders and their apologists, unlike the old dog, can learn new tricks. Public interests, not the "public be damned," is now the guiding criterion, social responsibility the underlying premise. But the inadvertent comments of old-fashioned captains of industry, such as Charles E. Wilson, and the brusque remarks of hard-shell Republicans, such as Governor J. Bracken Lee of Utah, indicate unmistakable nostalgia for the freedom and irresponsibility of the 1920's. Secretary Wilson's clumsy fulminations have been publicized enough.[47] Governor Lee's

[47] The most widely publicized example of Wilson's frank reversion to old values occurred on October 11, 1954, when he said: "I've always liked bird dogs better than kennel-fed dogs" (*New York Times*, Oct. 12, 1954, p. 13). Previously the Secretary had revealed his outlook in a less offhand fashion. Testifying in 1953 before a Senate committee investigating his fitness to serve as Secretary of Defense, Wilson found himself entangled with that old 1873 statute requiring would-be officers to rid themselves of stocks of any company with which their official duties might involve them. Mr. Wilson, before the Senate committee, insisting that an exception might be made in his case, engaged in this illuminating exchange:

"*Senator Hendrickson.* Mr. Wilson, you have told the Committee . . . more than once this morning, that you see no area of conflict between your interest in the General Motors Corp. . . . and the position you are about to assume. . . . Well, now, I am interested to know whether if a situation did arise where you had to make a decision which was extremely adverse to the interests of your stock and General Motors Corporation . . . [and] in the interests of the United States Government, could you make that decision?

"*Mr. Wilson.* Yes, sir; I could. I cannot conceive of one [any conflict of interest] because for years I thought what was good for our country was good for General Motors, and vice versa. The difference did not exist. . . .

"I do not think we are going to get into any foolishness like seizing the properties or anything like that," Wilson said. "The

pronouncements are less well known. President Eisenhower, the Republican Governor believes, has allowed himself to be caught up in the evil forces of "political momentum."

"We have gone farther to the left in the last two years than in any other period in our history," the Governor blurted out in mid-February 1955. Then and there he served notice on the Eisenhower Administration that if it "fails to get on the side of Constitutional Government we've got to do something about it and intend to do something about it." [48]

In a forthright article, published in *Fortune*, August 1952, John Knox Jessup asked whether we "can survive and win the struggle [with Communism] without putting our essential liberties in escrow, in the untrustworthy hands of our Government?" Jessup did not think so. Therefore he "nominated" the modern corporation for "a major and growing role in the political economy of a free nation." The need, as he sees it, is for "a focus of self-government with an economic base." The modern business corporation must perform a political role, must employ the methods of "private self-government." "In doing this job," Jessup hopefully concludes, "business is erecting a new basis of economic power that is *beyond the reach of Government.*"

The monster corporation is now accepted as a desirable and permanent feature of American life, as indispensable to economic prosperity, social welfare, and national security. "Bigness is with us," Berle writes, "and the technicians tell us it is necessary." [49] Berle adopts this assumption.

---

people are not afraid of businessmen like me right now" (Hearings before the Committee on Armed Services, U.S. Senate, 83d Cong., 1st Sess., Jan. 15, 1953, pp. 25–26).

[48] *New York Times*, Feb. 13, 1955, p. 54, col. 3.

[49] Address before the Brandeis Lawyers Society, p. 4.

Overlooked is Brandeis' tireless stress on the belittling effects of industrial bigness on human beings—not only the little men at the bottom but also the big men at the top. In all the talk about a revitalized sense of responsibility the aspect Brandeis so strongly emphasized, while it is not ignored, is passed over lightly.

Brandeis had commented in 1915:

We must bear in mind all the time that however much we may desire material improvement and must desire it for the comfort of the individual, that the United States is a democracy, and that we must have, above all things, men. . . . We are committed primarily to democracy. . . . Profit sharing, however liberal, can not meet the situation. . . . There must be a division not only of profits, but a division also of responsibilities.[50]

In industry, Brandeis explained, problems "arise from day to day, or from month to month, or from year to year." They come up "for consideration and solution as they come up in our political government." The workers must share this responsibility. " 'Men cannot live by bread alone.' Men must have industrial liberty as well as good wages." "Concentration of power," Brandeis remarked, "has been shown to be dangerous in a democracy, even though that power may be used beneficently."[51] This view still has defenders in 1955.

Justice Douglas observed in a recent Supreme Court opinion:

Size in steel is the measure of the power of a handful of men over our economy. That power can be utilized with lightning speed. It can be benign or it can be dangerous. The philosophy

[50] Testimony before the U.S. Commission on Industrial Relations, Jan. 23, 1915, *Sen. Doc.*, No. 415, 64th Cong., 1st Sess., XXVI, 7659–7660.

[51] Testimony of L. D. Brandeis, *ibid.*, pp. 7662–7663.

of the Sherman Act is that it should not exist. For all power tends to develop into a government in itself. Power that controls the economy should be in the hands of elected representatives of the people, not in the hands of an industrial oligarchy. Industrial power should be decentralized. It should be scattered into many hands so that the fortunes of the people will not be dependent on the whim or caprice, the political prejudices, the emotional stability of a few self-appointed men. The fact that they are not vicious men but respectable and social-minded is irrelevant. That is the philosophy and the command of the Sherman Act. It is founded on a theory of hostility to the concentration in private hands of power so great that only a government of the people should have it.[52]

The basic flaw in the more flamboyant versions of welfare capitalism is that they ignore the fact, cited by Berle, that "power has laws of its own."[53] At no point does either Johnson or Davenport take into account the revolutionary effect of the modern corporation on business practices and conventional economic concepts. Corporate action is still seen as private action; the rights of man are considered "just as safe in corporate as they are in individual hands." In urging business enterprise to annex welfare functions, Johnson and Davenport do not broach the leading question of how so-called free enterprise is to be held politically accountable. Ignoring the basic difference between government and other forms of social and economic organization, they disregard the certain risk that the businessman, however competent in production, profit-seeking affairs, may not be qualified to carry large social responsibilities. The narrowing experience of profit making, perforce the pri-

[52] Justice Douglas, joined by Justices Black, Murphy, and Rutledge, dissenting in *U.S.* v. *Columbia Steel Co.*, 334 U.S. 495 (1948), pp. 536–537.
[53] Berle, *Twentieth Century Capitalist Revolution*, p. 172.

mary concern of business, may prevent him from achieving that breadth of view necessary for encompassing the public welfare.

Davenport says that the old slogan, "What helps business helps you," is no longer tenable. Businessmen must think less of profits, more of goods and services and of human beings. But can one reasonably expect unselfish effort from management under a specific obligation to stockholders, but without any enforceable responsibility to society? In 1913 Brooks Adams asserted categorically that "the capitalist seems incapable of feeling his responsibility, as a member of the governing class." [54] It is at this point that Mr. Berle detects "the greatest current weakness of the corporate system."

In practice [he writes] institutional corporations are guided by tiny self-perpetuating oligarchies. These in turn are drawn from and judged by the group opinion of a small fragment of America—its business and financial community. Change of mangement by contesting for stockholders' votes is extremely rare, and increasingly difficult and expensive to the point of impossibility. The legal presumption in favor of management, and the natural unwillingness of courts to control or reverse management action save in cases of the more elementary types of dishonesty or fraud, leaves management with substantially absolute power. Thus the only real control which guides or limits their economic and social action is the real, though undefined and tacit, philosophy of the men who compose them.[55]

"He that is to govern a whole nation," Thomas Hobbes observed in 1651, "must read in himself, not this or that particular man, but mankind." When "the meanest interest brazenly lays hold of the sacred name of 'public good,' "

[54] Adams, *op. cit.*, p. 213.
[55] Berle, *Twentieth Century Capitalist Revolution*, p. 180.

Rousseau commented in his *Social Contract* of 1762, "the general will becomes mute." Can the businessman, or any other special interest group, rise to the Hobbesian standard? Can any self-appointed guardian of the public welfare avoid the blighting consequences the "Citizen of Geneva" noted? "The Widsom of the Few," James Harrington observed in his *Oceana*, "may be the Light of Mankind; but the Interest of the Few is not the Profit of Mankind nor of a Commonwealth." [56] "Men come easily to believe," Albert Venn Dicey observed, "that arrangements agreeable to themselves are beneficial to others";[57] and "theories of the public good, which turn out on inspection to be an elegant disguise for some particular interest, are common . . . in national affairs." [58]

[56] *Oceana*, 3d ed. (London, 1747), p. 48.
[57] Dicey, *Law and Opinion in England*, 2d ed. (London: Macmillan), pp. 14–15; quoted in E. H. Carr, *Twenty Years' Crisis* (London: Macmillan, 1939), p. 96.
[58] Carr, *op. cit.*, p. 96.
The drive for welfare capitalism seems but a single aspect of what Arthur Schlesinger, Jr., calls "The New Conservatism: Politics of Nostalgia."

"The deeper passion of the New Conservatives" Schlesinger writes, "is for the rich, humane, and somber sentiments of European conservatives, based on culture, morality, and tradition, not on the accumulation of money. They want a ruling class, but one composed of responsible patricians, not of successful shopkeepers." Professor Schlesinger believes that it will take a lot of doing to transform the American plutocracy into a socially sensitive ruling class on the model of British aristocracy. "For better or worse, our upper-classes base their position not on land or tradition or a sense of social responsibility, but on the folding stuff. . . . The very qualities of unbridled and creative acquisitiveness that account for the economic contributions of American business seem to disqualify it as a governing class. Very little that has happened since January 20, 1953 would render obsolete Henry Cabot Lodge's observation of half a century ago: 'The businessman dealing with a large political

Is not the Johnson-Davenport concept of welfare capitalism essentially a reversion to ill-fated NRA, with government excluded from the scheme, not only in creating the regulation, but in enforcing it? Does not this latest version of "self-government in industry" suggest John Locke's original state of nature, a condition marked by the absence of a common power over all, a situation in which each man was his own executive? But, alas, in Locke's "great and natural community," "all being king," and "the greater part no strict observer of equity and justice, the enjoyment of property" became "very unsafe, very insecure." Each man in deciding controversies involving his own interests proved incapable of transcending the narrow bounds of self, so essential to the process of governing. Might, rather than right, held sway; men were driven to establish government —to set up a common power over all. For Locke this was the "inconvenience incapable of a remedy."

Our own history affords telling examples in support of Locke's hypothesis. During the 1920's the modern corporation possessed a freedom of action much like that which Locke's men enjoyed in the state of nature. True self-government, as Herbert Hoover defined it, was then an accomplished fact. Industry was free to do then what Johnson and Davenport insist it should do now—"cure its own abuses." In 1930 Hoover indignantly repulsed the popular clamor for government intervention as the "specious claim that hired representatives of a hundred million people can do better than the people themselves, in thinking and

---

question is really a painful sight. It does seem to me that businessmen, with a few exceptions, are worse when they come to deal with politics than men of any other class'" (Arthur Schlesinger, Jr., "The New Conservatism: Politics of Nostalgia," *Reporter*, June 16, 1955).

planning their daily life." [59] Like the advocates of welfare capitalism today, Mr. Hoover then urged business to organize voluntarily, take steps of their own to increase production and thus create jobs. This was not, he insisted, goverment interference in business. It was "a request from the government" to businessmen to co-operate in solving a national problem. The federal government thus "asserted leadership only to pass it along to others." [60] But Mr. Hoover's theory proved altogether untenable—indeed, well-nigh disastrous. The year 1929 stands as a terrible warning of the "inconveniences," to use Locke's mild phrase, that followed in the wake of our own variant of the state of nature. And, in 1932, American businessmen turned as helplessly and imploringly to government as Locke's men did in his mythical state of nature. It was then abundantly proved that free enterprise, far from having an eye single to the public interest, was blind even to its own interest.

Finally, is the Johnson-Davenport alternative in accord, as claimed, with the American heritage? To a certain extent it undoubtedly is. The Founding Fathers feared democracy, distrusted government as such. Political power was, it is true, rooted in and derived from the people. Government was made politically responsible to them. But in addition to "dependence on the people," which the framers considered as "the primary control on government," they insisted on certain "auxiliary precautions" for obliging government to control itself—separation of powers, checks and balances, federalism, judicial review. In achieving the power to govern, the New Deal weakened these auxiliary

[59] Gordon Harrison, *Road to the Right: The Tradition and Hope of American Conservatism* (New York: Morrow, 1954), p. 278.
[60] *Ibid.*, p. 276.

devices. Though elimination of traditional safeguards did not add up, as President Roosevelt's critics would have us believe, to a deliberate design to create an absolute despotism of alien origin, their breakdown does create grounds for serious concern. The distrustful attitude of businessmen toward the expansion of government thus reflects the fears of those who framed the Constitution of 1787. The strange thing is that so many Americans are not equally sensitive to the enormous power of what T. K. Quinn called "uncaged tigers or elephants," [61] such as General Motors and United States Steel.

The British anthropologist Geoffrey Gorer sees this divergence of attitude as a quaint American "fantasy." It

[61] Theodore K. Quinn, *I Quit Monster Business: An Appeal for Independent, Decentralized Enterprise—To Save Individual Opportunity and Freedom in America*, (New York: Public Relations, Inc., 522 Fifth Avenue, 1948), p. 6. "I quit monster business," Mr. Quinn explains, "because it is undemocratic, because it is inhuman and not socially responsible, because most of it is big only for the sake of bigness or for purposes of concentrated power and control, because it is inefficient and corruptive, because it is causing a dependent society where only masses count, genuine individual freedom languishes and opportunity and expression are restricted, because it glorifies leaders whose interest is too much in themselves, and because, through its essentially collectivistic forms and methods and mockery of 'free enterprise,' it is leading our country, just as surely as the sun sets to a brand of totalitarianism which is a perversion as far from individualism, civil liberties and the democratic process as Russian communism." For an elaboration of this thesis, see T. K. Quinn, *Giant Business: Threat to Democracy:* The Autobiography of an Insider (New York: Exposition Press, 1953).

For a compilation of recent criticisms, such as Mr. Quinn's, and a brief attempt to answer them, see J. D. Glover, *The Attack on Big Business* (Boston: Graduate School of Business Administration, Harvard University, 1954). Louis M. Hacker has written a discriminating review of the book in the *New York Times Book Review*, Nov. 14, 1954, p. 41.

174

can be explained, he thinks, as a "subtle distinction" between *authority* and *power:* "Control of people—authority—is always morally bad; control over things . . . (natural resources, goods, services, money, chattels)—power—is morally neutral and even, within certain ill-defined limits, highly praiseworthy." [62] Thus corporate power continues its unabated aggrandizement without rousing any acute sense of danger to freedom. Increase in government authority, on the other hand, must be justified step by step—even in cases, such as the Tennessee Valley Authority, where large-scale government planning has proved highly successful. By the same token, initiation of welfare programs by government is strenuously opposed as "statism," while implementation of the same program by free enterprise was seen by Russell Davenport as capable of awakening "everywhere new hope for the perpetuation of Freedom."

Americans appear less sensitive than was Thomas Hobbes to the tendency of individuals to break off from society and form private power enclaves of their own, at war with society itself. This evil loomed so perilously before *The Leviathan's* author that he would have none of it. Corporations were denounced as "worms" in the entrails of the body politic. [63] Enduring peace demanded that they be

[62] Geoffrey Gorer, *The American People: A Study in National Character* (New York: Norton, 1948), pp. 39-40.

[63] See Thomas Hobbes, *Leviathan* (Everyman ed.; New York, 1928), ch. 29.

Rousseau was equally suspicious of individual and group temptation to break off from civil society, and for the same reason: "Each individual, as a man, may have a particular will contrary or dissimilar to the general will which he has as a citizen. His particular interest may speak to him quite differently from the common interest: his absolute and naturally independent existence may make him look upon what he owes to the common cause as a gratuitous

drastically purged away. Latter-day absolutists, whether Fascists or Communists, follow the same ruthless policy. James Madison confronted himself with this dilemma. Like Hobbes, he saw faction (especially that of a majority) as the evil to which popular government is peculiarly addicted. And yet he rejected the absolutist solution on the theory that, though liberty is to faction what air is to fire, it would be as foolish to destroy liberty because it nourishes faction as to annihilate air because it gives to fire its destructive quality.

Surely Madison's principles of free government now face a grueling test. The Father of the Constitution took less stock than do the advocates of welfare capitalism in the "perfectibility of man and the illimitable progress of society." [64] For him class-and-interest struggles are characteristic of a free society. Its future depended on the preservation of competitive pluralism. Freedom required a wide distribution of power in both society and in government; power alone constitutes an effective check on power. The greater the number of factions, the better the chances of freedom. In 1789 the prospect for continuance of the conditions Madison considered requisite for free government, though not unclouded, were reassuring. A "Utopia," he observed optimistically, "exhibiting a perfect homo-

---

contribution, the loss of which will do less harm to others than the payment of it is burdensome to himself; and, regarding the moral person which constitutes the State as a *persona ficta*, because not a man, he may wish to enjoy the rights of citizenship without being ready to fulfil the duties of a subject. The continuance of such an injustice could not but prove the undoing of the body politic" (*The Social Contract* [Everyman ed.; New York, 1938], pp. 17–18; see also p. 91).

[64] See Neal Riemer, "James Madison and the Current Conservative Vogue," *Antioch Review*, 14 (Winter 1954–55), 458–470.

geneousness of interests, opinions and feelings [has] nowhere yet [been] found in civilized communities." [65]

Conditions in 1787, however, are one thing, in 1955, something else. In modern society it is increasingly difficult to maintain this complexus of forces, this self-adjusting pluralism, either in society or in government. Accentuating our difficulties is the current trend toward coerced conformity, deemed to be essential to national security. So, the fate of free government still hangs in the balance.

"We only know," Reinhold Niebuhr remarks tentatively, "that a completely free market lacks the self-regulating power once ascribed to it, and that too inclusive [government] planning destroys the flexibility which a healthy economy requires." [66] Liberty, thus doubly imperiled, stimulates pessimism. Professor Robert S. Lynd sees the systematic effort of big business to get a strangle hold on various opinion-forming groups as striking at the essentials of free government. He goes so far as to suggest that the present-day conflict between public power and private right may have reached the point where the age in which we live will go down in history as the one in which "Western man at last recognized the contradiction between capitalism and democracy—accepted the fact that the middle way straddle called 'liberalism' was no longer workable." [67]

Certain it is that increasing government control and regulation, however essential or praiseworthy, combined

[65] Quoted in *ibid.*, p. 461.

[66] Reinhold Niebuhr, "Halfway to What?" *Nation*, 170 (Jan. 14, 1950), 28.

[67] Robert S. Lynd, "Can Liberalism Do It?" *New Century*, 1 (May 1948; published by the Princeton Liberal Union). Berle also notes how "concentration of economic power" creates a "dampening cloud" over "free-ranging thought." *Annals American Academy of Political and Social Science*, 300 (July 1955) 21, 24.

with the obstinate determination of big business to evade or end that trend or to replace government with a power system of its own, raises arresting questions: How far may government safely go into areas formerly considered immune from such control? How much more government planning can society employ without losing its "free" character? How much social power can a free society permit individuals and groups to annex and hold without depriving government of the authority essential for maintaining order and security? [68]

Of one thing we may be certain: government alone can create and re-create the broad firmament of order under which individuals and groups, including so-called free enterprise, can function for the good of all. "Neither the claims of ownership nor those of control can stand against the paramount interests of the community." [69] The vast extension of government power has not come as a result of some evil, alien force; it has been in response to long-felt necessity, or, as Justice Stone tried to explain to Herbert

[68] For the late Senator Robert A. Taft the answers were clear: "We are close to the line where government expansion must stop, or our free enterprise system is lost." See an elaboration of this view in "How Much Government Can Free Enterprise Stand?" *Collier's*, 124 (Oct. 22, 1949), pp. 16 ff.

[69] Berle and Means, *op. cit.*, p. 356. "It is my basic view," Justice Jackson has written, "that whenever any organization or combination of individuals, whether in a corporation, a labor union or other body, obtains such economic or legal advantage that it can control or, in effect, govern the lives of other people, it is subject to the control of the Government, be it state or federal, for the Government can suffer no rivals in the field of coercion. Liberty requires that coercion be applied to the individual, not by other individuals, but by the Government after full inquiry into the justification" (Robert H. Jackson, *The Supreme Court in the American System of Government*, p. 69).

178

Hoover in 1934, to preserve order in the broad sense.[70] Twentieth-century issues cannot, as Stone suggested, "be settled by an appeal to the eighteenth century philosophy of individualism in the abstract, for that philosophy cannot be completely adapted" to modern conditions.

Although Mr. Eisenhower, as a private citizen, had been highly critical of the bureaucratic trend,[71] as President, he

[70] President Roosevelt, at the outset, had toyed with President Hoover's approach—let business "cure its own abuses." If this had proved practical, he might have established welfare capitalism, instead of a sprawling, wasteful social welfare program under government auspices. In 1932 he had said: "The responsible heads of finance and industry, instead of acting each for himself, must work together to achieve the common end. They must . . . sacrifice . . . private advantage; and in reciprocal self-denial, . . . seek a general advantage. It is here that formal Government—political Government, comes in" (*Public Papers and Addresses*, I, 754–755). He recognized that the "relations between Government and business will be necessarily in process of redefinition during the coming years," but warned that the nature of that relationship would depend on how "business leaders . . . assume the responsibilities which accompany their power" (p. 785).

But there had always been lurking doubts. In his campaign address of Nov. 1, 1928, "Is Hoover Human?" F.D.R. had begun to wage war on the notion that a business elite knows how to run the country (*Public Papers and Addresses*, I, 68). On Sept. 23, 1932, he spoke of economic interests as a threat to liberty and said that government would have "to intervene, not to destroy individualism, but to protect it" (p. 746).

[71] In 1949 General Eisenhower had condemned government as "bureaucratic," as paving "the road to despotism." He then analyzed the remedy for current ills in terms of "voluntary cooperative" effort that will "bind labor and management in every productive enterprise."

"You must not bow your necks to a centralized government," the great World War II general admonished a Texas audience. You must "not trade the principles that made this nation great for some panaceas dished out by a bureaucrat sitting in an easy chair in

179

has not turned his back on either the achievements or the theory of the New Deal. On the contrary, the Republican President recognizes that "government must use its vast power to maintain employment and purchasing power as well as to maintain reasonably stable prices"; "must be alert and sensitive to economic developments, including its own myriad activities"; "must be prepared to take preventive as well as remedial action"; "must be ready to cope with new situations that may arise." "This is not," the President said, "a start-and-stop responsibility, but a continuous one." In words that smack of Franklin D. Roosevelt himself, President Eisenhower boldly proclaimed: "The arsenal of weapons at the disposal of Government for maintaining economic stability is formidable. . . . We shall not hesitate to use any or all of these weapons as the situation may require." [72]

In his State of the Union message, January 1955, the President went further, endorsing the basic structure of the entire New Deal program. This astounding evidence of well-nigh complete conversion indicates that the dream of automatic progress remains only as a fixation of "the wild-eyed Utopian capitalists." [73]

To escape anarchy, politics must be dominant over

Washington." If all that Americans want is security, they can go to prison (address, combined Luncheon Clubs, Galveston, Tex.; quoted in *New York Times*, Dec. 9, 1949, p. 23). These sentiments are a far cry from those Mr. Eisenhower has voiced as President. No wonder extreme GOP critics, such as Governor J. Bracken Lee, express bitter disillusionment.

[72] *New York Times*, Jan. 29, 1954, p. 10, col. 1. See also *Economic Report of the President*, transmitted to the Congress of the United States, Jan. 28, 1954, 83d Cong., 2d Sess. (Washington, D. C.: Government Printing Office, 1954), p. iv.

[73] C. Wright Mills, *The New Men of Power* (New York: Harcourt, Brace, 1948), p. 24.

economics. Official, politically responsible government must insist on monopolizing coercive power, as against any and all private aspirants for such power. It must do this, not because there is special virtue in established authority or because government is or can be omniscient, but because this is the only way of avoiding chaos, the only way, as Locke's men discovered in a state of nature, to prevent individuals and groups from taking law into their own hands.

* VI *

Can Freedom Conquer Fear?

AMERICAN political society, as portrayed in these pages, exhibits conflict, instability, and change as the normal pattern. Foreign and domestic issues have always agitated our politics. Social calm and the golden age have been disturbed, on the one hand, by the incessant human drive for freedom, property, and equality, on the other by the stubborn determination of privilege to maintain the status quo. Running through our tradition is a basic ambivalence, a persistent antinomy that expresses itself in many ways: numbers versus interests, public power versus private rights, majority rule versus minority rights, constitution of powers versus constitution of rights, political versus judicial restraints on government.[1]

[1] Louis Hartz describes our polar contradictions more broadly as: "pragmatism and absolutism, historicism and rationalism, optimism and pessimism, materialism and idealism, individualism and conformism." "The task of the cultural analyst," Hartz says, "is not to discover simplicity, or even to discover unity, for simplicity and unity do not exist, but to drive a wedge of rationality through the pathetic indecisions of social thought" ("American Political Thought and the American Revolution," *American Political Science Review*, 46 [June 1952], 339-340).

The Founding Fathers inherited the axiom that property is the firm basis of politics, the true measure of power. Alexander Hamilton and James Madison agreed that liberty itself leads to inequality.[2] Their guiding principles rested on this assumption. For them the primary function of government was to safeguard the fruits of this inequality, i.e., property against the ever-present threat of "mere numbers." In 1829 John Randolph of Roanoke saw the property-rulership relation so inextricably linked as to make it impossible, by universal suffrage or otherwise, to break the tie. "The two sexes do not, more certainly, nor by a more unerring law,

[2] "It was certainly true," Hamilton remarked on the floor of the Philadelphia Convention, June 26, 1787, "that nothing like an equality of property existed: that an inequality would exist as long as liberty existed, and that it would unavoidably result from that very liberty itself. This inequality of property constituted the great and fundamental distinction in Society" (ed. by Max Farrand; *The Records of the Federal Convention of 1787* [New Haven: Yale University Press, 1911], I, 424).

In *Federalist*, No. 10, Madison said: "The diversity in the faculties of men, from which the rights of property originate, is not less an insuperable obstacle to an uniformity of interests. The protection of these faculties is the first object of government. From the protection of different and unequal faculties of acquiring property, the possession of different degrees and kinds of property immediately results; and from the influence of these on the sentiments and views of the respective proprietors, ensues a division of the society into different interests and parties" (Max Beloff, ed., *The Federalist*, p. 42).

"It is a great and dangerous error," Calhoun wrote in 1857, "to suppose that all people are equally entitled to liberty. It is a reward to be earned, not a blessing to be gratuitously lavished on all alike. . . . There is another error not less great and dangerous . . . that liberty and equality are so intimately united, that liberty cannot be perfect without perfect equality. . . . Inequality of condition, while it is a necessary consequence of liberty, is, at the same time, indispensable to progress" (R. K. Crallé, ed., *The Works of John C. Calhoun* [New York: Appleton, 1883], I, 55-56).

gravitate to each other, than power and property. You cannot cause them to change hands." [3] James Kent, agreeing with Randolph, insisted that universal manhood suffrage is "incompatible with government and security to property," and he confidently predicted that with its achievement "the government and character of this country are going to ruin." [4]

Latter-day Americans furbished this doctrine even brighter and promoted it as the most distinctive facet in our culture. Joseph H. Choate said in his successful argument of 1895 against the federal income tax:

I have thought that one of the fundamental objects of all civilized government was the preservation of the rights of private property. I have thought that it was the very keystone of the arch upon which all civilized government rests, and that this once abandoned, everything was at stake and in danger . . . and I supposed all educated, civilized men believed in that.[5]

In 1922 a Federal District Court Judge commented that "of the three fundamental principles which underlie government, and for which government exists, the protection of life, liberty and property, the chief of these is property." [6] Constitutions themselves have been valued as "checks upon

[3] *Proceedings and Debates of the Virginia State Convention of 1829–30* (Richmond, 1830), p. 319.

[4] *Reports of the Debates and Proceedings of the Convention of the State of New York, 1920,* p. 219–222, passim.

[5] *Pollock* v. *Farmer's Loan & Trust Co.,* 157 U.S. 429 (1895), p. 534.

[6] Justice Van Orsdel in *Children's Hospital* v. *Adkins,* 284 F., 613 (Nov. 6, 1922), p. 622. In similar vein, Paul Elmer More declared: "To the civilized man *the rights of property are more important than the right to life*" (italics are More's, *Shelburne Essays,* 9th series [Boston: Houghton Mifflin, 1915], p. 136).

the hasty action of the majority," [7] as a "set of limitations on the political power of the majority in favor of the political power of the property owner." [8]

From the very outset, however, exponents of the property-power nexus have been confronted by those upholding the sovereign authority of government, by those stressing the role of public power rooted in persons, in numbers, by those who would make politics dominant over—not subordinate to—economics. The Declaration of Independence dedicated the American people to the doctrine that just governments rest on the consent of the governed. We are committed, in some measure, to the principle of majority rule, and to the idea that government is a positive, creative force in society. In the preamble to our Constitution, government is instituted to promote the general welfare. Writing in 1826, Edward Livingston declared: "Political society owes perfect protection to all its members in their persons, reputations and property; and it also owes necessary subsistence to those who cannot procure it for themselves. . . . The preservation of life is the first object, property is only a secondary one." "Can it be supposed," Livingston inquired, "that any just contract could stipulate that one of the con-

---

[7] Special message of President William Howard Taft, objecting to a provision in the proposed Arizona Constitution for the recall of judges, in *House Doc.*, No. 106, 62d Cong., 1st Sess., Aug. 15, 1911, p. 4.

"The prescriptions in favor of liberty," Madison declared, "ought to be leveled against that quarter where the greatest danger lies, namely, that which possesses the highest prerogative of power. But this is not found in neither the executive or legislative departments of Government, but in the body of the people, *operating* by the majority against the minority" (Madison, *Annals of Congress*, I, 454–455).

[8] Arthur Twining Hadley, "The Constitutional Position of Property in America," *Independent*, 64 (April 16, 1908), 838.

tracting parties should die of hunger, in order that the others might enjoy, without deduction, the whole of their property?" [9] "This Court from the early days," Justice Roberts said in 1934, "affirmed that the power to promote the general welfare is inherent in government." [10]

At every turning point in our history, spokesmen for property have met rebuttal from those who valued the human personality. The dominant trend has been democratic. "We march and rest and march again," [11] Henry Demarest Lloyd observed in 1893. Defenders of economic privilege have found to their chagrin the truth of Disraeli's aphorism: Democracy, "like death, gives back nothing." [12] This radical strain in our tradition has not been, however, an unmixed

[9] Edward Livingston, Introductory Report to the Code of Reform of Prison Discipline, 1826, in *Criminal Jurisprudence* (New York, 1873), I, 528–529, 533, *passim.*

[10] *Nebbia* v. *New York*, 291 U.S. 502 (1934), p. 524.

Following Locke, Justice Johnson wrote: "The right of the owner to traffic in his property never was, since the institution of society, a right independent of the control of government. It is a right surrendered necessarily to the government, by every one when he enters into society and becomes one of its members. A government which does not possess the power to make all needful regulations in respect to its internal trade and commerce, to impose such restrictions upon it as may be deemed necessary for the good of all, and even to prohibit and suppress entirely any particular traffic which is found to be injurious and demoralizing in its tendencies and consequences, is no government. It must lack that essential element of sovereignty, indispensably necessary to render it capable of accomplishing the primary object for which governments are instituted, that of affording security, protection and redress to all interests and all classes and conditions of persons within their limits" (Justice T. A. Johnson, dissenting in *Wynehamer* v. *New York*, 13 New York [Court of Appeals] Reports, 378 [1856], pp. 474–475).

[11] H. D. Lloyd, *Wealth against Commonwealth* (New York: Harper, 1894), p. 533.

[12] Quoted in W. J. Ghent, "Benevolent Feudalism," *Independent*, 54 (April 3, 1902), 783.

blessing. If reformers and revolutionists have been necessary to counterbalance the inertness and fossilism of those who "refuse to move altogether for fear of being moved too far," adherents of the status quo have been indispensable as a safeguard against reformers who, as Burke said, "by hating vices too much, they come to love men too little." [13] It was a reformer who said that "the greatest dangers to liberty lurk in insidious encroachment by men of zeal, well-meaning but without understanding." [14]

These divergent interwoven strands constitute the strength of American politics. Whether one reads Madisons's notes of the debates in the Philadelphia Convention of 1787, or the recorded discussions held in the 1820's in Massachusetts, New York, and Virginia then engaged in broadening the constitutional base of power, or the long and bitter wranglings that preceded Lincoln's Emancipation Proclamation, or the nation-wide controversy F.D.R.'s Court-packing proposal aroused, one notes a baffling and continuing paradox. Pitted against each other are the moral ideals of freedom and stubborn determination to keep economic inequality intact by means of immutable constitutional safeguards. "The government of our country, instead of a Democracy the most simple, is" as John Quincy Adams said, "the most complicated government on the face of the globe." [15] Polar contradictions, not unity and simplicity, are its essence.

"A great equality of condition," Webster declared in 1820, is the "true basis, most certainly, of popular govern-

[13] Edmund Burke, *Reflections on the French Revolution* (Maynard's English Classic Series; New York: Merrill, n.d.), p. 109.

[14] Justice Brandeis dissenting in *Olmstead* v. *U.S.* 277 U.S. 438 (1928), p. 479.

[15] John Quincy Adams, *Jubilee of the Constitution* (New York, 1839), p. 115.

ment" [16] and the surest safeguard against its decay. After about 1850, as political power became increasingly diffused, industrial and financial power became steadily more concentrated, ever more aggressive and dominant. Meanwhile, the people refusing, as De Tocqueville had foreseen, "to be miserable and sovereign," asserted their authority in corrective legislation. By 1890 the juxtaposition of political democracy and economic oligarchy had set the stage for our present political-economic antinomy. It was not until the election of 1932 that America emphatically rejected the eighteenth-century commonplace that political power inevitably follows economic power. President Roosevelt's New Deal is significant in making political power dominant, economic power subordinate and submissive. Ironical as it may seem, it remained for an alleged radical to disprove the economic determinism implicit in the dogmas adhered to from the beginning.

But President Roosevelt's successive triumphs were never absolute or unchallenged. Just as in the years prior to 1932 free enterprise had to vie with the sporadic effort of government to restrain its power and correct its abuses, so, in the years that followed, reformist zeal faced constitutional and other obstacles defiantly interposed by the economic elite. President Roosevelt's showdown with the Supreme Court in 1937 did not finally resolve the issue of political versus judicial restraints on government. The Justices did not abdicate, nor is it desirable that they should do so. For with the displacement of judicial control as auxiliary to political restraints on government, our democracy would demand less accommodation, adjustment, ten-

[16] *Journal of Debates & Proceedings in the Convention of Delegates Chosen to Revise the Constitution of Massachusetts* (Boston, 1853), p. 245.

sion, balance, compromise—less conscientious effort to preserve all the manifold elements in our culture.

In America no one dogma, no single interest, no particular group, has succeeded in mastering all others or in embracing the full flavor of our political complexity. Harold Laski wrote:

Americanism is multiform, and it is also, at its very roots, nonconformist. No one can fully shape it the way he wants it to go—no President and no millionaire, no labour leader and no intellectual; and it is not even shaped by all the objective consequences of its mass production system. Something is always escaping to be itself; something is always emerging to protest that things must be done another way; there is always an ardent clash between traditionalist and reformer which makes the consequential Americanism different from what either of them dared both to hope and to fear.[17]

Conflict has been, and is endemic. Our choice today is not between progress with conflict and progress without conflict. The alternative is between conflict and stagnation.[18] The real peril is lest at some point in the quest for freedom, for security against ever-emerging tyrannies, we become so weary of disorder, so weighted down with the responsibilities freedom inevitably entails, so troubled by domestic turmoil verging on chaos, so fearful of external aggression and foreign creeds, as to yield to the lure of that phantom no free society can possibly attain, the status quo. In a

[17] Harold J. Laski, *The American Democracy: A Commentary and Interpretation* (New York: Viking, 1948), p. 719. In a similar vein Henry Steele Commager observed: "Every effort to confine Americanism to a single pattern, to constrain it to a single formula, is disloyalty to everything that is valid in Americanism" (*Freedom, Loyalty and Dissent* [New York: Oxford, 1954], p. 155).

[18] Arthur M. Schlesinger, Jr., *The Vital Center* (Boston: Houghton Mifflin, 1949), p. 255.

wartime generation driven, like ours, by the adolescent urge for conformity, Randolph Bourne observed how "the strain of being an adult human being weighs heavily on us all." Amid national crisis, he wrote, "the slack is taken up, the cross-currents fade out, and the nation moves lumberingly . . . towards that 'peacefulness of being at war.' " [19] Overlooked is the abiding truth Rousseau put in his query of 1762: "Tranquillity is found in dungeons; but is that enough to make them desirable places to live in? What do they gain, if the very tranquillity they enjoy is one of their miseries?" [20]

Each generation, including our own, thinks of itself as having to decide its fate, to save or lose free government. The experience is not new; only the context changes within which that decision must be made. In his *Song of the Open Road* (1856) the poet Whitman reminds us: "It is provided in the very essence of things that from any fruition of success, no matter what, shall come forth something to make a greater struggle necessaary."

Today the "something" which has come forth to test the enduring power of our tradition is national insecurity. The paradoxical fact is that whatever measure of success we achieve in overcoming it raises new dangers to freedom. Security means spending up to half the national income on defense, thus elevating the role of the military; it means the intrusion of government into sectors heretofore exempt. Channels of public information must be blocked so that in our desperate attempt to ward off the hostile threat we risk cutting the jugular vein of free government

[19] Randolph Bourne, *Untimely Papers* (New York: Huebsch, 1919), p. 142.

[20] J. J. Rousseau, *The Social Contract* (Everyman ed.; New York, 1947), bk. 1, ch. 4, p. 9, *passim.*

—discussion, dissent, opposition, nonconformity. These essential attitudes and processes, always hard to maintain, labor under impossible difficulty in national crisis. Writing in 1787 at a time perhaps calmer than ours, Alexander Hamilton noted that "safety from external danger is the most powerful director of national conduct. Even the ardent love of liberty will, after a time, give way to its dictates. . . . To be more safe [nations,] at length, become willing to run the risk of being less free." [21] "It is a sobering fact," Justice Frankfurter commented in the Communist conspiracy case of 1950, "that in sustaining the conviction before us we can hardly escape restriction on the interchange of ideas." [22]

[21] Beloff, ed., *op. cit.*, No. 8, p. 32.

[22] Concurring in *Dennis* v. *U.S.*, 341 U.S. 494 (1951), p. 549. Nor is the Court any sure reliance for the preservation of freedom. "The dominant lesson of our history in the relation of the judiciary to repressions is that courts love liberty most when it is under pressure least" (John P. Frank, "Review and Basic Liberties," in Edmond N. Cahn, ed., *Supreme Court and Supreme Law* [Bloomington: Indiana University Press, 1954], p. 114). For documentation of this proposition, see Richard L. Sklar, "The Fiction of the First Freedom," *Western Political Quarterly*, 6 (June 1953), 302–319.

Said the late Justice Jackson: "I know of no modern instance in which any judiciary has saved a whole people from the great currents of intolerance, passion, usurpation, and tyranny which have threatened liberty and free institutions. . . . It is not idle speculation to inquire which comes first, either in time or importance, an independent and enlightened judiciary or a free and tolerant society. Must we just maintain a system of free political government to assure a free judiciary, or can we rely on an aggressive, activist judiciary to guarantee free government? While each undoubtedly is a support for the other, and the two are frequently found together, it is my belief that the attitude of a society and of its organized political forces, rather than its legal machinery, is the controlling force in the character of free institutions" (Jackson, *The Supreme Court in the American System of Government*, pp. 80–81).

Politics now prevails over economics. The crucial issue is whether, to achieve national security, government is to invade all other activities. Even as the Supreme Court announced the demise of laissez-faire in economics, the Justices exhibited sharp divergence on legislative control of thought, speech, and religious belief. Widely different judicial views illustrate disagreement among men of high competence and unquestioned loyalty as to the permissible range of government in the delicate realms of mind and soul. The issue is the more baffling in that it poses a conflict between two valid interests—the demands of national security and the claims of individual freedom. If neither can be presumed to be exclusive, the contradiction itself may be a part of the mystery, as well as the measure of the difficulty.[23]

"To make a government requires no great prudence," Burke wrote in his *Reflections on the French Revolution*, "Settle the seat of power; teach obedience; and the work is done. To give freedom is still more easy. It is not necessary to guide; it only requires to let go the rein. But to form a

---

The lengths to which the Court has gone in sustaining legislative curbs on freedom of speech is indicated by Justice Black's harsh words, dissenting in *Feiner* v. *New York*, 340 U.S. 315, 1951: "In my judgment, today's holding means that as a practical matter, minority speakers can be silenced in any city. Hereafter, despite the First and Fourteenth Amendments, the policeman's club can take heavy toll of a current administration's public critics" (p. 328).

[23] "When, in any field of human observation, two truths appear in conflict it is wiser to assume that neither is exclusive, and that their contradiction, though it may be hard to bear, is part of the mystery of things" (from *London Times Literary Supplement;* quoted by Felix Frankfurter, *New York Times Magazine*, Nov. 28, 1954, p. 14). See also Frankfurter, "Some Observations on the Nature of the Judicial Process of Supreme Court Litigation," *Proceedings of the American Philosophical Society*, 98 (Aug. 16, 1954), p. 234.

free government; that is, to temper together these opposite elements of liberty and restraint in one consistent work, requires much thought; deep reflection; a sagacious, powerful, and combining mind." Small wonder that neither government policy nor court decisions provides clear-cut answers.

The Communist menace is real. No reasonable man can deny its existence as an external threat to our peace and security or question the necessity of rigorous law enforcement. But we dare not jump to the conclusion that the dictator's way is more effective than any we can devise. Much less can one condone use of the Communist threat, great as it is, as a cosmic taboo to enforce conformity and discourage all criticism of things as they are. The obstructive strategy is familiar. De Tocqueville commented on how vested interests "regard every new theory as a peril, every innovation as an irksome toil, every social improvement as a stepping stone to revolution." Felix Frankfurter observed in 1938:

That a majority of the [Supreme] Court which frequently disallowed restraints on economic power should so consistently have sanctioned restraints of the mind is perhaps only a surface paradox. There is an underlying unity between fear of ample experimentation in economics and fear of expression of heretical ideas.[24]

Today, however, the radical smear so widely and effectively used is not, as formerly, a bugaboo. The diabolical fact is that the beneficiaries of the status quo are able to convert this mortal danger to their own purposes. Vague reference to a person's subversive activities or left-wing associations is enough to brand him "controversial." An

[24] Felix Frankfurter in *Mr. Justice Holmes and the Supreme Court* (Cambridge: *Harvard University Press,* 1938), p. 62.

organized minority or a politically ambitious demagogue can thus destroy or impair the usefulness of "men whose habits of mind, or whose honest research, or whose speculations, or whose artistic expression tend to conflict with the even tenor of current operations, or are antagonistic to current business thought." [25] Thus the task of safeguarding society against a danger that is real is tremendously complicated by the feverish clamor of our own nostrum vendors, busily engaged in ferreting out some special enemy of democracy and in asserting their own peculiar claim to its sanction. In fighting subversives, we must be on guard lest we be unwittingly joined in a broad-gauged assault on merely unpopular views. How, then, can we maintain national security based on and protecting our freedom?

A first step toward a more enlightened approach may be to recognize differences, divergences, opposition, and dissent as the peculiar hallmarks of free government. We might recognize negotiation, discussion, debate, compromise, as the essence of our politics—as in fact it has always been—and face the fact that when this process ends, statesmanship is bankrupt, civilization gone.[26] Disunity and dissent, rooted in idealism, have been ever-present aspects of our politics. The right to speak freely and to promote diversity of ideas is "one of the chief distinctions that set us apart from totalitarian regimes." "Thought control," the late Justice Jackson remarked, "is a copyright of totalitarianism, and we have no claim to it." [27] "Compulsory unification of opinion achieves only the unanimity of the graveyard. . . . Authority here is to be controlled by public opinion not

[25] Words of Adolf Berle, Jr., *New York Times*, April 2, 1955.

[26] See J. S. Mill, *Utilitarianism, Liberty and Representative Government* (Everyman ed.; New York), p. 149.

[27] Justice Jackson in *American Communications Assoc. v. Douds*, 339 U.S. 382 (1950), p. 442.

public opinion by authority." [28] The very liberty a free society recognizes and guarantees makes for disorder, "induces a condition of unrest," encourages criticism, "stirs people to anger." [29] "We believe that ideas can be dangerous," the American Library Association declared in 1953, "but that the suppression of ideas is fatal to a democratic society. Freedom itself is a dangerous way of life, but it is ours." "All discussion, all debate, all dissidence," Judge Learned Hand commented in a recent address, "tends to question, and in consequence to upset, existing convictions: that is precisely its purpose and its justification." [30]

"Agitation and a plentiful degree of speculative license [is] to political and moral sanity," Walt Whitman tells us, what "circulation [is] to air." [31] In any event, effort to make a better world by change constitutes an endemic strain in our heritage.[32] It is the American way. Likewise endemic and continuous have been the blundering efforts of stand-patters to save free government from alleged radicalism. By use of the "subversive" label, we suppress arguments that dis-

[28] Justice Jackson in *West Virginia State Board of Education* v. *Barnette*, 319 U.S. 624 (1942), p. 641.

[29] Justice Douglas in *Terminiello* v. *Chicago*, 337 U.S. 1 (1949), p. 4.

[30] Judge Learned Hand, address before forty-eighth Annual Meeting of the American Jewish Committee, in *New York Times*, Jan. 30, 1955, p. 68, col. 4.

[31] Walt Whitman, *Democratic Vistas* (Washington, D.C.: Redfield, 1871), pp. 26–27.

[32] The Englishman J. B. Priestly wrote in the January 1950 *Coronet:* "An American is brought up with the high burning phrases of great revolutionaries, themselves starry-eyed, forever ringing in his ears. To forget them, to act against their hope and faith in men, is to take an axe to his own roots. There is in the American mind just because it is an American mind, an idealism that cannot be quenched, a small voice of conscience that all the hokum in the world cannot drown."

turb our complacency and then, as Judge Hand has commented, we "congratulate ourselves on keeping the faith
as we have received it from the founding fathers." [33] Around
1800 reactionary forces tried to quench Jeffersonian idealism and block change by stimulating fear of Jacobin Republicans. Jefferson and his followers were accused of subversive
allegiance to France. American abolitionists of the 1830's
were so bitterly assailed that William Ellery Channing paid
tribute to them, lauded their courage in proclaiming their
cause amid menace and insults:

Of such men, I do not hesitate to say, that they have rendered to
freedom a more essential service than any body of men among
us. The defenders of freedom are not those who claim and
exercise rights which no one assails, or who win shouts of ap-
plause by well-turned compliments to liberty in the days of her
triumph. They are those who stand up for rights which mobs,
conspiracies, or single tyrants put in jeopardy.[34]

When, during the latter part of the nineteenth century,
various popular movements advocated regulation and control of economic power, an industrial elite and their lawyers
denounced all such crusades as communistic, socialistic,
populistic, anarchistic. When fear of this "vague terror,"
as Justice Holmes described it, "went over the earth and
the word socialism began to be heard," "the comfortable
classes of the community were a good deal frightened." That
fear "was translated," he said, "into doctrines that had no
proper place in the Constitution or the Common law."
Holmes went further, suggesting that fear of socialism had

[33] Hand, *op. cit.*, col. 5.
[34] W. E. Channing, Tribute to the Abolitionists, 1836, The
American Anti-Slavery Society, 1861, p. 4.

led people who no longer hope to control the legislatures to look to the courts as expounders of the Constitutions, and that in some courts new principles have been discovered outside the bodies of those instruments, which may be generalized into acceptance of the economic doctrines which prevailed about fifty years ago. . . .

Justice Holmes declared flatly that judges were in politics, "taking sides upon debatable and often burning issues." [35]

America retraced this familiar pattern during and after World War I.[36] Suppression of dissenting radicals reached a notorious high on January 7, 1920, when the New York Assembly refused to seat five duly elected socialist members. Now, however, "the fury is breaking against the rock of deeper developments," leading one reflective student of American history to wonder "how many orgies of McCarthyism the United States can stand and still remain a nation capable of adjusting to the continuing revolution of our times."

Each wave of frenzied atavism has left weaker the chief instruments that make the adjustment possible. The outbursts have cut down the ability of the American educational system to teach a fluid approach to human problems. They have besmirched pragmatic thinking as a form of submission to the Devil. They have permeated workaday idealism with hostility to the aspirations that are the eternal stuff of democratic living.[37]

[35] O. W. Holmes, *Collected Legal Papers* (New York: Harcourt, Brace, 1920), pp. 184, 295 *passim*.

[36] See Robert K. Murray, *Red Scare: A Study in National Hysteria, 1919–1920* (Minneapolis: University of Minnesota Press, 1955).

[37] Eric Goldman, "There's Nothing New about McCarthyism," *Reporter*, Sept. 14, 1954, p. 30.

By 1952 fear of the unorthodox had developed into a frenzy such as to prompt Justice William O. Douglas to declare:

The great danger of this period is not inflation, nor the national debt, nor atomic warfare. The great, the critical danger is that we will so limit or narrow the range of permissible discussion and permissible thought that we will become victims of the orthodox school. . . . Our real power is our spiritual strength, and that spiritual strength stems from our civil liberties.[38]

Unease in American scientific circles drove the late Dr. Einstein, in November 1954, to say that if he had his life to live over again, he would "rather choose to be a plumber or a peddler" than a "scientist or scholar or teacher." [39] This from a man who had come to the land of freedom to escape the Nazis.

Today we are fearful of revolution. Yesterday Jefferson feared the absence of revolution. Freedom used to be considered prerequisite to security; today we are in danger of losing sight of how freedom serves to promote it. The

[38] William O. Douglas, "The Black Silence of Fear," *New York Times Magazine*, Jan. 13, 1952, p. 38. See also *To Secure These Rights* (The Report of the President's Committee on Civil Rights; Washington, D.C.: Government Printing Office, 1947), p. 49, and George F. Kennan, "Seek the Finer Flavor," in *Is the Common Man Too Common?*" (Norman: University of Oklahoma Press, 1955), pp. 123–130.

On July 4, 1951, the *Capital Times* (Wisconsin) found that only one person out of 112 approached would sign a petition composed exclusively of sections from the Declaration of Independence and the Bill of Rights. "That may be the Russian Declaration of Independence," one frantic nonsigner said, "but you can't tell me its ours." "You can't get me to sign that," another timid nonsigner commented. "I'm trying to get loyalty clearance for a government job" (*Capital Times*, July 5, 1951).

[39] Editorial, *New York Times*, Nov. 11, 1954, p. 30.

contrasting views are sharpened by Jefferson's query: "What country can preserve its liberties, if its rulers are not warned from time to time that this people preserve the spirit of resistance?" [40] Madison, Hamilton, John Adams, and Lincoln recognized the right of revolution as the last refuge, the extra constitutional right of a tyrannized people. Madison wrote:

If there be a principle that ought not to be questioned within the United States, it is that every nation has a right to abolish an old government and establish a new one. This principle is not only recorded in every public archive, written in every American heart, and sealed with the blood of a host of American martyrs, but is the only lawful tenure by which the United States hold their existence as a nation.[41]

Madison, like Locke, believed that this reserve right in the community was a formula for avoiding, not promoting, revolution. Similarly the First Amendment rests on the strong conviction that the progress of political freedom gives better assurance of national security than does any program of political repression and enslavement.[42] Jefferson

[40] Thomas Jefferson to William S. Smith, Nov. 13, 1787, in *Writings of Thomas Jefferson* (ed. by Henry A. Washington; Washington, D. C.: Taylor and Maury, 1853), II, 318–319.

[41] Madison, in answer to "Pacificus," April 22, 1793; quoted in Saul Padover, *The Complete Madison* (New York: Harper, 1953), p. 48. See Alexander Meiklejohn, "What Does the First Amendment Mean?" *University of Chicago Law Review*, 20 (Spring 1953), 461–479.

[42] Justice Douglas elaborated this theme in *Dennis v. U.S.*, 341 U.S. 494 (1951), pp. 581–591, and *Beauharnais v. Ill.*, 343 U.S. 250 (1951), pp. 284–288.

"The authors of the First Amendment," Richard L. Sklar observes, "hoped to prevent the punishment of political blasphemy. They believed in government by persuasion, and sought to deny entrenched values access to any weapon against dissenting opinion

had this close relation between freedom and security in mind when he spoke of America as an "Empire of Liberty." It was this same relationship that prompted him to describe republican government as the "strongest on earth." [43]

Though internal disorder or foreign aggression may, under certain circumstances, tip the scales in favor of purposes other than free exchange of ideas, freedom of speech is sanctified, as Madison suggested, in formal declarations and in the Constitution itself. Among the subjects on which the Congress is forbidden to enact restrictive legislation is freedom of speech. This constitutional injunction is based on the conviction that no one man, no group has, or can have, any exclusive rendezvous with truth. It rests on Justice Holmes's belief that "the wisest are but blind guides." [44]

---

save argument alone. Such a policy seems to embrace the highest measure of political acumen. Change is inevitable. Free discussion is the avenue of peaceful change; suppression drives change into revolutionary channels" ("The Fiction of the First Freedom," *Western Political Quarterly*, 6 [June 1953], 319).

[43] See, in this connection, Julian P. Boyd, "Thomas Jefferson's 'Empire Liberty,'" *Virginia Quarterly Review*, 24 (Autumn 1948).

[44] On his appointment to the Supreme Court in 1902, Justice Holmes observed: "I have tried to see the law as an organic whole. I also have tried to see it as a reaction between tradition on the one side and the changing desires and needs of a community on the other. I have studied tradition in order that I might understand how it came to be what it is, and to estimate its worth with regard to our present needs; . . . I have considered the present tendencies and desires of society and have tried to realize that its different portions want different things, and that my business was to express not my personal wish, but the resultant, as nearly as I could guess, of the pressure of the past and the conflicting wills of the present. I have considered the social and economic postulates on which we frame the conception of our needs, and I have tried to see them in a dry light. It has seemed to me that certainty is an illusion, that we have few scientific data on which to affirm that one rule rather than another has the sanction of the universe, that we rarely could be sure that one

It enforces the conviction that "the great body of insights, . . . touching life and the world, comes in large part from an unknown multitude, not mentioned in the histories of philosophy." [45] "The best test of truth," Holmes commented in a much-quoted judicial opinion, "is the power of the thought to get itself accepted in the competition of the market." [46] Truth was to be "strived for on the tacit understanding that it will not be reached." [47] "I therefore define the truth," Holmes wrote, "as the system of my limitations, and leave absolute truth for those who are better equipped." [48]

There must be wide latitude for political freedom because our notion of the common interest tends to be realistic only as it emerges from the cross fires of conflict. All opinions must be accorded freedom not on the basis of whether they are "right" or "wrong," but because they are relevant to

---

tends more distinctly than its opposite to the survival and welfare of society where it is practised, and that the wisest are but blind guides" (from an unpublished speech delivered to the Bar Association of Middlesex County, Dec. 3, 1902, and included in a bound volume of miscellanies at the Harvard Law School).

Even "if the ideas of the very wisest were by a miracle to be fixed on the race," Bagehot observed, "the certain result would be to stereotype monsterous error" (*Works and Life of Walter Bagehot*, ed. by Barrington [New York: Longman's, 1915], p. 225).

"We protect freedom in order to discover truth," but truth can never be confidently and conclusively labeled (H. S. Commager, *Freedom, Loyalty and Dissent* [1954], p. 14). "We can never walk surely but by being sensible of our blindness" (Edmund Burke; quoted in Adlai Stevenson, *Call to Greatness* [New York: Harper, 1954], p. 37).

[45] Mark de Wolfe Howe, ed., *Holmes-Pollock Letters* (Cambridge: Harvard University Press, 1941), I, 261 (March 1, 1918).

[46] *Abrams* v. *U.S.*, 250 U.S. 616 (1919), p. 630.

[47] Mark de Wolfe Howe, ed., *Holmes-Laski Letters* (Cambridge: Harvard University Press, 1953), I, 259.

[48] *Collected Legal Papers*, pp. 304–305.

attaining a full understanding of public issues and to reaching informed decisions thereon. This arduous process of bringing different points of view into constructive accord constitutes the high art of politics. "If there were no different interests," Rousseau wrote in his *Social Contract*, "the common interest would be barely felt, as it would encounter no obstacle; all would go on of its own accord, and politics would cease to be an art." [49]

[49] J. J. Rousseau, *The Social Contract and Discourses* (Everyman ed.; New York, 1947), bk. 2, ch. 3, p. 25.

"When you adopt one way of looking at things, you destroy at the same moment some alternative way of seeing them. This is the reason why open controversy is deliberately used as a method of discovering truth. In a courtroom, for example, counsels for the prosecution and for the defense are each required to take one side of the question at issue. It is supposed that only by committing themselves in opposite directions can they discover all that can be found in favor of each side. If, instead, the judge would enter into friendly consultation with counsel for both sides and seek to establish agreement between them, this would be considered a gross miscarriage of justice" (Michael Polanyi, *The Logic of Liberty* [London: Routledge and Kegan Paul Ltd., 1951], p .20).

In his personal testament, *This I Do Believe* (New York: Harper, 1949), David Lilienthal wrote: "One of the most beautiful phrases in our language are the words an American uses when he says to those with whom he has been in disagreement: 'I'll go along with you. That's not the way I see it, but I'll go along.' Out of this precept of reasonableness and respect for the opinions of others often issues one of the finest fruits of thought: a composite judgment, the product of many minds.

"The considered judgment of men who reason together embodies more than 'tolerance' which is, after all, a somewhat thin and negative concept. It is rather based on an affirmative belief in the value of blending diverse experiences, diverse backgrounds. Such a composite or group judgment can be sturdier than any one of the individual or separate judgments that makes it up. This harmonizing of conflicting views into a common conclusion is not merely the trader's 'splitting the difference'; it is not compromise for its own sake. It is a doctrine in exact contradiction to the growing fanaticism and dogmatism in the world, in which differ-

Freedom of speech is an American birthright.[50] It is a right which men have because they are men, a right the exercise of which should redound not only to the benefit of the individual but also to the good of all. The evidence assembled at the Nuremberg trials proved the idiocy of suppression. It showed conclusively that "the seeds of eventual annihilation for Hitler's power were sown when he began burning books, exiling scholars, persecuting scientists and closing down on information." In reply to Prosecutor Robert H. Jackson's cross-examination about German experiments with atomic energy, Albert Speer, Reich Minister for Armament and Munitions, the most intelligent of the defendants at Nuremberg, said, "Unfortunately, because the best experts we had in atom research had gone to America, we hadn't advanced as far as we wanted

---

ences from an official party line are dealt with as traitorous and in which the accommodation of conflicting ideas is regarded as a sign of weakness rather than what it is in fact: a mark of strength" (pp. 35–36).

Similarly Adlai Stevenson wrote: "Compromise is not immoral or treasonable. It is the objective of negotiation, and negotiation is the means of resolving conflict peacefully. . . . Keeping an open, flexible mind, shedding our passion for crusades and our taste for absolutes that equate compromise with immorality will be another hard and useful exercise" (*op. cit.*, pp. 101, 103).

For a contrasting view, see John H. Hollowell, *Moral Foundations of Democracy* (Chicago: University of Chicago Press, 1954), ch. 2.

[50] See Archibald MacLeish, "Freedom to End Freedom," *Survey Graphic* ("Calling America"), Feb. 1939, pp. 117–118.

"It cannot be the duty, because it is not the right, of the State to protect the public against false doctrine. The very purpose of the First Amendment is to foreclose public authority from assuming a guardianship of the public mind through regulating the press, speech, and religion. In this field every person must be his own watchman for truth, because the forefathers did not trust any government to separate the true from the false for us" (Justice Jackson in *Thomas* v. *Collins*, 323 U.S. 516 [1945], p. 545).

to; we suffered set-backs in atom research and were about one to two years from achieving results—the splitting of the atom." Jackson then asked: "The policy of driving people out who didn't agree with Germany hasn't produced very good dividends, has it?" "That, as far as we were concerned," Speer replied, "had a very decisive disadvantage."

"The Soviet lawyers were present," Jackson commented, "and they might have made this testimony the subject of a special cable to Moscow, but I doubt if they did." [51]

"The fitting remedy for evil counsels," Justice Brandeis wrote in a notable judicial opinion, "is good ones." "It is the function of speech to free men from the bondage of irrational fears. . . . Those who won our independence by revolution were not cowards. They did not fear political change. . . . Only an emergency can justify repression. Such must be the rule if authority is to be reconciled with freedom." [52]

---

[51] Justice Jackson, address before the New York County Lawyers' Association; reported in the *New York Times*, Dec. 9, 1948, p. 2, cols. 2–3.

[52] *Whitney* v. *California*, 274 U.S. 357 (1927), pp. 375–377 *passim*. John Stuart Mill elaborated this theme in his famous essay *On Liberty*, and Woodrow Wilson expressed much the same thought: "I have always been among those who believed that the greatest freedom of speech was the greatest safety, because, if a man is a fool, the best thing to do is to encourage him to advertise the fact by speaking. It cannot be so easily discovered if you allow him to remain silent and look wise, but if you let him speak, the secret is out and the world knows that he is a fool. So it is by the exposure of folly that it is defeated; not by the seclusion of folly, and in this free air of free speech men get into that sort of communication with one another which constitutes the basis of all common achievement" (address at the Institute of France, Paris, May 10, 1919; in *Selected Literary and Political Papers and Addresses of Woodrow Wilson* [New York: Grosset, 1927], II, 333).

If there is any single tenet on which the success of free government depends more than on any other, if there be a central core within the truly liberal creed, it is tolerance —tolerance not only of views we like, but tolerance of views we detest. "Freedom to differ," a Supreme Court majority opinion declared, "is not limited to things that do not matter much. That would be a mere shadow of freedom. The test of its substance is the right to differ as to things that touch the heart of the existing order." [53]

But tolerance means more than open-mindedness; it means not only willingness to be persuaded but inclination to practice the difficult art of persuasion. "As a free society, we must rely primarily on persuasion." [54] In its practice, "time is amongst the assistants." [55] "It takes time to persuade men to do even what is for their own good." [56] The collapse of innumerable conferences, domestic and international, the mania for quick (and final) solutions, the "take it or leave it" attitude of our leaders in presenting controversial policy to uncommitted nations—all this suggests both unwillingness to persuade or be persuaded. Here, indeed, is solid ground for fear, certainly for thoughtful concern, tending to support the fatalistic French author, Albert Camus: "Mankind's long dialogue has come to an end," [57] and we face again the grim fact that men who will not reason, or be reasoned with, are men to be feared.

[53] Justice Jackson in *West Virginia State Board of Education* v. *Barnette*, 319 U.S. 624 (1942), p. 642.

[54] Stevenson, *op. cit.*, p. 103.   [55] Burke, *op. cit.*, p. 107.

[56] Saul Padover, ed., *Thomas Jefferson on Democracy* (New York: Appleton-Century, 1953), p. 154. "There is a snail-paced gate for the advance of new ideas on the general mind, under which we must acquiesce. . . . You must give [the people] time for every step you take" (*ibid.*, p. 162).

[57] Quoted by J. Donald Adams, *New York Times Book Review*, March 27, 1955, p. 2.

The great lesson of our tradition is that the current threat can and must be met in the realm of the free man's mind and will and by our own social and political processes.[58] That lesson has still to be learned.

"I am not in love with any particular methods," President Franklin Roosevelt commented offhandedly on September 23, 1937, "but I am in love with particular . . . objectives." [59] When the national objective becomes, as

[58] "Our freedom and liberty will be easy to redeem if we remember the fundamentals. First, our way of life is greatly concerned with *method* and *means*. The history of man's struggle to be free is in large degree a struggle to be free of oppressive procedures. . . . Second, we have principles or articles of faith to which we are committed. Of these, none is more important than the right to speak and to write freely; the right to worship God as one chooses; the sanctity of the conscience; the right to be let alone; the dependency of government on 'the consent of the governed' " (From *An Almanac of Liberty*, by William O. Douglas. Copyright 1954 by William O. Douglas, reprinted by permission of Doubleday & Company, Inc., p. viii).

[59] Quoted in the *New York Times*, Sept. 24, 1937, p. 3, col. 4. On F.D.R.'s lack of concern for traditional democratic processes, see Anne O'Hare McCormick, "As He Sees Himself," *New York Times Magazine*, Oct. 16, 1938, p. 1. This article might be read in connection with Harold Ickes' diary (*The Inside Struggle, 1936–1939*). Ickes contends that by 1938 the President had grown weary of the liberal chase and was about ready to capitulate to the reactionaries. And Edgar Kemler has observed: "President Roosevelt has prided himself on the amount of discussion that he has provoked and on the thorough grounding in political and economic fundamentals that he has given the voters in pursuance of his program. And yet he is palpably more interested in having them consent to and participate in his *faits accomplis* than in having them share in the preliminary deliberations. . . . He is no more interested in stimulating strategic thought among the citizens than the General Staff of the United States Army is interested in stimulating strategic thought among the soldiers" (*The Deflation of American Ideals: An Ethical Guide for New Dealers*. [Washington, D.C.: American Council on Public Affairs, 1941], p. 109).

now, security from external danger, free institutions are put under special strain. The President's comment, made well in advance of World War II, overlooks free society's most distinctive feature. Free government stands or falls on an attitude of mind, on the methods employed, on the individual's opportunity to dissent and oppose. No opposition means no democracy. "One can never be sure of ends—political, social, economic," Brandeis once remarked. "There must always be doubt and difference of opinion; at best one can be 51 per cent sure. There is not the same margin of doubt as to means." Here "fundamentals do not change;

R. G. Tugwell's general explanation of how pressure forces the President to "blur the distinction between ends and means" appears especially applicable to F.D.R. "There is a serious problem of ends and means in political life: nowhere does it focus with more significance than in the American Presidency. Ends tend to become especially enlarged for the President since he seems to be the only agent in the government who is expected to accomplish what has to be done in the general interest, or even to effectuate those policies to which commitment has been made.

"Because of this compulsion—which comes to be more and more strongly felt as the President struggles toward shaping a program and meets inevitable opposition in carrying it out—there is constant temptation to resort to the means readiest at hand for getting his way in the exigencies of struggle. There is the further necessity, felt by every president, to perpetuate the policies he has labored to establish; and this turns usually into an urge for re-election, or for the continuation in power of his party and of those in it who will see his policies through.

"Short-run tactics are in the usual circumstances a ready resort, irresistibly attractive because of their convenience and relative certainty. Since the President has great ends in view, means he would not attempt to justify philosophically seem to diminish in significance. Because they cannot be justified, he tends to employ these means either secretly or without linking them into a system related to the body of his principles" ("The Compromising Roosevelt," *Western Political Quarterly*, 6 [June 1953], 320).

centuries of thought have established standards." [60] Those standards are so widely recognized as to reveal the fraud lurking in the most subtle effort to pervert them.

Consider, for example, the elementary requirements of balloting and majority rule. These essential procedural devices have all been appropriated by the totalitarians, proving that these may mean something or nothing at all, depending on the atmosphere in which they are used. What must prevail in any free society is not so much the will of the people identified by a majority, or even by unanimous vote, but cool reason, the weight of evidence, of argument, leading to judgments in which the minority can freely and willingly acquiesce. If consent is all that is wanted in government there is plenty of experience, not only in totalitarian systems but also in Puritan Massachusetts and the Deep South, showing how dissenting minorities may be taught to agree, to conform, to be unanimous. In a free society there must be willingness to test any and all preferred conclusions, desire to hear the other side. The will of the majority must, of course, eventually prevail, but the minority must always have and use the right freely to criticize and oppose. The liberty of the majority to govern is limited by this right of the minority to dissent and to persuade others to join in their efforts. But the right to oppose is limited by the right of the majority to rule, as well as by the duty of the minority to accept that rule, in a *peaceful* and *law-abiding* spirit, so long as it is thus in operation. Any other theory makes it in fact impossible to govern at all. These essential attitudes of mind and spirit must be ingrained in the habits and traditions of the people. No constitution, no bill of rights, no court can provide or guar-

[60] A. T. Mason, *Brandeis: A Free Man's Life* (New York: Viking, 1946), p. 569.

antee them.[61] Nor can their achievement be a finished work.

Liberty [Woodrow Wilson said] is not something that . . . can be laid away in a document a completed work. It is an organic principle,—a principle of life, renewing and being renewed. Democratic institutions are never done; they are like living tissue—always a-making. It is a strenuous thing, this living the life of a free people.[62]

A distinguished mathematician, Vaclav Hlavaty, commenting on man's effort to understand the universe, said: "The farther we go the more the ultimate explanation recedes from us, and all we have left is faith." [63] John Stuart Mill, Thomas Jefferson, Justice Holmes had that kind of faith—faith in political freedom, in reason and persuasion, in the power of truth to conquer error.

If civilisation [Mill wrote] has got the better of barbarism when barbarism had the world to itself, it is too much to profess to be afraid lest barbarism, after having been fairly got under, should revive and conquer civilisation. A civilisation that can

[61] "I submit," Judge Learned Hand declared, "that it is only by trial and error, by insistent scrutiny and by readiness to re-examine presently accredited conclusions that we have risen, so far in fact as we have risen, from our brutish ancestors, and I believe that in our loyalty to these habits lies our only chance, not merely of progress, but even of survival." Principles of civil liberties "lie in habits, customs—conventions, if you will—that tolerate dissent and can live without irrefragable certainties; that are ready to overhaul existing assumptions; that recognize that we never see save through a glass, darkly, and that at long last we shall succeed only so far as we continue to undertake 'the intolerable labor of thought'—that most distasteful of all our activities" ("A Plea for the Freedom of Dissent," *New York Times Magazine*, Feb. 6, 1955).

[62] W. Wilson, *An Old Master and Other Political Essays* (New York: Scribner's, 1893), pp. 115–116.

[63] Quoted in Douglas, *An Almanac of Liberty*, p. 383.

thus succumb to its vanquished enemy, must first have become so degenerate, that neither its appointed priests and teachers, nor anybody else, has the capacity, or will take the trouble to stand up for it. If this be so the sooner such a civilization receives notice to quit the better. It can only go on from bad to worse, until destroyed and regenerated . . . by energetic barbarians.[64]

. . . that the truth is great and will prevail, if left to herself [runs the awkward language of Jefferson's Virginia Statute of Religious Liberty] that she is the proper and sufficient antagonist to error, and has nothing to fear from conflict, unless human interposition, disarmed of her natural weapons, free argument and debate, errors ceasing to be dangerous when it is permitted freely to contradict them.[65]

Justice Holmes did not fear that in a free and open fight, the forces of evil would prevail. "If in the long run," he commented calmly, "the beliefs expressed in proletarian dictatorship are destined to be accepted by the dominant forces of the community, the only meaning of free speech is that they should be given their chance and have their way." [66]

[64] J. S. Mill, *Utilitarianism, Liberty and Representative Government*, p. 149.

[65] Jefferson draft of an act of 1786 for establishing religous freedom in Virginia; quoted in Mason, *Free Government in the Making*, p. 363.

[66] Justice Holmes concurring in *Gitlow* v. *U.S.*, 268 U.S. 652 (1925), p. 673. Similarly Justice Jackson wrote in 1942: "We apply the limitations of the Constitution [against government encroachments on freedom] with no fear that freedom to be intellectually and spiritually diverse or even contrary will disintegrate the social organization. To believe that patriotism will not flourish if patriotic ceremonies are voluntary and spontaneous is to make an unflattering estimate of the appeal of our institutions to free minds" (*West Virginia State Board of Education* v. *Barnette*, 319 U.S. 624 [1942], pp. 641–642).

The foundations of our heritage are at stake.[67] Repression repudiates the "great postulate of democracy," betrays the First Amendment's implicit trust in the "common sense of our people and their maturity." [68] By resorting to it, we discredit our creed and offer the world "proof," as Jefferson said, of "the imbecility of republican government, in times of pressing danger, to shield [us] from harm." [69] We must conquer fear or else pay a gratuitous compliment to the sworn enemies of freedom and thus tell the world that free government is defective, outmoded, in these times when the future of western civilization depends on a persuasive demonstration of its vitality.

American experience shows that the vitality of free government depends primarily on the people themselves. Free elections and political controls, rather than Bills of Rights and courts are, ultimately, the only means we have for obliging the government to control itself. If the political process is to serve this all-important purpose, any action that impedes its functioning or attacks its integrity must, as Justice Stone said, be subjected to "more searching judicial scrutiny." [70] But informal action and attitudes can under-

[67] "Freedom to speak and write about public questions is as important to the life of our government as is the heart to the human body. In fact, this privilege is the heart of our government. If that heart be weakened, the result is debilitation; if it be stilled, the result is death" (Justice Black in *Drivers Union* v. *Meadowmoor Dairies*, 312 U.S. 287 [1941], pp. 301–302).

"Fundamental personal rights and liberties," Justice Roberts said in *Schneider* v. *Irvington* (308 U.S. 147 [1939], p. 161), reflect "the belief of the Framers of the Constitution that the exercise of these rights lies at the foundation of free government by free men."

[68] *Dennis* v. *U.S.*, 341 U.S. 494 (1951), p. 590.

[69] *Writings of Jefferson*, VIII, 391; quoted in Mason, *Free Government in the Making*, p. 169.

[70] "Mr. Justice Stone brings the germ [of the original procedural conception of due process] to maturity in a due process for democ-

mine—even destroy—effective operation of the political process—worse still, strike at the fundamentals that give uniqueness to the American adventure.

George F. Kennan, whose opportunity to appraise the Communist danger is considerable, rates the damage we may inflict on ourselves and on our habits and ways of life as of more serious concern than the external threat of

---

racy in action. He would keep open the right of intellectual search and maintain a free forum for the interchange of ideas and the resulting action" (Walton H. Hamilton and George D. Braden, "The Special Competence of the Supreme Court," *Yale Law Journal*, 50 [1941], 1353).

"There is a national interest," Louis Lusky observed, "not only in preserving a form of government in which men can control their own destinies, but in enabling the common man to see its advantages and know its feasibility. It is an interest in quelling doubts as to the practical efficiency of our system to accomplish essential justice. It is an interest in preventing deviations from our national ideal, . . . because deviations create such doubts. In short, it is an interest in making a belief in our system a part of the American creed" ("Minority Rights and the Public Interest," *Yale Law Journal*, 52 [1942], 18–19).

"The Court," Lusky continued, "thus performs an important part in the maintenance of the basic conditions of just legislation. By preserving the hope that bad laws can and will be changed, the Court preserves the basis for the technique of political obligation, minimizing extra-legal opposition to the government by making it unnecessary. . . . Where the regular corrective processes are interfered with, the Court must remove the interference; where the dislike of minorities renders those processes ineffective to accomplish their underlying purpose of holding out a real hope that unwise laws will be changed, the Court must itself step in." Lusky sees such judicial intervention as a contribution to security for "if every person has an equal opportunity to take part in controlling the government which in turn controls him, there will be a general confidence that the laws are designed to serve the needs of the entire community, by making a fair adjustment between the conflicting interests of groups within the community and advancing as far as possible the welfare of the community as a whole" (pp. 20–21, 5).

Communism. "That our country is beset with external dangers," Kennan wrote, "I readily concede." The internal danger is, he believes, of "a different order."

If our handling of the problem of Communist influence in our midst is not carefully moderated—if we permit it, that is, to become an emotional preoccupation and blind us to the more important positive tasks before us—we can do a damage to our national purpose beyond comparison greater than anything that threatens us from the Communist side. . . . The subjective emotional stresses and temptations to which we are exposed in our attempt to deal with this domestic problem are not an external danger: they represent a danger within ourselves—a danger that something may occur in our own minds and souls which will make us no longer like the persons by whose efforts this republic was founded and held together, but rather like the representatives of that very power we are trying to combat: intolerant, secretive, suspicious, cruel, and terrified of internal dissensions because we have lost our own belief in ourselves and in the power of our ideals. The worst thing that our Communists could do to us, and the thing we have most to fear from their activities, is that we should become like them.

America [Kennan concluded] is not just territory and people. . . . America is something in our minds and our habits of outlook which causes us to believe in certain things and to behave in certain ways, and by which, in its totality, we hold ourselves distinguished from others. If that once goes there will be no America to defend.[71]

The notion that security can be found in repression is false. History demonstrates that security rests primarily on individual freedom of mind.[72] The view that order means

[71] George F. Kennan, "Where Do You Stand on Communism?" *New York Times Magazine*, May 27, 1951, pp. 53, 55.

[72] "Assurance that rights are secure tends to diminish fear and jealousy of strong government, and by making us feel safe to live under it makes for better support. Without promise of a limiting

absence of change is also in error.[73] The quest for human betterment would still confront us with complexities, with issues not easily resolved, not capable of any final solution, even if all Communist taint were scoured from this continent. Though Russia were defeated and her dictatorial government destroyed, there still would be plenty of discords among ourselves. This is not to underestimate the external danger, but rather to stress the values and methods that have made this nation a human force of incalculable

Bill of Rights it is doubtful if our Constitution would have mustered enough strength to enable its ratification. To enforce those rights today is not to choose weak government over strong government. It is only to adhere as a means of strength to individual freedom of mind in preference to officially disciplined uniformity for which history indicates a disappointing and disastrous end" (Justice Jackson in *West Virginia State Board of Education* v. *Barnette*, 319 U.S. 624 [1942], pp. 636–637).

[73] Said De Tocqueville: "Men who are possessed by the passion for physical gratification generally find out that the turmoil of freedom disturbs their welfare before they discover how freedom itself serves to promote it. If the slightest rumor of public commotion intrudes into the petty pleasures of private life, they are aroused and alarmed by it. The fear of anarchy perpetually haunts them, and they are ready to fling away their freedom at the first disturbance. . . .

"When the love of property becomes so restless and ardent, I cannot but fear that men may arrive at such a state as to regard every new theory as a peril, every innovation as an irksome toil, every social improvement as a stepping stone to revolution, and so refuse to move altogether for fear of being moved too far" (quoted by Henry Steele Commager, "Democracy in America: One Hundred Years After," *New York Times Magazine*, Dec. 15, 1935, p. 15).

"If anyone [De Tocqueville wrote] could point out an intermediate and yet tenable position between the complete independence and entire servitude of opinion, I should perhaps be inclined to adopt it, but the difficulty is to discover this intermediate position." For his discussion of the point, see *Democracy in America* (Vintage Book, 1954), I, 188–189.

strength. It is to emphasize the urgent necessity of ameliorative measures corrective of social misery as a substitute for coercive action that would suppress complaints of its existence.

The problem now, as always, is to combine individual freedom with social justice, to fuse that degree of initiative necessary for progress with the social cohesion needed for survival. No adjustment will ever be perfectly and finally achieved. It is the tediousness of its method and the stress on human values rather than efficiency that places free government at seeming disadvantage. "The wastes of democracy are," as Justice Brandeis said, "among the most obvious wastes." [74] So many minds have to be consulted, informed, and brought into agreement. But that, when done, is democracy's great strength, the only assurance that whatever course it may have to take, freedom may endure.

[74] "But we have compensations in democracy," Brandeis added, "which may far outweigh the wastes, and make it more efficient than absolutism" ("Efficiency and Trusts," address delivered before the Four Criers, Providence, Oct. 7, 1912; quoted in Mason, *Brandeis: A Free Man's Life*, p. 382).

"Democracy does not give the people the most skilful government," De Tocqueville observed, "but it produces what the ablest governments are frequently unable to create; namely, an all-pervading and restless activity, a superabundant force, and an energy which is inseparable from it, and which may, however unfavorable circumstances may be, produce wonders. These are the true advantages of democracy" (*Democracy in America* [tr. by Henry Reeve; Boston: Allyn, 1882], I, 321).

"The worth of the State," John Stuart Mill wrote in his classic essay *On Liberty*, "in the long run, is the worth of the individuals composing it; and a State which postpones . . . *their* mental expansion and elevation to a little more of administrative skill, . . . a State which dwarfs its men, in order that they may be more docile instruments in its hands even for beneficial purposes—will find that with small men no great thing can really be accomplished" (*Utilitarianism, Liberty and Representative Government*, p. 170).

The Messenger Lectures

IN ITS original form this book consisted of six lectures delivered at Cornell University in March 1955, namely, the Messenger Lectures on the Evolution of Civilization. That series was founded and its title prescribed by Hiram J. Messenger, B.Litt., Ph.D., of Hartford, Connecticut, who directed in his will that a portion of his estate be given to Cornell University and used to provide annually a "course or courses of lectures on the evolution of civilization, for the special purpose of raising the moral standard of our political, business, and social life." The lectureship was established in 1923.

Appendix

SUPREME COURT OF THE UNITED STATES
WASHINGTON, D.C.
CHAMBERS OF
JUSTICE FELIX FRANKFURTER

May 27, 1940

Dear Stone:

Were No. 690 an ordinary case, I should let the opinion speak for itself. But that you should entertain doubts has naturally stirred me to an anxious re-examination of my own views, even though I can assure you that nothing has weighed as much on my conscience, since I have come on this Court, as has this case. Your doubts have stirred me to a reconsideration of the whole matter, because I am not happy that you should entertain doubts that I cannot share or meet in a domain where constitutional power is on one side and my private notions of liberty and toleration and good sense are on the other. After all, the vulgar intrusion of law in the domain of conscience is for me a very sensitive area. For various reasons—I suspect the most dominant one is the old colored man's explanation that Moses was just raised that way—a good part of my mature life has thrown whatever weight it has had against foolish and harsh manifestations of coercion and for the amplest expression of dissident views, however absurd or offensive these may have been to my own notions of rationality and decency. I say this merely to indicate that all my bias and predisposition are in favor of giving the fullest elbow room to every variety of religious, political, and economic view.

But no one has more clearly in his mind than you, that even when it comes to these ultimate civil liberties, insofar as they are protected by the Constitution, we are not in the domain of absolutes. Here, also, we have an illustration of what the Greeks thousands of years ago recognized as a tragic issue, namely, the clash of rights, not the clash of wrongs. For resolving such clash we have no calculus. But there is for me, and I know also for you, a great makeweight for dealing with this problem, namely, that we are not the primary resolvers of the clash. We are not exercising an independent judgment; we are sitting in judgment upon the judgment of the legislature. I am aware of the important distinction which you so skillfully adumbrated in your footnote 4 (particularly the second paragraph of it) in the *Carolene Products Co.* case. I agree with that distinction; I regard it as basic. I have taken over that distinction in its central aspect, however inadequately, in the present opinion by insisting on the importance of keeping open all those channels of free expression by which undesirable legislation may be removed, and keeping unobstructed all forms of protest against what are deemed invasions of conscience, however much the invasion may be justified on the score of the deepest interests of national wellbeing.

What weighs with me strongly in this case is my anxiety that, while we lean in the direction of the libertarian aspect, we do not exercise our judicial power unduly, and as though we ourselves were legislators by holding with too tight a rein the organs of popular government. In other words, I want to avoid the mistake comparable to that made by those whom we criticized when dealing with the control of property. I hope I am aware of the different interests that are compendiously summarized by opposing "liberty" to "property." But I also know that the generalizations implied in these summaries are also inaccurate and hardly correspond to the complicated realities of an advanced society. I cannot rid myself of the notion that it is not fantastic, although I think foolish and perhaps worse, for school authorities to believe—as the record in this case explicitly shows the school authorities to have believed—that to allow exemption to some of the children goes far towards disrupting the whole patriotic exercise. And since certainly we must admit the general right of the school authorities to have such flag-saluting exercises, it seems to me that we do not trench on an undebatable territory of libertarian immunity to permit the school authorities a judgment as to the effect of this exemption in the particular setting of our time and circumstances.

For time and circumstances are surely not irrelevant considerations in resolving the conflicts that we do have to resolve in this particular case. Contingencies that may determine the fate of the constitutionality of a rent act (*Chastleton Corp.* v. *Sinclair*, 264 U.S. 543) may also be operative in the adjustment between legislatively allowable pursuit of national security and the right to stand on individual idiosyncracies. You may have noticed that in my opinion I did not rely on the prior adjudications by this Court of this question. I dealt with the matter as I believe it should have been dealt with, as though it were a new question. But certainly it is relevant to make the adjustment that we have to make within the framework of present circumstances and those that are clearly ahead of us. I had many talks with Holmes about his espionage opinions and he always recognized that he had a right to take into account the things that he did take into account when he wrote Debs and the others, and the different emphasis he gave the matter in the *Abrams* case. After all, despite some of the jurisprudential "realists" a decision decides not merely the particular case. Just as *Adkins* v. *Children's Hospital* had consequences not merely as to the minimum wage laws but in its radiations and in its psychological effects, so this case would have a tail of implications as to legislative power that is certainly debatable and might easily be invoked far beyond the size of the immediate kite, were it to deny the very minimum exaction, however foolish as to the Gobitis children, of an expression of faith in the heritage and purposes of our country.

APPENDIX

For my intention—and I hope my execution did not lag too far behind—was to use this opinion as a vehicle for preaching the true democratic faith of not relying on the Court for the impossible task of assuring a vigorous, mature, self-protecting and tolerant democracy by bringing the responsibility for a combination of firmness and toleration directly home where it belongs—to the people and their representatives themselves.

I have tried in this opinion really to act on what will, as a matter of history, be a lodestar for due regard between legislative and judicial powers, to wit, your dissent in the *Butler* case. For please bear in mind how very little this case authorizes and how wholly free it leaves us for the future. This is not a case where confinement either of children or of parents is the consequence of non-conformity. It is not a case where conformity is exacted for something that you and I regard as foolish—namely, a gesture of respect for the symbol of our national being—even though we deem it foolish to exact it from Jehovah's Witnesses. It is not a case, for instance, of compelling children to partake in a school dance or other scholastic exercise that may run counter to this or that faith. And, above all, it is not a case where the slightest restriction is involved against the fullest opportunity to disavow—either on the part of the children or their parents—the meaning that ordinary people attach to the gesture of respect. The duty of compulsion being as minimal as it is for an act, the normal legislative authorization of which certainly cannot be denied, and all channels of affirmative free expression being open to both children and parents, I cannot resist the conviction that we ought to let the legislative judgment stand and put the responsibility for its exercise where it belongs. In any event, I hope you will be good enough to give me the benefit of what you think should be omitted or added to the opinion.

Faithfully yours
s/Felix Frankfurter

Mr. Justice Stone.

Index

INDEX

Bagehot, Walter, 201n
Baldwin, Simeon, 62
Baltimore Sun, 56
Batchelor, Bronson, 150
Beauharnais v. *Illinois*, 199
Bedford, A. C., 47n
Bellamy, Edward, 42
Bentham, Jeremy, 165
Berle, Adolf, Jr., 159ff, 177, 194
Big business: philosophy of, 46; interest of, 59; government intervention of, 70
Bill of Rights, *see* Civil liberties
Bituminous coal industry, 92
Black, Hugo: on due process, 119n; on judicial self-restraint, 137ff; on role of Court, 137ff; in *Dennis* v. *U.S.*, 143; in *Feiner* v. *New York*, 192
Bolsheviks, 62f
Bourguin, George M., 59n
Bourne, Randolph, 190
Boyd, Julian P., 200n
Braden, George, 127f, 145n, 212n
Bradley, Justice, 37, 124
Brady, Ralph A., 151n
Brandeis, Louis D: on industrial absolutism, 43; as liberal constructionist, 58f, 66; as progressive, 62; moratorium decision, 88; and NIRA, 90; and Court-packing plan, 104f; on First Amendment, 129; on capitalist democracy, 148, 160, 168, 215; on bigness, 162, 168; on dangers to liberty, 187; on free speech, 204; on fallibility, 207f
Brant, Irving, 109n
Brewer, David J., 35, 39f, 68, 82
Brookings Institute, 48
Brown, Henry Billings, 39
Bruce, W. C., 8n
Bryan, William Jennings, 73n
Bryce, James, 83
Bureaucracy, 87, 154, 157, 165
Burke, Edmund, 187, 192

Burleson, Postmaster General, 46
Bursk, Edward C., 157n
Business: in government, 51; leadership, 56; ideology, 149f; reaction to popular power, 151ff; advertising, 151ff; politics of, 155; accommodation to New Deal, 155; responsibility of, 156ff; advantages of, 159
Business Week, 155
Butler, Justice, 59, 98

Calder v. *Bull*, 18
Calhoun, John C., 183
Camus, Albert, 205
Capitalism: delusion of, 149; twentieth-century, 156; pride in, 164; responsibility of, 170; and democracy, 177; "Utopian Capitalists," 180; *see also* Welfare capitalism
Cardozo, Justice, 88, 91, 106f
Carr, E. H., 171n
Cartels, 53
Carter v. *Carter Coal Co.*, 92
Challenge to Liberty, 81
Chamber of Commerce, 52
Channing, William Ellery, 196
Chase, Justice, 19, 28
Chastleton Corp. v. *Sinclair*, 219
Chesapeake and Ohio Railroad, 152
Chester, Colby M., 150
Chicago, Milwaukee and St. Paul R.R. v. *Minnesota*, 37, 124
Children's Hospital v. *Adkins*, 55, 184
Choate, Joseph H., 85n, 184
Civil liberties: under special protection, 125ff; recent Supreme Court decisions, 191ff; and security, 198ff
Clark, Charles E., 108f
Clarke, John H., 58
Clayton Act, 80
Coercion, 177, 181, 215
Colegrove v. *Green*, 143

INDEX

Colgate v. *Harvey*, 98
Collective bargaining, 121
Collectivism: political, 43; socialist, 162; private, 162
Commager, H. S., 46n, 201n
Commerce, Department of, 53f
Commerce clause: limitation on states, 61; and reform, 88; expansion of, 107, 139
Commonwealth Club speech, 71
Communism, 42, 85, 167, 176, 191, 193, 196, 212ff
Competition, 33, 153
Compromise, theory of, 203, 208
Conformity: urge for, 190; enforcing of, 193, 208
Congress: Seventy-first, 63; impasse with Court, 66; control of commerce and industry, 73, 137f; control of agriculture, 91; limitations on, 113, 200; expansion of power, 123
Congress of Industrial Organizations, 110
Conkling, Roscoe, 33f
Conscientious objectors, 46
Constitution: resting on "*The Consent of the People*," 13; basic rights under, 18, 200; and legislative supremacy, 26; as safeguard against popular power, 31f, 43, 187; and laissez-faire, 38; as battle cry, 94; and Democratic Party platform, 99; mechanistic theory of interpretation, 116ff, 117n, 144; judicial construction of, 121; restraints on economic legislation, 126; and social welfare legislation, 157; reflecting fear of the framers, 174
Constitutional conventions, state, 20ff, 187
Constitutionalism: in Locke, 7; and revolution, 12
Contract, freedom of, 44, 61
Contract clause, 18

Conwell, Russell H., 50, 165
Cooley, Thomas M., 28, 31f, 117
Coolidge, Calvin, 46, 54, 56f
Co-operation and coexistence, 160
Corporation: rise of, 24; as person, 33; role in modern society, 159ff; as dominant social form, 160ff; separation of ownership from control, 161; in praise of, 163, 167; revolutionary effect, 169
Corwin, Edward S., 10n, 17, 60n, 67, 90n, 125n
"Court-packing plan": proposal of, 100f; explanation of, 101; and the Constitution, 100; inconclusive outcome of, 103; and newspapers, 103; traditional significance of, 103, 187; and judicial power, 123-124; hearings on, 146
"Critical period," 9, 16
Cummings, Attorney General, 146
Curtis, Charles P., 122n

Darwin, Charles, 31
Davenport, Russell, 153ff
David, Donald K., 156
Declaration of Independence: and Locke, 4; Jacksonian Period, 22; and progress, 87; consent theory of, 185
Demagogue, 51
Democracy: evils of, 16; Jacksonian, 22, 25; and industrial absolutism, 25; social, 43; fear of, 82, 100, 173; increased, 86; dangers of, 87, 150; preserving democratic process, 128; opposed, 149; and private enterprise, 152ff; trend of, 186; requires opposition, 207
Democratic liberals, 64
Democratic Party, 99
Demosthenes, 72
Dennis v. *United States*, 126, 142f, 191, 199, 211

INDEX

Depression: economic, 52, 55, 63, 70, 173; and governmental power, 77

Desvernine, Raoul E., 96

Dicey, Albert V., 171

Dill, Senator, 65, 69

Diplomacy, dollar, 45

Di Santo v. *Pa.*, 61

Disarmament, 45

Disraeli, Benjamin, 186

Dissent, hallmark of free government, 194, 207

Dos Passos, John, 53n

Douglas, William O., 168, 195n, 198f, 206n

Dowling, Noel T., 142

Dred Scott case, 36, 92

Drivers Union v. *Meadowmoor Dairies*, 211

Due process: 26; as constitutional basis for judicial control, 27, 41, 59; and police power, 28; narrow interpretation of, 29; drafting of, 33-34; decline of substantive, 118n; expansion of, 139

Economic determinism, 188

Edgerton, John E., 49, 55f, 164

Eighteenth Amendment, 93

Einstein, Albert, 198

Eisenhower, Dwight D., 165f, 179ff

Emancipation Proclamation, 187

Emerson, Ralph Waldo, 87

"Empire of Liberty," 200

Ex post facto laws, 18-19

Fairman, Charles, 38

Farmers, 52

Fascists, 176

Fay, Charles N., 47n, 48

Fay, S. B., 52n

Feather, W., 47

Federalism, 140

Federalists, 18, 98

Federal Power Commission v. *Hope National Gas Co.*, 120

Feiner v. *New York*, 192

Fernandez v. *Weiner*, 143

Feudalism, benevolent, 43, 164f

Field, Justice, 28, 30, 34ff, 61

Fifteenth Amendment, 128

First Amendment: under special protection, 125ff, 200; "preferred freedoms" doctrine, 135f; restoration of, 211; *see also* Civil liberties

Fish, Hamilton, 92

Flag salute cases, 125, 130ff

Ford, Henry, 50, 73

Fortune magazine, 155, 167

Forum magazine, 68

Fourteenth Amendment, 28-29, 33, 35, 84, 116, 127

France, 196

Frank, John P., 191n

Frankfurter, Felix: on laissez-faire judges, 38f; on judicial supremacy, 67; criticism of the Court, 68; on substantive due process, 120n; "preferred freedoms," 126, 141f; in *Minersville School District* v. *Gobitis*, 130ff; on role of the Court, 131ff; against injection of personal values in judging, 132; conception of judicial review, 132, 142f; on judicial self-restraint, 142; on precedent, 143; in *Dennis* v. *U.S.*, 191; on freedom of expression, 193; letter to Justice Stone concerning Gobitis case, 217ff

Franklin, Benjamin, 16

Freedom: and revolution, 12; diversity and stability, 13; conflict with economic inequality, 22; restraints on, 80; and social organization, 121; "preferred," 126, 135f; of modern corporation, 172; and inequality, 183, 187; and security, 190ff; arguments for, 201ff; *see also* Civil liberties

Freedom of speech, *see* Civil lib-

INDEX

Journal of Commerce, 52
Judicial control: expansion of, 61; and Republicans, 92; auxiliary to political control, 188
Judicial restraint, 27, 103, 113
Judicial review: and free government, 10; restraint of legislative majorities, 17; as dispensing power, 26, 67; of rate fixing, 37; of Congress, 60; personal preferences of judges, 116, 118, 121, 130ff, 145; as oligarchic, 132
Judicial self-restraint, 69, 113ff, 122ff, 131ff

Kellogg-Briand Pact, 45
Kemler, Edger, 206n
Kennan, George F., 198n, 212f
Kent, James, 20f, 41, 184
Keynes, John Maynard, 1-2, 111n
Knights of Labor, 42
Kovacs v. *Cooper*, 126
Ku-Klux Klan, 46

Labor, 51f, 59, 107, 108
La Follette, Robert M., 60
Laissez-faire, 56, 79, 83, 85, 124, 144, 157
Lamar, Justice, 37
Land policy, 22
Laski, Harold J., 85, 189
Law: as barrier to power, 5; as binding government, 12; corporate organization, 24, 160ff, common, 29, 36, 60, 196; higher, 36; natural, 41, 50, 96; fair trade, 53; as a method of social control, 57; judge-made, 66, 69; foundation of, 145; of scarcity, 158; "intracorporate common law," 160ff; of power, 169
Lawyers: on the side of property, 30; Soviet, 204
League of Nations, 45
Lee, J. Bracken, 166f
Legislative majorities: need to re-

strain, 9, 17f, 40, 140; danger to property, 30
Legislative repeal, 13
Legislative supremacy, 26; remedy for, 41
Legislatures, state, infringements on property, 15
Lerner, Max, 111n
Lewis, Sinclair, 47
Liberalism, 177
Lilienthal, David, 159ff, 202n
Lincoln, Abraham, 187, 199
Lincoln Federal Labor Union v. *Northwestern Iron and Metal Co.*, 119
Literary Digest, 45n, 54
Livingston, Edward, 185
Livingston, P. R., 21
Lloyd, Henry Demarest, 42, 186
Lochner v. *New York*, 44
Locke, John: on individualism, 3; on state of nature, 3f, 172f, 181; on social contract, 4; and *Second Treatise of Civil Government*, 4ff, 17; application to America of, 10f; and liberty, 4; on authority, 4, 6; on equality, 4; on restraints on government, 5; on separation of powers, 5; on natural law, 5; on revolution, 5, 199; on natural right, 5; on prerogative, 5; on property, 6, 35; on mercantilism, 7; on constitutionalism, 7; faith in reason of, 7, 20; on majority rule, 14; on legislative supremacy, 41
Lodge, Henry C., 171n
Lusky, Louis, 127-128
Lynd, Robert S., 177

McBain, Howard L., 113, 115
McCarthyism, 197
McCormick, Anne O'Hare, 206n
McKenna, Justice, 59
McReynolds, Justice, 58f, 98, 108, 121f

227

INDEX

INDEX

United States v. Butler, 91, 98,
112ff, 131, 220
United States v. Carolene Products
Company, 126ff, 131ff, 218
United States v. Columbia Steel
Co., 169
United States v. Rabinowitz, 143
United States of America v. Rompel, 143

Van Devanter, Justice, 59, 98
Van Horne's Lessee v. Dorrance,
18
Van Orsdel, Justice, 55, 184
Vauclain, Samuel, 49
Vaughan, C. E., 6n
Veblen, Thorstein, 44
Viner, Jacob, 7n
Virginia Statute of Religious Liberty, 210
Voice of America, 3

Wagner, Robert F., 65n
Wagner Labor Relations Act, 107
Waite, Chief Justice, 29, 38, 60, 124
Walker, S. H., 151n
Wallace, Henry, 85n
Wall Street, 73
Ward, Lester, 84
Warsoff, Louis A., 130
Washington Naval Conference, 45
Wealth: concentration of, 23f; influence of, 65
Webster, Daniel: on threat to

property, 20, 23, 25; on equality,
187
Wechsler, Herbert, 125
Welfare: responsibility for, 25, 33,
153ff; general, 89; demand for,
155f; under the Constitution, 157,
185
Welfare capitalism, 156ff
Welfare state, 153ff
West Coast Hotel v. Parrish, 117,
121f
West Virginia v. Sims, 142
West Virginia State Board of Education v. Barnette, 135f, 149, 195,
205, 210, 214
Wheeler, Burton K., 104
White, William Allen, 92
Whitehead, Alfred North, 2
Whitman, Walt, 190, 195
Whitney v. California, 129, 204
Whyte, William Holley, 154n
Wilson, Charles E., 166
Wilson, Edmund, 57n
Wilson, Woodrow, 48, 56, 58, 204n,
209
Wolff Packing Co. v. Ct. of Industrial Relations, 60
Work, as remedy for radicalism,
49
Workmen's Compensation, 80
World War I, 78, 197
Wynehamer v. New York, 25, 27,
29

Yale University, 43